TONY GALE

That's Entertainment

'If you can't laugh at yourself, don't laugh at anyone else.'

– Peter Gale, Tony's dad

I'm dedicating this book to my dad, Peter and my mum, Valerie, who supported me from as young as I could kick a ball and right throughout my football career.

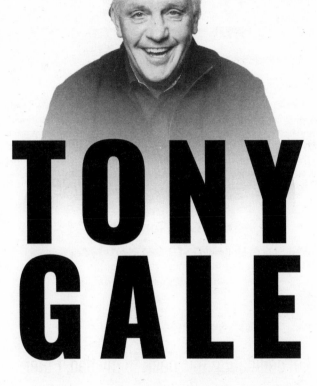

TONY GALE

That's Entertainment

Reach Sport

www.reachsport.com

Reach Sport

www.reachsport.com

Written with Paul Zanon.

Published in Great Britain and Ireland in 2023 by Reach Sport.

www.reachsport.com
@Reach_Sport

Reach Sport is a part of Reach PLC.

Hardback ISBN: 9781914197802
eBook ISBN: 9781914197819

Photographic acknowledgements:
Tony Gale personal collection,
Alamy, Reach Plc.
Thanks to Ken 'Mr Fulham' Coton, Dick Pelham,
and Richard Shenton.

Editing and production: Simon Monk, Adam Oldfield.

Every effort has been made to trace copyright.
Any oversight will be rectified in future editions.

Printed and bound by CPI Group (UK) Ltd,
Croydon, CR0 4YY.

CONTENTS

CONTENTS

PREFACE
Tony Gale – January 2023

3 August 2022 – Soho restaurant.
Paul Zanon & Danny Imray having lunch

DANNY (TONY'S friend) and I were having a nice lunch in the summer sun, when suddenly his phone rang. He answered, 'Alright Tony. How ya doing?' Two minutes later Danny wrapped up the conversation and said, 'Yeah, yeah, sounds good Tone. See you at the golf club at the weekend.' The moment he came off the phone he said to me, 'Would you write Tony Gale's book?' I replied, 'Yes,' expecting nothing more to be said about the subject and for us to tuck into our lunch. Within 30 seconds Danny called Tony back and had arranged for all three of us to meet in Essex a few days later.

From that first session with Galey, it soon became very apparent why he's loved by so many people. He always makes himself available for you, irrespective of the request, and makes it feel like you're doing him the favour when most of the time it's genuinely the other way round. He's also that very same guy that hates to see anybody on their own in a room and will be the first person his friends call in a moment of crisis. As far as human beings go, he's genuinely one of the best. His contribution to football over the last 50 years is a nostalgic masterclass on so many fronts and the anecdotes to accompany that half century will have you laughing, shaking your head and on occasions welling up. Enjoy the ride.

Paul Zanon – January 2023

1

FOREWORD

By Jonathan Pearce

IT WAS a wet and windy December 1986 morning at West Ham's Chadwell Heath training ground when I first met Tony Gale. His smile lit up my day and we've been laughing together around the world ever since.

I had not long joined the BT Clubcall service as the editor for the Arsenal, Birmingham City, Chelsea and West Ham club premium rate phone service where you could dial up information, commentary and player interviews for a fair amount of money. One of my tasks was to grab interviews that lasted as long as possible to keep the listener hooked and paying out the dosh. I quickly found Tony was ideal for the purpose.

He'd missed the Christmas defeats against Tottenham and Wimbledon as the Hammers' season took a downturn and was therefore one of the few players readily available at Chadwell that day. He should have been downcast I guess when I approached him for a few words, but he gleefully grabbed at the chance to talk football and to take the mick out of a new victim with his infamous acidic but brilliant sense of humour. In fact, he never stopped talking. If he was the perfect interviewee, then I was the perfect fall-guy. In between insightful comments about the club and the game in general he ripped it out of me! We ended up in hysterics.

The smile is infectious. The eyes have a devilment in them. The character is immense. He played with character. He played with a wisdom instilled by his mentor at Fulham, Bobby Moore, and his great West Ham hero Billy Bonds, not forgetting his mum and dad who taught him to respect those around in life and to enjoy every moment of that life.

How many mistakes did he make in those 300 cultured league games for West Ham? Very few. How many interceptions did he make or long raking passes did he play out from the back? Countless. Of course, he should have played for England. He was better than many who were picked ahead of him. He won the title with Blackburn and a poor refereeing decision cost him an FA Cup final for West Ham. I watched that infamous semi-final against Forest because I was commentating on the other FA Cup last four clash that day for Capital Gold – the Gazza-inspired Tottenham win over Arsenal. I phoned Tony that night. He was furious and distraught. I'll never forget it.

We promised to keep our conversations going and as the autumn of his playing days arrived we discussed the possibilities of joining the Capital Gold team. I always felt he'd be a natural and it proved to be true. At the 1998 World Cup finals he was wonderful company in and out of the commentary box. With his intuitive understanding of the game, I soon realised he could predict what was going to happen in a game well in advance. Tony has never been a 'co-comm' who simply rehashes what the commentator has said. He gives the listener a discerning perception of the game from the tactical eye of a very, very good former player. That's why he's a very, very good pundit – 'The People's Pundit' as he styles himself with self-deprecating humour.

We travelled to games all over Europe giggling our way through silly pranks and football quizzes. I adored working with him and they were great days. I wished we'd had the chance to replicate the partnership on TV, but it never happened. The bosses would have had to risk having two people having a laugh and celebrating life on air. They tend to shy away from such exuberance!

TONY GALE – THAT'S ENTERTAINMENT

Tony has always had that understanding of where football sits in life. It's helped him through the sad and bad times and enabled him to meet such glorious people. I'm so glad I met him. We have continued our close friendship and he has been a huge and generous supporter of the Lily Foundation, set up by myself and my sister-in-law Liz in memory of her baby daughter. We meet at Lily events or at games. We talk football. We moan and groan like any old fans of the game.

Most of all though we chuckle at life. When I'm down, I see his smile in my mind's eye. It always cheers me up. He's kept me going during some black spells I have been forced to endure.

It was a wet and windy day at Chadwell Heath when I first met Tony Gale. He has lit up my life with sunshine ever since. I am proud and lucky to call him my friend.

Good luck with the book, 'Peoples'!

Jonathan Pearce

Chapter 1

PASSPORT FROM PIMLICO

'We shape our buildings and afterwards our buildings shape us.'
– Sir Winston Churchill

KICK-OFF WAS at Westminster hospital on 19 November 1959, right round the corner from where I lived on Page Street, Millbank. Shortly afterwards we moved to a flat on the Churchill Gardens Estate, also in Pimlico, on Lupus Street, which was a big housing estate made up of 36 tower blocks named after poets. The estate had been developed soon after the Second World War to replace rows of Victorian houses that had been bombed during the Blitz. At first we lived at 4 Ripley House, which was a two-bedroom flat on the first floor, then when my sister was born in 1966, we moved to 70 Chaucer House, which was a three-bed on the seventh floor.

My parents, Valerie and Peter, were very hard-working, well-respected people who made sure my sister and I had a good quality of life. Whatever we lacked in, they more than made up for with their time they gave us. My mum was a full-time civil servant and worked in Westminster, which was convenient as she would walk there. Before that she was in the catering business at St Ermin's Hotel where she worked under her mum. My mum brought up her three younger brothers while her mum and dad were at work, and when I came along, it was another boy for her to look after. She really is the hardest person in the world. If you messed with her, you'd had it.

My dad used to be a lorry driver for Schweppes until he did The Knowledge and then he became a cabbie. When he was doing his research he'd have this big map of London on the living room floor with all these pins in it and he'd ask me to write down the routes for him. Let's say, to go from Big Ben to Wimbledon, he would need to take such and such route and I'd be writing it down. That's how I kind of started learning how to read and write. My best memories of all that though was riding on the back of his old moped while he was doing The Knowledge and then going to watch him play five-a-side.

They had two schools on the estate and our flat was right in the middle of them. There was Churchill Gardens Primary School, where I went, and the other was St Gabriel's. There was always gang fights going on to prove who was the best fighter from both schools, but I never got involved in all that because football always got me out of it. The other kids would be like, 'Don't beat him up, he's in our team.' My mate Andrew Dickie didn't mind a row though, but he came out of a big family with three big brothers, two of whom went on to become top men in the police, not to mention his dad was quite high up in the force.

My dad was a bit of a ducker and diver and the first time Andrew knocked for me, my dad answered the door. Andrew's said, 'I've come to see if Tony wants to come for a kickabout.' My dad's replied, 'Just a minute.' He pushed the door to, but didn't shut it. He's come over to me and said, 'That Dickie boy's here. You tell him fuck all. His old man's a copper.' Andrew always says, 'That was the start of a lifelong friendship between me and Peter,' and it was.

Growing up on the estate was brilliant and I got to know about 50 or 60 kids from there. Right outside the front of our flat we had a bit of grass, which you weren't allowed to play on, but my mum didn't mind me going on there because she could keep an eye on me from the balcony. However, the moment we started to play, the estate porters were constantly chucking us off. Didn't stop us though. As soon as they went, we were straight back on.

My nan on my dad's side, Helen Mooney, who everyone used to call Nelly, died when I was very young and she was married to my granddad Sid Gale, who lived a bit longer and managed to come and watch me play Sunday morning football with my dad. Sid would get picked up by my dad, then after we'd go back to the club at lunchtime and they'd have a drink while my nan used to look after me, because my mum would be working. That was like a day out for Sid.

* * * * *

I ALSO used to travel to Tachbrook Estate with my dad where my mum's parents, nanny Eileen and granddad Bill lived on the sixth floor. It was only about half a mile away from ours and that estate is where I grew up playing football with the older boys. There was a concrete football pitch and that's where everybody used to gather to play, which is all you really used to do back then. There was no PlayStations or any of that shit.

A good mate of mine, Richard Quartly, who I've known since about eight, is about five years older than me and his parents lived on the ground floor, directly beneath my nan. His mum always used to moan, because there was a little tarmac square outside her door and we used to try and keep the ball with one-touch football in this square. She'd come running out shouting, 'Why don't you go down to the pitch?', because she was worried about us breaking the windows. Again, it didn't stop us though and we still broke our fair share of windows all over the estate. My nickname for Richard later on was '10 to 2,' because his feet used to stick out, but not at that age though as I wouldn't have been brave enough.

*****

CERTAIN FOOTBALL memories stick in your head as a kid. I remember watching the 1966 World Cup final indoors with my dad on a black and white telly as if it was yesterday. Watching Bobby Moore collecting the World Cup was something else, especially as he was always my hero. Who'd have thought our paths would cross a few years down the line.

My earliest recollection of playing team football was for the 60th Pack cubs when I was about eight, which was also based on the estate I lived on. I had the silly green cap and all the badges on my shirt like the running ones, explorer, swimming and all that, but it was playing competitive football against other packs that I loved. In fact, I think I set a record once scoring nine times in one game.

My dad was a natural swimmer and I took after him, but he never really got the chance to compete, whereas I broke a number of records in the London swimming trials doing freestyle. I used to train at St George's baths down Buckingham Palace Road and the lady that was training Olympians down there said to me, 'You've got a really good chance of being an outstanding swimmer.' The problem was, I couldn't juggle the swimming and the football, so I had to make a choice and went with football. Also, I didn't like having to get up at 5am to do the swimming training. You never know, I could have been a professional swimmer.

After cubs, my first organised football was playing at the Chelsea Boys Club, which was down at the World's End estate, where Teddy Weston used to coach us. We won loads of silverware at Chelsea Boys Club in five-a-side competitions and 11-a-side. I say silverware, not in terms of trophies, but medals. You'd get a box with a load of hooks on and you'd hang them all in that. My mum still has that box.

We used to have a lot of games at Battersea Park by the Chelsea Pensioners, but we called it the Old Man's Gardens. We played against some really strong boys teams, and there was always a competitive edge to the games. I came from a good background with a strong mum and dad, but some of them who grew up on the World's End estate didn't have mums and dads and that's where Teddy Weston was incredible. He'd pick them up, take them home or take them back to his house for a bit of lunch and made sure they got home. He genuinely cared for them.

Out of a small group at Chelsea Boys Club, four of us went on to become professional. Me, Robert Wilson, Tommy Mason and Perry Digweed, who was Teddy's nephew. Not that he got any preferential treatment from Uncle Ted though. Perry became a successful professional goalkeeper, but back then he started as a centre-back. When Teddy eventually put him in goal, he had Perry dribbling out with the ball. Those were the days you could pass the ball back and the keeper could pick it up, but Perry would come out, draw someone in and pass it out wide to a full-back.

Teddy was a mad Chelsea supporter and was my first and best footballing mentor. He never had a football badge or anything, but his football knowledge was unbelievable. Teddy's philosophy would have still been great today. He taught us to pass it quick, pass it early and never hang on to the ball too long. One thing I learned early on with him was to receive the ball on the half-turn when I was in the middle of the park. That's something which stuck with me throughout my career.

Playing at Chelsea swimming baths was particularly memorable because they used to put boards over the swimming pool and it converted into a five-a-side pitch. They'd have posts, as swimming baths do and you'd be running and dribbling around them, playing off the walls, which all added to the technicalities.

As the years ticked on it was obvious we were too good for the kids leagues on Sunday morning, so Teddy put us in an adult league. Our team consisted of about three or four adults, including Teddy, and we'd play down at Regent's Park, Wormwood Scrubs and the Old Man's Gardens. We used to get the shit kicked out of us, but it taught us how to play quick and early. I loved Sunday morning football and back then it was a really high standard. That's gone out the window now where everyone meets down the pub and then off they go to football. Back then, that's how I proper hardened up. Our dads were on the line supporting us, so if it all kicked off, they were all ready to jump in.

The 1970 FA Cup final stands out for me, because at the time I was a Chelsea fan. My dad used to take me along with my cousin Steven Collins and his dad, my uncle Jimmy, who had season tickets. We used to walk down the Embankment to Chelsea and then Jimmy used to bunk us in on the season tickets going through the turnstiles and then they'd sit us in on their laps at the old north stand.

Back at Pimlico though, we had it all on our doorstep. Battersea Park was the place to be because it had everything you wanted. Athletics track, football pitch, big pool with fountains and a permanent funfair. Back then, kids could go out in the morning and come back in the evening, but the rule was that we couldn't leave the estate. We did though. We used to go across Chelsea Bridge, over into the park, sneak under the fence into the funfair and then bunk on the rides like the big dipper, dodgems and the water chute. Battersea Park wouldn't get away with the health and safety now with some of those rides, but we didn't give a shit.

Me and Steven used to get up to some stupid things, such as climbing up over the bridges that crossed the Thames. We could have been killed. There's one railway bridge you go under when you go to Chelsea Bridge and we climbed up a ladder which had a hatch at the top. We opened it and as we popped our heads up, we suddenly realised we were on the railway tracks. If a train had come we'd have been history. We didn't think like that though. We closed the hatch, carried on walking over the bridge and went over to Battersea Park.

One of Andrew Dickie's brothers, Paul, used to work at ITN House as a cameraman, which meant we could go in as kids and watch all the European matches during the week. You have to remember that back in those days there were only three channels on TV and we didn't have coverage for those games like we do now, so we used to go there from 6pm until about 10.30pm while Paul was working and we'd be watching all the Dutch football with the likes of Johan Cruyff playing. Tuesdays and Wednesdays every week we'd watch the lot, which was a great insight into the foreign football. There was another guy at the time called Mickey Ingles, who was Paul's best pal and they ended up going to Sky down the line doing all the parliamentary camera work, so I ended up meeting them later in life as well, but on the Sky News side instead of the Sky Sports side.

Watching the stuff on ITN was a real treat, but I also remember at that time there was something called 'Pay-TV', where you could watch films. You'd put a few shillings in a slot and twist it round and you'd get access to stuff like *Planet Of The Apes* and *Ben-Hur*. Crazy when you think about what we have access to now.

* * * * *

WE HAD some good lads on the estate who I played football with. Some went on to become good football players, whereas others either lacked the discipline, became successful in something else or had bad luck. Here's a few examples. Phil Nutt, who we called Peanut (P. Nutt), lived in the area and shortly after turning 16 was playing in QPR's first team. Then weeks later he snapped his cruciate ligament and his career was over before it had started. Nowadays, with the advancement in medical care he would have been playing again within 12 months and might have gone on to have a good career.

Another couple of lads who used to enjoy playing football on the estates were Steve Walsh, who lived on the Tachbrook estate and was good mates with my cousin Steven and the other was Paul Hardcastle, who went on to become a massive name in the music industry. Steve was a big, big guy who tended to play in goal and went on to become one of the UK's most famous DJs. Remember that track, *I Found Lovin*'? That was him. Paul, whose nickname at the time was 'Curly,' because of his hair, was a decent player up front and who knows how he might have done if he'd have followed that route. Everyone remembers him for the song *19*, but he's had around 40 Number 1s, all over the world. I lost touch with him and then years later my mate Jonathan Pearce along with Terry Alderton started a podcast called *The Football Friendly* and me and Paul were among the first guests on it in August 2022. We kind of followed each other's careers without either of us knowing and reconnecting again years later was a nice touch.

My family also had a number of good footballers. My dad, my cousins Terry and Steven and then down the line, the son of one of my cousins, Scott Fitzgerald, who went on to play for

Wimbledon, Brentford and Millwall – not to mention he ended up playing in my testimonial at West Ham. However, when I was a kid, I was the first one in my family to progress through as a pro footballer. I was single-minded on playing the game and never saw a future in anything else.

petaChapter 2

TRIALS AND ERRORS

'There's no Plan B for your A-Game.
Be the best in the world at what you do.'

–Bo Eason

MY FIRST day of secondary school was at Pimlico School. You walked into this big hall and you had a much wider geographical reach, with kids from parts of South London, Brixton, Battersea etc, all coming together. Andrew Dickie was in the corridor trying to look half-intelligent and half-hard with his briefcase and I walked over from the other side of the hall and spotted him. I went and sat next to him with my own briefcase, which was a little bit flasher, because it had a clip-down buckle at the front. There we were sitting down and I asked him, 'What you got in your briefcase? Your books?' and he's said, 'Nah. Me mum's put me sandwiches in there.' I said, 'Same here. What the fuck are we doing with briefcases?'

My nickname at school was 'honey boy,' because of 'Gale's Honey,' but I was maybe best remembered for my ability to flip a coin. Me and Andrew used to be partners in crime with the 2p and 10p 'up the wall game.' At the end of break we used to rope a few boys into it and whoever got closest to the wall won the money. We cleared up most of the time, but now and then we did get our trousers pulled down by a few hustlers. It's quite funny, because later in my life, Jack Walker, who owned Blackburn Rovers, used to come into the dressing room and play 50p up the wall with Ray Harford before every game. I never jumped in or told them how good I was because it was the boss and assistant manager, so I thought best to keep out of that one.

Outside of school, we used to go to the Wimpy Bar and I loved a Brown Derby, which was like a donut with whipped cream, nuts and chocolate, although I got into a strange habit of eating it with tomato ketchup after my mates one day dared me to try it. The tomato ketchup in the Wimpy was special because it came in a plastic squeezy bottle in the shape of a big tomato and I squeezed a load on. Not only did I eat the lot, I became addicted to that combination.

I had good memories from that Wimpy, but I also remember the record shop next door to it. I bought my first ever single from there and it was Wendy Richard who starred in *Are You Being Served?* and *EastEnders*, and the song was *Come Outside*. The first LP I bought was *Innervisions* by Stevie Wonder. Seems like a million years ago.

Me and Andrew also used to go to the pictures and play snooker on Sundays. At the corner of Ecclestone Street and Buckingham Palace Road there used to be a garage and underneath was the snooker hall. When we first started to go, my dad or someone older than us would come with us because there were so many dodgy characters there. Everyone thinks snooker halls are shit, but it was a good way to grow up with adults and if you had a couple of quid left after you'd put money in the meter for the snooker lights, then they did a lovely crusty cheese and onion roll down there. My dad was a right-footed footballer, played darts and table tennis with his right hand, he wrote with his left hand, was a right-handed cricket player, a left-handed snooker player and left-handed golfer. How does that work?

As a teenage kid, it was a bit different for me, because I wanted to become a professional footballer and didn't really go out as much as all the other kids my age. Nobody forced me to do that, it was always my choice and my friends and family respected that. Andrew was a great friend in that he'd sit in with me when he didn't need to. For about three years, on Sunday afternoons we used to play a card game called Kalooki with my mum, dad and Andrew and he used to call it 'Gale's school of card playing'. He was shit at cards and if we won any money off him, my mum and dad would always give it back, because they felt sorry for him.

Say what you want about Andrew, but everybody thought he was funny as fuck and as a friend, you couldn't find a better one. As a person, I've always confided in him, whatever the circumstances have been. Love, money, work, family, whatever it might be. We might have a difference in opinion, but we've never had cross words or fallen out with each other in all these years.

***** *

IT WAS my dad who took me to Fulham for my trial when I was 11. A mate of his called John Fluskey, also a cab driver, was one of the coaches for the team and back then, if you did alright in the trials they'd offer you to sign schoolboy forms. They started to recognise that I was a good player when I started representing Pimlico school, then as I got to about 13 or 14 years old, I had a bit of a growth spurt and that's when I really started to progress with football. I hardly played in any school matches, as it was mainly county – as in representing schools in different areas, like West London, then Middlesex, Inner London, London and then England trials. Because of my height, I probably found it easier to play with older people than other 14-year-olds would have done.

There was one teacher in particular at Pimlico called Bob Fisher, who I'll be eternally grateful for. West London trials is the first district you play for and he knew I was pulling up trees for the school team and said, 'You've got to go and have your West London trial.' I said, 'But I've got to get down there and all that.' He said, 'I'll take you.' From then on he used to take me down to the trials and my dad would pick me up afterwards, or sometimes I'd get the bus home. There was also another couple of teachers called Bob Fox and John Ianson who encouraged me. The PE department at Pimlico was brilliant. If there was a little bit of talent, they'd recognise it and help you. We had some proper wrong-uns at Pimlico, but I'll always be grateful for those teachers who helped me improve and develop my football.

Apart from football, I didn't have a backup plan. I can remember going to see the careers advice person and thinking, 'They're going to ask you what you want to do in life and you have no idea.' If I said, 'I want to be a footballer,' they would have thought I was taking the piss. As I'm queuing up to see this careers guy, a friend of mine in my class called Clive Collins was in front of me and I asked him, 'What are you going to do?' and he said, 'I want to be a pharmacist.' I thought, 'That will do. I'll say the same'. That's exactly what I said and I didn't have a clue what a pharmacist even was. All I knew was that they worked in a chemist.

My last year at school in 1976 was a bit of a write-off for me. I was in the top class in our year, but I was kind of blagging it because all my spare time I was practising football. If I wasn't doing the Tuesdays and Thursdays training sessions at Elliott School or Richardson Evans with Fulham, then I was training with Chelsea Boys Club or down the playground kicking balls up against the wall. When it came to the O Levels, I was sitting there at one of those wooden desks in a massive gymnasium and I could see everybody had their head down. It was that really hot summer and I remember sitting there for an hour thinking, 'I haven't written anything on the page.' All I could think about was, 'Who's playing up front for Fulham this week,' or 'Who's in the team I'm playing against this weekend.' I wasn't thinking about geography, history, maths, English, humanities, religious education or science. In fact, what the fuck was humanities even about? The only thing I liked was science, because I could mess about with Bunsen burners with the other lads.

My head was spinning and I thought, 'Fuck it. Leave.' Me and Andrew got 'Unclassified,' grades. I'm not proud that I didn't get any qualifications, but my university of life was about to start at Fulham and I couldn't wait to get started.

Chapter 3

THE APPRENTICE

'You'd go for a drink in the pub and they'd all be telling you about how they were contenders. The thing is, they might have been good football players, but they didn't make the same sacrifices that Tony did. They were pissheads and drugged up. People who'd got in with the wrong crowd. Could have been a contender? Yeah, you could have, but you didn't, mate.'

– Andrew Dickie

AFTER THREE years of training with Fulham, I signed school-boy forms with them. However, I'd also been offered terms with QPR, Leeds and Chelsea. All the scouts from these teams were going to these representative games and Fulham must have realised, 'Fuck me, he's 14 and been training with us for three years. Let's sign him up before the others try and poach him.' That's how I officially ended up at Craven Cottage.

The Fulham manager who signed me as an apprentice was Alec Stock. After the 1975 final, he retired as first team manager and Bobby Campbell came in to replace him. Talk about mentors, I was so lucky. Teddy Weston was one, Ken Craggs was my youth team manager who was brilliant with me and the third one was Bobby Campbell, who had every faith in me during my time at Fulham.

I'd like to give a special mention to Ken. Around 1975, I first met Tony Mahoney at a trial match at the Richardson Evans training ground, down the A3 which weren't proper pitches, but more like Wimbledon Common extensions. Tony lived in East London and we were both there to play Reading and neither of us knew that many people. We ended up winning 2-1 and after the game, we're all standing about and there was this big fella, wearing a big trench coat and wellington boots. We all thought he was the groundsman, but he introduced himself as Ken Craggs, the Fulham youth team manager. He turned out to be a big part of our lives during those early years at Fulham, encouraging and developing us as players and people. Ken sadly passed in 2021 and me and Les Strong did the eulogy at the funeral. RIP mate.

Part of my incentive in signing as an apprentice with Fulham was two free tickets to the 1975 Cup final against West Ham and to also go to the ball after. I'd been to the League Cup final between Stoke City and Chelsea in 1972, but this was totally different. I remember looking around Wembley thinking, 'Wow. This is incredible.' There was a band playing, not fireworks and pop music like nowadays, and you'd hear the fans singing for an hour and a half before the game. Then seeing the teams coming out and being presented to the royalty was something else. It's probably every kid's dream to want to play at Wembley and I would have never thought I'd get the chance to play there about 20 years down the line.

I went to the Fulham banquet afterwards at the Grosvenor Hotel with my dad, and all the West Ham players turned up to come and have a drink with Bobby Moore even though he was playing for Fulham. I thought that spoke volumes for what the man was about. I was only 15 and we were sat at one of the main tables, as my dad's getting pissed as a fart enjoying meeting all the footballers and I'm sitting there thinking, 'I hope you're having a nice time!'

THE APPRENTICE

Back to Fulham. Three of us signed up as apprentices at the same time. Me, Perry Digweed and Tony Mahoney and I'm still close mates with them now. The day we signed, we booked a dinner that evening at some restaurant in Battersea to go with our parents. However, at the time they had something called the *Evening Standard* London Five-A-Side tournament at the Wembley Arena and just as we're thinking we're off out we're told by Bobby Campbell, 'Sorry. You're playing in the five-a-side tonight.' It was all the stars playing like Liam Brady and Glenn Hoddle, which was a great baptism for us. We didn't win it that year, but a few years later, I won it with Jim Stannard in goal, myself, Robert Wilson, Gordon Davies, Ray Houghton and Tony Finnegan.

Being an apprentice back then was very different to a teenager entering the system these days. If you're an apprentice now, they'll put you through a programme with schooling, money management courses, you name it. Back then there wasn't any education or life skill coaching, it was our parents who gave us life skills.

Here's what a typical day was like for me. I'd leave home from Pimlico around 7am and then get a train from there to Victoria and change to get the District Line to Putney Bridge. When we first started travelling to Craven Cottage we used to buy weekly passes, but one of the next influx of apprentices had a lad called Robert Wilson and his dad Pat was a ticket collector at Putney. When he saw us coming he used to let us through the barrier and on the way back he used to give us tickets to get home, no matter where you lived. We obviously claimed expenses both ways, which gave us a couple of extra quid to put in our pockets every week.

Then as you came out of Putney train station there was a fruit and veg shop run by Perry's parents, Harry and Monica. When

Harry used to see us coming out, he'd put the kettle on and make us a cup of tea and ask, 'Do you want an apple, orange, pear?' Robert Wilson's dad, Pat and Harry became good pals and would often go to the working men's café next door, and they'd also come along to as many of our youth team games as they could.

After leaving Perry's parents' greengrocers, we'd walk under Putney Bridge through an archway and there's a church on your right called All Saints, just by the bridge and that's where they filmed *The Omen*, which is one of the scariest films ever. When they were filming around 1974, I used to shit myself, because it was dark in the mornings and they used to have wind machines to create storm effects and there would be leaves flying everywhere. When we saw that film and the cross came off the church and it hit the geezer in the chest, that was scary. We used to run through the archway and if you've seen that film, you'd understand why!

Then we'd walk through the park to the football ground, where we started our chores. All the kit was cleaned by the washing lady the night before, so we had to pack it all into skips and then we had to go down to the training ground, which was in Tolworth. A skip is a big metal container like you see on Soccer AM which they all sit on. They had great big clips on them and if you got your hand stuck in them, it hurt to say the least. That's basically where all the kit went into. For example – you might have to pack 16 first team shirts, shorts, socks, all the boots. Then the physio's stuff went into another skip. What always happened was, you'd packed the skips and then someone would always say something like, 'Did you pack Bobby Moore's spare socks?' Even though you probably had, you'd always think, 'Fuck. Did I pack them?' If you forgot anything, you'd get crucified by the players. So, you'd have to empty the whole skip out, only to realise you had actually packed them.

After sorting the skips we got on a minibus and Ken Craggs drove us to the training ground, where we'd unload the skips, put all the kit out for all the players, then do our training. Afterwards we'd put all the kit away into dirty bags, head back to the main ground and give the kit to the lady who did the washing in this giant washing machine. Then we'd clean the boots which took ages because there was about 30 pros playing at the time and only three of us cleaning.

Boot boys don't exist these days because the modern boots are made of laminated leather, and they just hose them off. Back in our days, we had to wash the mud off, let them dry for a little bit and then rub polish into the leather. Once you'd done that, you took the laces out, cleaned them, then put them back in. On match days, you'd ask the players, 'Which boots do you want?' and you'd get them out, took the studs out and Vaseline'd them. Being a boot boy was a trade that took time to master and we weren't always the most patient.

One day we were fed up with it because it was taking so long to clean all the boots and Tony Mahoney had this great idea. 'Right lads – there's a quicker way to do this. Fill that bath with water and chuck all the boots in.' This was the giant communal bath and Tony jumped in, wearing a pair of briefs, and started scrubbing these boots. He'd then pass them to me and I'd towel dry them, then I'd pass them to Perry who was in charge of throwing them into the washing lady's massive tumble dryer.

Well, the boots came out like fucking rocks and we had to do the whole lot again. Not only that, when Tony was in the bath scrubbing the boots, all the mud that came off ended up blocking the drains. It took us about two days to clear everything up from this brainwave we had.

* * * * *

I HAD some of the best days of my life as an apprentice at Fulham, but it wasn't always easy cruising, because we had a hard taskmaster in our groundsman. Bobby Moore used to give him all his leftover clothes, which made him the smartest dressed groundsman in the world, but very few realised what a fucker he was with us.

First day at work, he's said, 'Get your arses out here and start shifting that fucking sand.' There must have been 100 tons of sand and we had to spread it all over the pitch. There we were, three 16-year-olds and six old age pensioners breaking our backs to move this sand, while he just watched. We hadn't done a day's labour like that in our lives and at the end of the afternoon our hands were covered in blisters. He said, 'I tell you how you stop getting any blisters. Piss on your hands.'

He'd also have us painting, cleaning toilets and doing all the stuff that maintenance staff would now be in charge of. We also used to sweep the terraces, which we admittedly used to take the piss with. We used to sweep all the rubbish into the middle by the big steps and then set fire to it instead of putting it in plastic bags. Within minutes you couldn't see Craven Cottage because of all this black smoke and shortly after you'd hear someone on the microphone upstairs shouting, 'Who's lit that fucking fire?'

Whatever the duties were on the day, if you hadn't finished them, you couldn't train. As apprentices, we were just like schoolboys among some bigger lads. When you first turn up, you tend to be a bit quiet and reserved until you got your feet under the table, but once we got a little bit more established, our characters started to appear. When you join a football club, all your inhibitions go. There was some strong characters in there and some very good football players, so it wasn't a case of sink or swim, but you had to stand your ground.

THE APPRENTICE

There were initiation ceremonies that wouldn't be allowed these days. It was more the culture of football, but that groundsman always had a part of it and always thought it was hilarious. You had to sing songs at Christmas that the players had nominated, stark bollock naked with a bucket on your head and a mop in your hand, while standing on the treatment table pretending to play the mop like a guitar. If they didn't like what you were singing they'd lob something at you, like a flannel or something like that. Was it right? Probably not. We just inherited that culture and then passed it on because we didn't know any better.

Here's another one. We had boot brushes and you'd put them in the Kiwi boot polish, then they got you on a bed and smeared the boot polish all over your body. The groundsman would then say, 'In order to get that boot polish off, you have to put paraffin on it.' He brought a big can in and you'd think it was paraffin, but it was just water. You'd be trying to get it off and then he'd come up to you with a box of matches and would light them and flick them at you, just to make you shit yourself. We'd all run to the bath and dive in.

We never used to tell our parents when we got home because we were worried how they would react and we also didn't want to rock the boat at Fulham. Mine, Perry and Tony's mum's used to come and watch us at youth games when we were playing southeast counties and they had quite the reputation for expressing themselves to the officials. Southeast counties football was brilliant. That's where all the parents got to know each other watching all the games on the sidelines together. It was such a competitively brilliant league and I remember our mums terrorising the linesmen, standing behind them with their handbags, shouting, 'That wasn't offside.' Ken Craggs had to warn mine and Tony Mahoney's mum for getting on to the linesman.

We all thought the groundsman was a bit of a bully, but we were always afraid to take our concerns to the management as we might have been seen as grassing. Sometimes he just took it too far though. Once we were on the pitch sorting out the divots and he came in and was in a bad mood. He shouted, 'Oi, you, Galey.' I said, 'What's the matter?' He'd say, 'Get up there and clean them fucking lights.' I said, 'What lights?' and he replied, 'The floodlights,' which were hanging over the river at Fulham.

He handed me a duster and said, 'Go on. Get up there.' I said, 'I can't go up there.' It was one of those ladders with railings all around your body. He said, 'Them lights need dusting. They were a bit dim the other day. Up you go.' I went about a quarter of the way up, shitting myself and he said laughing, 'I was only joking!' Prick.

Some of the stuff he put us through back then, he'd be nicked for these days, like aiming or shooting an air rifle at us from up in the stand when we weren't doing the divoting properly. You'd sometimes be on the pitch and hear a crack and a pellet would fly past you. The worst memory I have of the grounds-man was that he made us fight between ourselves. It was called a slap fight and you'd put a hooded wet top on and pull the hood up and you had to slap each other. Of course, it would generally end up in a full-blown fight and this geezer was standing there laughing. Once he got Perry and Tony to fight and it quickly got out of hand. Perry ended up with a busted lip and the second the groundsman saw the blood, he really panicked. That was horrible to see him make two mates fight. When Bobby Campbell came along, he wouldn't have stood for it. In fact, Bobby probably would have lamped him, because, despite being a tough manager, he was very protective of the younger players and hated bullies.

Just need to say, being an apprentice at Fulham, despite all the crap the groundsman put us through, they were some of the best days of my life. I'd be getting home around 7pm, later during pre-season because the first team would be doing morning and afternoon sessions. Some people moaned about that, but I wouldn't have swapped it for the world. The experiences and people I played with in the coming seasons were the stuff dreams are made from.

Chapter 4

THE THREE AMIGOS

*'When we arrived in Copenhagen, there was about
five thousand screaming girls as we came off the plane.
It was crazy when you think about it.'*
– Rodney Marsh

WHEN I made my debut in the 1976/77 season, George Best, Bobby Moore and Rodney Marsh were playing in America – that was part of the reason I got my chance when I did. Marshy was playing for the Tampa Bay Rowdies, Bestie for Los Angeles Aztecs and Mooro was at San Antonio Thunder. Then Bestie's agent Ken Adam, along with Fulham chairman Ernie Clay and board director Sir Eric Miller, put together a deal to get all three of them back to the UK to play for Fulham. They were soon known as The Three Musketeers.

While Bestie and Marshy were back for the beginning of the season, Mooro was a couple of weeks behind, finishing off his time with San Antonio Thunder. Fulham were now missing a defender for the No.6 shirt and that's when Bobby Campbell came and had a chat with me. 'You will be playing in the Anglo-Scottish Cup until Mooro gets back.' I was delighted. I'd just left school and had only just done three or four weeks of pre-season training and here I was playing first team football. Perry and Tony were supposed to put my kit out for me and I remember them putting all the kit out for the players and when it came to my No.6, they said, 'Alright lucky bollocks. Put your own fucking kit out. You're still an apprentice!'

My first game in the Anglo-Scottish Cup was against Leyton Orient on 11 August 1976 and I had no nerves whatsoever. I sorted the tickets out for my mum and my dad and had about 100 family and friends who came for the match. The team talk was good and the sound or the size of the crowd didn't affect me. As we were running out, I was thinking, 'Right. This is it. Let's do this.' Then the centre-forward Viv Busby tapped me on the shoulder and said, 'I hope you've enjoyed all this,' and I said, 'What's that Viv?' He said, 'The team talks, the time with your family and all that, but you do know we're playing for money today.' I said, 'Yeah, yeah,' thinking he was talking about our salaries. Then he said, 'It's £25 bonus for a draw and £75 for a win.' I was on £16 a week and said, 'Fucking hell!' He then said, 'I've got a wife, family and kids and most of the other players here also have families. That extra money means a lot for us. So enjoy your evening, but don't go making any silly mistakes.' The result was 0-0, but the whole experience was far more valuable.

Leyton Orient had two great goalscorers in Gerry Queen and Derek Possee, who were household names at the time. Queen had played for Crystal Palace all his career and Possee for Millwall, then they both came to Leyton to finish off their careers. Laurie Cunningham was also in that team and what a player he was. He's the only footballer I've seen who used to take corners on the right-hand side with the outside of his right foot. Unbelievable talent and such a shame he died so young in a car crash a few years later. We lost that game 2-1 and Leyton Orient went on to become runners-up, losing 4-0 to Nottingham Forest in the final.

When I played in that game, I was the second youngest player to have played in the first team at 16 years and 266 days. Tony Barton held the record at 16 years and 259 days when he made his appearance in 1954 and that's since been beaten by Harvey Elliott who played at 15 in 2018. However, I was the youngest goalscorer when I scored against Hull City later on, although Ryan Sessegnon then beat that many years later.

The second game was on 14 August against Norwich, at home. They had a renowned partnership up front with Ted MacDougal and Phil Boyer, but we managed to hold our own and come away with a 1-1 draw. A few days later, Bobby Moore returned from America and I was playing back in the reserves again. However, it's worth mentioning that my year out of the squad was a massive learning curve on so many fronts, one of them being 'combination football,' which unfortunately doesn't exist anymore.

First time I played combination football was when I was 15. I was dragged out of school by Fulham to go and play for the reserves against Swindon, away. They had to come and get permission from my headmaster, Mr Roberts at Pimlico secondary school. Fulham said, 'We'd really like Tony to play for the reserves, because we really think he's got good prospects as a footballer. It would be a great experience for him as a kid to be playing against seasoned professionals.' Thankfully he agreed.

Combination was basically reserve team football that was played at the grounds, but in a league format. The football was that good, I used to bunk off from school to watch it. If a player like Peter Osgood was in the reserves because they were looking to regain fitness or were out of form, you could go to a combination game and see the likes of him wanting to bang a few goals in. You got used to playing at all the grounds like Highbury, White Hart Lane, Stamford Bridge, instead of the training grounds and you got to actually play the players in the main squad. I remember playing against the great Ipswich side which had players like Alan Brazil, Eric Gates, John Wark, Russell Osman, Kevin Beattie and Terry Butcher, who were all homegrown players.

Admittedly, you were playing in front of the staff, not 60,000 fans, which was kind of like playing during lockdown, however, when people got an inkling there was going to be first team players playing, sometimes you got a decent crowd. You also met every first team manager from every London club and all the clubs in the various counties in the south. For them, it was a great way to see how we could cope as youngsters up against adults and whether we were ready to compete at that first team level yet. Some players were signed from their performance in reserve team football before they'd even played in the pros, just because some managers could see the promise of the players at that level.

Combination football was the breeding ground of breeding grounds and it was so much better than academy football now, where it's all Under-23s or Under-18s playing against each other at the same age. The problem then comes when they get into the first team and they don't know what's hit them. Whereas if you prepare for first team football and for what goes on in the dressing room and the type of banter at a higher level and how seasoned professionals prepare for games, your mindset is rock solid. By the time I was 19, I'd played in over 100 first team games. That experience you can't get in a restricted academy setting. It's amazing how it's changed now and not for the better either. Most of the learning should be with good pros. I only played combination football for just over a year, but it made a massive impact on me.

When Mooro came back from America, Bobby Campbell said to him, 'You've just come back and need a bit of a run out to get your fitness up. I'll put you in against Bristol City, against the reserves.' My highlight in combination football was playing with Bobby Moore for that one game at Craven Cottage against Bristol, only a few weeks after the Anglo-Scottish games. It was a baking hot day and as we were all running around warming up in the sunshine, Mooro was the only one in the shade warming up, as relaxed as you like. How sensible was that?

I learned more in that one game than I did in a whole season playing for someone else. How to communicate to a full-back and my midfield players, when to stay up, when to drop off when one or either of you attack the first ball. And what he did with offsides was brilliant. He'd be waving his arm to me behind his back to stay up as he was running along. Also his positioning from opposing crosses, taking a space from the near post, was impeccable. He's the first player I've seen do that.

I was captain of the reserves for the rest of that season and outside of that one game, every time he was in training I would watch him and learn. Everything he said was brilliant, from his poise to his elegance on and off the pitch. I don't think I heard him say a bad word about anyone and I don't think I ever saw him get angry. He was coming to the end of his career and all the other teams held him in such high esteem and respected him so much because he was the 1966 World Cup winning captain, but I nevertheless did see people try to rattle him. He never reacted though. I saw him have a nightmare at one game and he still wanted the ball and still kept accepting it and kept going. That attitude of never giving up was contagious.

For the rest of that season Bobby played and I was his understudy. I was down to be sub once for him at Stamford Bridge and there must have been 50,000 people in attendance. There were even people sitting on top of the old scoreboards, where you used to have some old geezer behind it changing numbers whenever a goal was scored. I never did come on and Chelsea were the winners that day, but what an experience.

* * * * *

SHORTLY AFTER Alan Mullery left Fulham, Bobby Moore kind of became a star on his own from the World Cup, but with Bestie and Marshy also in the mix, the whole fucking place took off. It was like the Three Amigos of Fulham. Although I was playing in the reserves, I was still very lucky to be able to play in friendlies with the first team throughout the 1976/77 season and additionally, they used to take the apprentices to the first team away games to suck in the experience of the evening and the atmosphere in the dressing room.

We were going on pre-season trips all over the place and even having exhibition games during the season. I remember going to Copenhagen to play in a five-a-side tournament and in addition to the three musketeers, we also had some really experienced players which Bobby Campbell signed, like Peter Storey who played for Arsenal and England, Les Strong, Alan Slough, John Mitchell, John Evanson, Gerry Peyton and Chris Guthrie.

I was a 17-year-old kid tagging along and wherever we went in Copenhagen, I've never seen women flock around men as I saw them flock around Bestie, Marshy and Mooro – particularly Bestie. You'd see women leaving their boyfriends and run over to George just to say hello. There were no photos then, unless someone happened to be walking around with a proper camera and definitely no selfies or any of that shit.

Being around them was incredible. It was like Bestie was the out and out superstar, Marshy was the maverick and Bobby was football's king of England. Three players, who played in totally different positions, with totally different characters, who all got on so well. Not just with us, but with everyone they crossed paths with. And just by being around them, you got caught in their slipstream, which meant I was also getting these pretty blonde Danish girls coming up to me asking me for my autograph, not having a clue who I was. It was just great to be a part of it all.

Playing with this lot in the five-a-side tournament was the stuff dreams were made of. The game itself was pretty one-sided and at one point we were winning 5-0, so Marshy decided to jump up in the penalty area, catch the ball and put it down on the penalty spot. Bobby Campbell absolutely slaughtered him. I don't think Marshy would have done it if it was 1-0 down at Chelsea, it was just a bit of fun and we went on to win about 8-1. He didn't worry about the consequences, because he was Marshy! What a talent. I saw him doing the Johan Cruyff turn before Cruyff was even known for it and I genuinely believe he should have got more England caps.

After the games in Copenhagen, we'd all go out with Bestie, Marshy and Mooro, and they would make us young-uns feel really welcome. Memories of sitting in bars and clubs, listening to Tom Jones and Elvis Presley music, drinking with these guys was priceless. Even when we were back in Fulham they'd do the same. Sometimes after a training session we'd go to the Duke of Wellington pub in Chelsea and Mooro would be up the bar, leading the way. I only went in there a couple of times, because I was too young and not drinking, but the fact that they never left anyone out from the invitations always made you feel special.

All the tournaments and games we took part in were in the public eye, but my favourite memories of the trio were what they did behind the scenes. Me, Tony Mahoney and Perry Digweed were boot boys for Marshy, Mooro and Bestie. We shared the duties between us and they were always very generous and appreciative. At Christmas time all three of them gave us a tip – something like a fiver or tenner, which back then was a lot of money, but I probably made my biggest money from the merchandise they gave us.

Marshy was arguably the most generous of the three, both with drinks at Christmas and gear. At the time, Ken Adam did a package deal for Marshy and Bestie with Puma where the both of them had to do a few promo bits using their stuff. As a result, they got sent loads of shirts, shorts, boots, bags, you name it. They already had all the gear and used to leave it at the ground for whoever wanted it. It didn't take me, Perry and Tony long to hoover that load up and move it on.

At the time there were boots that had come out called Puma King Pelé, which were wafer thin, made from some special leather, low at the back and either had a white or yellow Puma stripe on them. They looked the bollocks. Marshy used to get a new pair sent to him every couple of weeks and because we were the same size, he used to say, 'Wear them in training for me once and break them in for me.' They didn't need breaking in because they were soft as anything, but I never told him that. Then after two weeks he used to give them to me and I made more money selling my Puma King Pelé boots to all my mates on the estate than I made as an apprentice.

It was more than just gifts that we'll remember these three for. They all took the time to share their knowledge with us and also had some fun. Outside the manager's office there were big dustbins, which we used as a goal. Perry was goalie and me and Tony used to practise volleys. Marshy would sometimes come back in the afternoons and would come outside and give us a few tips. Things like, 'You don't want to do that, this is what I did when I was a kid.' Marshy would throw the ball on top of the corrugated roof of the turnstile, which was slanting towards you. The ball would roll down and then you'd have to volley it. It was brilliant that he'd come out and do that with us.

Marshy was also the master of doing tricks. He'd see us messing about sometimes in the changing room and say things like, 'When I was an apprentice, I'd do this,' then stick a broomstick on his foot and walk around the dressing room balancing it on his foot. Once you'd had a go at that and managed to master it, he'd say, 'Right then, try this,' and balance the broomstick on his head. However, his best trick was scoring from the tunnel. He'd say to us, 'Can you score a goal from here, inside the tunnel?' We'd reply, 'Do what?' He would throw it up and from a half-volley curl it out of the tunnel. After a few attempts it would end up in the goal. You have to remember this was on a slope and he'd be doing this in his trainers. We'd be trying for hours without getting one.

You hear stories of how some of the older players look down their noses at the apprentices or fans, but Bobby Moore was never one of them. Sometimes after training, the apprentice manager Ken Craggs would say to us, 'We're going to let you go home early today.' First time it happened I remember him saying to me, 'Mooro said he'd give you a lift home.' I lived in West London and Bobby Moore had to drive through there to get to East London. He had this yellow Jaguar E-Type and it was the absolute nuts. You have to remember that he'd met prime ministers, presidents, Frank Sinatra and I'm in this car listening to Tom Jones, who was also a mate of his, thinking, 'I wonder who else has sat in this seat?'

I'd be in the car with him for about 40 minutes and never had a word to say because I was so nervous. I just spoke when spoken to. Going home in that Jag with the windows down, I was hoping that absolutely everyone that knew me would spot me next to the World Cup-winning captain. I used to ask him to drop me by the shops next to the estate in Pimlico I lived on, where my friends used to sit on a wall, who'd all left school and were out of work. Bearing in mind I'd hardly said a word the whole trip, when I used to get out of the car in front of my mates, I'd say, 'Cheers Bob. Same time tomorrow mate?' Bobby would laugh and you'd hear people on the street saying, 'Was that Bobby Moore?'

Marshy was great with his tricks, but Bestie was another level. He'd ask you to point at a light switch in the changing room and then he'd kick a ball at the switch and turn it off first time. Then we'd try to do it and trash the dressing room to bits. Once, Ken Craggs walked in and he's seen the mirror smashed and bits of false ceiling were hanging down. Kenny's said, 'What the fuck's happened to this dressing room?' Tony Mahoney calmly said, 'We were just trying the tricks Bestie and Marshy had shown us.' Ken then replied, 'Well – you're not fucking George or Rodney, are you?' We then burst out laughing and he said, 'You think it's funny? You're staying for another couple of hours and you're paying for the damages.'

Everyone talks about how good Bestie was as a player and I can say, first hand, he really was unbelievable. At the time, it was no secret that he had problems and that's the only reason Fulham got him, otherwise he would have been playing at Man United. Bobby Campbell gave him carte blanche. 'If you don't turn up to training, make sure you're in this afternoon because you'll be running in Bishops Park.'

We used to get in at 8am, do our chores, get all the kit ready, go off to the training ground, come back, clean all the kit and boots for the next day, and then just as we were ready to go out the door, Bestie turned up. Bobby Campbell would come in and say, 'Hold on. Extra training for you lot. You're out in Bishops Park with Bestie.' At the time, we thought it was a hardship to go out and train again, but looking back on it, those were magical times.

You have to remember that Bishops Park wasn't a training ground. It was a communal park next to the stadium. We'd put our jumpers down for goalposts and around the park you had ladies walking around with prams. The other task was trying to find a bit of grass with no dog shit on it to have a game of football on.

We had one goalkeeper and three outfield players. Bobby used to go about 50 yards away with a bag of balls and say, 'You three against him,' pointing at Bestie. Basically, he had to get past all three of us to score a goal and that's exactly what he did. I defy anyone now to score the goals he scored in Bishops Park with dog shit, prams and still beat three fit 17-year-old players and score goal after goal. Bestie used to come off that pitch absolutely soaked. He worked his arse off and on his day he was one of the most talented players on the planet.

Bestie was also known for his playboy lifestyle and as teenage apprentices we used to wait for him to be dropped off to see which lady he'd be with that afternoon. Once, he was supposed to play, but didn't turn up. We were at the players' bar after and he turned up pissed, with Don Shanks and Miss World, Mary Stävin. It was like they had a cameo role. They walked into the bar, had a drink and left a few minutes later.

One pre-season game we ended up at a nightclub called Busby's in South London after playing a friendly against Crystal Palace and the Palace lads came out with us as well, just because they wanted to be around Marshy, Bestie and Mooro. After, we got on the coach and on it were friends of Bobby Campbell, comedian Jimmy Tarbuck and singer Kenny Lynch and the three amigos. In we went to Busby's and the red carpet was rolled out for us. I was just an apprentice and it was like my first introduction to nightclubs, full of people drinking and loads of beautiful women. It was like 'Wow! Fucking hell.' They always looked after us, but if you stepped out of line, maybe drank too much or was being flash, you'd soon be told.

Marshy and Bestie played some incredible football that season and it genuinely looked like they were having fun. One of the most memorable games was when they played against Hereford on 25 September 1976. I wasn't playing in the game, but there's a clip on YouTube where you can see them trying to tackle each other to get the ball. They were 4-1 up at the time and the crowd loved it and started to cheer them on. You'll never see that these days.

The football was entertaining and I was lucky to play with two managers Bobby Campbell and John Lyall who encouraged that style of play. Not every team is going to win the league and not every team is going to qualify for Europe, so why the fuck do supporters wanna go down there? The answer is, because you want to be entertained. You want to see a George Best, Rodney Marsh, Alan Devonshire or Paolo Di Canio. You want to see these guys do something you can't do. When I'm doing my commentary these days, I love to see the real players such as the Bergkamps, the Zolas, the Thierry Henrys, the De Bruynes and the Mo Salahs, and look at them and think, 'I couldn't see that pass happening.' About 99 per cent of the time you can see a pass before it happens, but it's those players that see the pass that you couldn't see who are the ones worth watching. They give you entertainment.

So, that was the Best, Moore, Marsh era. Incredible players, great personalities, but also great mentors, for which I'll have great memories I can cherish for life.

I had some of the best days of my life as an apprentice and in combination football, but as I entered my first full season in the first team, all eyes were on me to see if I could rise to the challenge.

Chapter 5

NO.6

'When he came to Fulham, I thought they likened him to Bobby Moore because he was slow and couldn't head the ball! However, it turned out Galey was a great player on the ball, a terrific force in defence and a fantastic addition to Fulham.'

– Les Strong

I MADE my full league debut in August 1977 and took over the No.6 shirt as Bobby Moore had retired. Yes, the pressure was on, but I was Bobby Campbell's blue-eyed boy to the extent where the other players would say, 'Here he comes. Golden bollocks can't do no wrong.' However, if I made a mistake in training, he'd stop the whole session and say something like, 'Listen. Bobby Moore got criticised for that. He made a mistake against Poland in a World Cup and it cost England. You can't make mistakes like that. I know you want to play the ball, but you can't play it every time. This is what you need to do,' and he'd explain the tactic. Mike Kelly was Bobby's assistant initially and between them it was kind of a good cop, bad cop routine, which they'd alternate.

Despite being a defender, we started playing a 4-3-3 formation and I went into midfield that season as a temporary measure. Looking back on it I think Bobby Campbell thought it was a good way for me to learn my responsibilities in different positions. You cannot make a mistake at the back, but you can take more of a risk when playing in midfield.

If you lose possession, you've got someone behind you, but if you lose possession as the last man at the back, you're done. My asset was that I was calm and composed on the ball and could find a pass. Bobby told me, 'You've got a knack of arriving at the right time. Don't ever lose that.'

My first league game was against Charlton at home on 20 August 1977. Derek Hales and Mike Flannagan were playing up front for Charlton and were one of the most prolific strike forces about. We drew that game 1-1, which was a great taster of first team football at that level.

Playing against Spurs at White Hart Lane on 10 September in front of a full house also stood out for me. We had this lovely red silky kit with black stripes down the shoulders and over the arms, which looked the absolute bollocks. Only problem is we lost 1-0, albeit against a strong Spurs side which featured a young Glenn Hoddle and Steve Perryman. However, a more memorable game was away at Crystal Palace on 1 October in front of a packed stadium at Selhurst Park.

Palace were managed by Terry Venables and I was playing midfield with Bestie that day and I scored the winner to make it 3-2. Bestie put me through and I lobbed the keeper, Tony Burns. Everyone ran over to celebrate and were jumping on top of me, which for a 17-year-old kid was something else. It was also a strange game because we all went off the pitch, thinking it was the final whistle, but we all had to come back and play the last three or four minutes because apparently it wasn't the ref's whistle that everyone heard.

After the game I managed to get my mum and dad into the players' bar, and we stayed there until long after the game had finished. I thought everyone had gone home, but as I came out I got mobbed and held up aloft by Fulham fans. I thought, 'Bloody hell. This is how much the game affects people's lives.'

From me being on the terraces as a kid, I never saw that side of things. It was a lot to take in. That itself was wealth and I had to manage it, but young players of today have much more of that to deal with. Yes, you want to be in that position these days, but you're going to get people wrapped around you who just want money, whereas we had people wrapped around us who just wanted love. Money can't buy you love.

As a family, I couldn't have asked for better support. From my first day in first team football at Fulham, my mum and dad, uncles, aunts, cousins and friends all came to support me, which was a group of between 20-30 at each match cheering me on. However, that also left me a problem of sourcing tickets as you only got a few comps. What I ended up doing from that season onwards was going around fishing for anybody who didn't want theirs and then give them to my family. If it was a big game and my allocation didn't cover everyone who wanted to go, everyone would split the costs of the tickets between them all to make it fair. They used to joke that it wasn't the Riverside Stand, it was the Tony Gale Stand. That was our Saturday day out and we wouldn't leave Craven Cottage until about 8pm.

I was part of a great Fulham team back then. Up in midfield there was me, Terry Bullivant, John Margerrison and later on Richard Money and Brian Greenaway. At the time, Bobby Campbell was getting a lot of older players out and new ones coming through. After Mooro and Marshy had left, Bestie was left behind and it was like a changing of the guards. I was lucky to play eight games in midfield alongside Bestie, which was incredible. He'd always say, 'If you're in trouble, gimme the ball.' That was also my brief from Bobby Campbell. 'Keep giving it to Bestie. Give him as much as the ball as you can,' which when you have a talent like that, made total sense. The problem was, when you gave the ball to Bestie he became like a magnet because you couldn't mark him one on one. Two or three players would get around him and when that happened, he'd give you the ball straight back, which gave you those vital couple of yards to be free from your markers.

I can always remember people giving him verbals on the pitch and him proper giving it back to them. In that Palace game, there was a sickening incident where centre-back Ian Evans broke his leg following a tackle from Bestie. It wasn't a particularly good challenge, but he always went in like that because he was the victim of many challenges like that himself.

Scoring against Hull City at home on 19 November 1977 was memorable for a couple of reasons, one of them being it was my 18th birthday. It was a dipping volley and that made me the youngest scorer at Fulham at the time. I was playing against the legend Billy Bremner in midfield who had all the experience in the world and when I scored, he came over and said, 'Great goal son, and happy birthday.' He must have read the programme before the game, otherwise I've no idea how he would have known it was my birthday.

In February 1978 we signed Gordon Davies, who went on to become Fulham's highest ever goalscorer, clocking up 178. I got on well with Gordon, but he never bought a drink! His nickname was, 'While you're there,' because every time you'd sneak up to the bar he'd be behind you and say, 'While you're there, can you get us...' That's an ongoing joke between me, Gordon and Robert Wilson, even 45 years later. Any time we can chuck it in conversation, we'll do it.

When Gordon arrived, his boots looked two sizes too big for him and he had this little tash. His clothes to this day still ain't the best. When Les Strong and Gordon are doing their ambassadorial roles at Fulham, I'm sure Gordon still wears the same pair of flares he had when he was in his playing days. On a serious note though, Fulham couldn't have made two better choices than them two as ambassadors in terms of what they've done for the club.

Gordon was right footed but could kick with his left and his pace was unbelievable. He was so quick to get off the mark and his variety of goals were something else. I had a great under-standing with Gordon, which was mainly down to eye contact. He may have just taken one step forward, but I knew that he was then going to turn and spin and go the opposite way. I'd flick it with the outside of my foot and curl it into his path, then bang, it was in the net. He'd time those runs superbly, get ahead of the defenders and hardly ever got offside. It's not just about that though, if you can't execute a goal at the end of that, it's not worth anything. Gordon delivered on the lot all the time.

I also respected him because he'd come up from non-league side Merthyr Tydfil and took a massive step up with no previous high level experience. He'd seen Fulham on *The Big Match* on telly a couple of times, but when he arrived he was petrified of training with us, because he didn't think he was as good as the other guys. We soon settled him into the team.

We were trying to get nicknames for Gordon over a period of weeks and nothing seemed to stick. Around this time, *Ivor the Engine* had just started being aired on telly at 5.55pm before the 6pm news and it was about a Welsh steam engine. Someone must have watched it and thought, 'That will do.' Then one day he walked into the training ground and as he was getting a cup of coffee, someone shouted, 'Ivor!' He turned around, because he thought, 'Is there another Welsh person that I don't know of, or maybe they've signed somebody else from Wales?' The lads said, 'That's it!'

Ivor became his name in training, but somehow the support-ers also got wind of it. Whether they thought it was his middle name or a nickname, but either way, he started scoring loads of goals and instead of them chanting, 'There's only one Gordon Davies,' it came out, 'Ivooooor, Ivooooor.' The Fulham fans loved him. All of that from a throwaway comment from us lot.

Another player I'd like to mention from that season is Terry Bullivant, who had been an apprentice a couple of years before me at Fulham and joined the first team in 1974. When I broke into the team in 1976, he was a great help to me, giving me knowledge and letting me bounce ideas off him. Bulli was a good leader and coach, a very good midfielder, a very good striker and passer of the ball, and I was always looking up to him because he was one of the ones who came up through the ranks and I wanted to be up there alongside him.

I was really pleased when Terry went to Aston Villa but was a little bit gutted because I would have liked to have played on with him for a few more years. I only found this out recently, but Villa showed an interest in me when Bulli went over. At the time, there was a lot of clubs watching our games at Fulham and when he got to Villa they put him up at a hotel and after sitting down for breakfast Ron Atkinson walked over and said to him, 'Come and have breakfast with me.' He quizzed him about me, Richard Money and Gordon. I wouldn't have left Fulham at that time, but it was nice to know that someone like Ron Atkinson showed an interest.

We finished 10th that season, I scored eight times in 38 league appearances and I was player of the year. The only person to score more goals than me that season was Johnny Mitchell. Considering I got 24 goals in my entire career, that was a good spell. A number of people who I played with over the years, such as Rodney Marsh, Gordon Davies and Ian Bishop, couldn't understand why I didn't play midfield for my entire career, but I can't complain with how things panned out over the next 15 years.

When I got player of the year, it was a work night and we all stayed in the Riverside Stand, then later that night we all went back to my mum and dad's flat, which included all the stars and a load of mates. You can't buy those experiences or memories and I've been lucky to have a few.

Chapter 6

EN-GER-LAND

'You've got to hold and give
But do it at the right time
You can be slow or fast
But you must get to the line'

– John Barnes and New Order, World in Motion

PEOPLE OFTEN ask me, 'Galey. How come you never played for the England squad?' Fact is, I did, just not for the over 21s! Not sure if my style of football didn't fit or the management didn't like me, but it's not something I like to dwell on. I was however captain for the England Under-18s for the 1977/78 season, which for a 17-year-old kid playing first team football at Fulham was all a bit of a dream, really.

Back then, the UEFA European Under-18 Championships were known by many as The Little World Cup and it was interesting to see how some of the players from that time went on to become massive names in football, but also how many didn't make the cut, either due to ability or injury.

In October 1977, we went out to Gran Canaria to take part in the Torneo Internacional Juvenil 'Copa Del Atlantico,' which roughly translated as the Youth Atlantic Cup. The competition acted as a warm-up for The Little World Cup and we played three games in four days, which was pretty full-on. The first game was on 9 October against Uruguay, at the Estádio Insular, Las Palmas. We had a pretty good squad, with the likes of Chris

Woods in goal and Terry Fenwick at the back, and managed to get a draw, with Jason Seacole scoring for us. The day after we beat Hungary 3-0 and then lost 2-1 to Las Palmas on 12 October in front of 15,000 fans. Thankfully, we'd done enough on goal difference and ended up winning the tournament.

Next day we headed to the airport to fly home. As we're waiting for our flight, I've decided to go for a piss and as I've perched up at the urinal, in walks this old geezer and stands next to me to take a pee. I've looked across and then did a double take and realised, 'Fuck me, it's Bing Crosby.' I didn't say anything to him, I just walked out and said to the lads, 'I've just seen Bing Crosby in the carsey.' They've all said, 'Fuck off.' Next thing Bing walks out and they've all gone silent. The day after he died and two days later I was playing alongside George Best for Fulham against Luton away. You couldn't make it up.

In order to qualify for the UEFA youth tournament in Poland, we had to play in a couple of preliminary matches earlier in the year. We had a few new players on the squad, like Bryan Klug and Vince Hilaire, who certainly made an impact. I'd known Vince from when I was about 14, playing regional football. He lived in East London and his school in Borough, Newham came under Essex, so we met a number of times along the way representing each other's counties. I always got on well with him and we've stayed in touch all these years, but as a kid, I remember Vince being a ducker and diver like George Cole out of *Minder* and was always classily dressed with the best gear. He had the latest shirts with medallions over the top and in the winter days he'd always have a nice sheepskin coat. I remember asking him, 'Where d'ya get that coat from? Love that,' and he said, 'If you come over to East London, I'll sort you out.' Me and my dad went over and Vince took us to some market, which is where I bought my first sheepskin coat. I thought it was the bollocks.

The first leg of the preliminaries was on 8 February 1978 at Selhurst Park against France. I had good memories of playing at Selhurst Park, because a few months earlier on 1 October 1977, we beat Palace 3-2 and I scored the winning goal. I particularly liked the lads at Palace who I grew up with through the school system, like Vince, Jerry Murphy and Billy Gilbert. Even though there was only a thousand people in attendance, the atmosphere was great and we beat France 3-1. Terry Fenwick, Jason Seacole and Vince scored, which was particularly nice for Vince because he was playing for Palace at the time. We drew the next leg 0-0 on 1 March in Paris at the Stade Jean-Bouin which meant we'd qualified for the Little World Cup in Poland.

At the time, Brian Clough had his eye on being England manager and they offered him the England youth manager's job. Ron Greenwood took over as assistant manager of England, but most of the country at the time wanted Cloughie in charge. Taking the England youth job brought him into the fold, which would have made it easier for him to go for the full squad manager's role in the future.

Apparently Cloughie had attended the tournament in Las Palmas, but none of us ever saw him. It was only when we were getting ready to head to Poland a couple of months later that he got us all together at some hotel in Lancaster Gate for a team talk that we actually met him face to face.

There we are at this hotel officially being told that Cloughie was going to take over. Alongside him was Peter Taylor and Ken Burton, who was the youth coach at the time and a really nice bloke. There was a couple of players on the team that had played under Cloughie and they said, 'If he takes over, it will be a nightmare.' When he walked in, we were shitting ourselves.

Cloughie starts his talk, which went something like this 'Well lads. You know what it's like to play for your country. I'm a patriot, so is Peter, so is that man there, Ken Burton.' Then he asked, 'Who's the captain?' I've stuck my hand up and he's said, 'What do you call the manager, young man?' I said, 'Ken.' He says, 'Well, you shouldn't call him Ken. There's no respect. You have to call him Gaffer, Manager or Boss. Got it, lad?' Talk about shitting myself. He's then asked again, 'You're captain of this team?' and I've replied, 'Yes, Mr Clough.' He says, 'Well I like my captains to smile.' I can see all the lads looking at me. It was like one of them films with the gangsters when they have a gun pointing at someone and shout at them to laugh, dance or sing. I was forcing out this uncomfortable smile.

Cloughie finishes his speech, walks out of the hotel and we never saw him again. He never came out to Poland with us and we never saw him in training. Honestly though, we weren't too upset.

★★★★★

OUR LAST game of the season at Fulham was on 29 April 1978 against Bolton, then a few days later, we were off to Poland to play in The Little World Cup. There's no other way to describe our accommodation apart from a total shithole. It was cold, grey, the food was shit, there was nothing to do and we hardly left the hotel, which felt more like a prison camp with the amount of soldiers around. However, we had to keep reminding ourselves that it was not a holiday and that we were there to play football and represent our country.

We had a strong squad going into this competition. In addition to Chris Woods, Terry Fenwick, Vince, Bryan Klug, there was also Steve Burke on the wing, Danny Salman who went on to play for Brentford and Andy Ritchie who had a great career at Man United and Oldham in particular. There was also Clive Allen, who was only 16 at the time and was already a serious talent. I played loads of youth team football against Clive when he was in his early days at QPR and he was already scoring goals for fun back then.

We were in a tough group alongside Turkey, Spain and Poland and knew we couldn't lose in the opening game. First up was Turkey on 5 May 1978 at the Stadion Odry, Wodzisław Śląski in front of 15,000 fans. We drew 1-1 and I scored the goal. Scoring for your country and being captain at the same time was very special, but I wish there was a bit of YouTube footage, because I can't remember the goal.

Two days later we played Spain. Bryan Klug came off and Clive Allen came on and scored the winning goal giving us a 1-0 victory. However, the game wasn't remembered so much for the win, but an injury Bryan suffered from a horrendous tackle. The medical support and treatment wasn't the best where we were staying and that injury put a real downer on the trip for us all. Bryan was a really talented midfield player, but back in those days you couldn't do the rehab people do now to get fit again. He came back and had a good career, but his movements may have been hampered by that old injury.

A couple of days later we were up against Poland. My first impression of the Polish team was, 'Bloody hell. These lads are fit.' It was like a team of bodybuilders or 100-metre sprinters. We played in front of 14,000 people, mainly Polish military, in a small stadium. Some players found the atmosphere was quite intimidating, but I loved it, because it brought out the best in me. It wasn't a pretty game and we ended up getting beaten 2-0 in a very tough, physical encounter. Poland finished third in the competition and the Soviet Union beat Yugoslavia to become champions.

The last time I played for England was on 17 March 1982. We played out in Warsaw, Poland in the European Under-21

Football Championship and they played me out in midfield. There was only a small crowd in attendance, which like last time I'd played in Poland four years before was mainly Polish military, but it didn't matter because we had a good team with the likes of Justin Fashanu, Steve McMahon and Gary Mabbutt. Paul Goddard scored after 10 minutes, they equalised early into the second half and then David Hodgson scored the winner a few minutes before the final whistle.

That was the end of my days playing for England. Great memories, but at this point, my focus was all about the 1978/79 season at Fulham.

Chapter 7

EL CAPITANO

*'We used him as a near post flick-on merchant. I'm sure his
hair helped him, because heading a ball was not in Tony Gale's
vocabulary. If he could bring it down and play from there, he'd do it.
He also had a great right foot, because I can't remember him even
passing five yards with his left. He was like Franz Beckenbauer. I
was astounded that he never got picked for the full England squad.'*
– Gordon Davies

THE 1978/79 season was memorable for a number of reasons, but the biggest highlight was Bobby Campbell making me first team captain at the age of 18. He called me to his office one day and said, 'You're leading the squad, son. You've got to take on the responsibility and believe in yourself and others around you.' My first reaction was 'Bloody hell.' I'd been captain for the Youth England team and Fulham reserves, so I wasn't afraid of the position, but this wasn't just a case of wearing an armband and leading a load of kids. I was in charge of a lot of experienced players and to my knowledge I was Fulham's youngest ever first team captain. At Arsenal, Bobby brought in youngsters at the time like Liam Brady, Frank Stapleton and David O'Leary. He did a similar thing at Fulham and maybe saw me as the one to pin his faith on, for which I'll be eternally grateful.

There were a few firsts that season. I'd passed my driving test and bought a bright canary yellow Ford Capri 1.6 Ghia that had electric windows and a black sunroof, which you had to open with a wind-around handle. At the time we used to train at the Bank of England sports ground in Roehampton which was lovely. The first day I had the Capri I drove to training, proud as punch, came out of the ground and to the right was a dead end. Cars never came from that way, but as I came out and turned left, a car came out from the right and I went into the side of it. Two geezers got out, both police cadets. I shook my head and thought, 'How's your luck?' Insurance job on the first day. I went home and told my dad and being a cab driver he couldn't wait to tell me, 'You soppy bastard! You've always got to look to the right even if it's a dead end.' However, it didn't take long for a bit of role reversal.

One day, I was at Fulham and my dad said to me, 'Me and Andrew are going up for the away game, but we've got to come back for this function later. You can get back to Craven Cottage on the coach, but can we take the Capri?' I said, 'Yeah. No problem.'

On the way back, the big end (connecting rod to the crank-shaft) went. The car was knackered and cost an absolute fortune to repair. I was back at this do in London before them and thought, 'How's that happened? I've been in the dressing room, had a bollocking, come out, come back in a 60-mile an hour coach and my dad's come back in a Capri and he's not here.' He rang me from the motorway and said, 'I've got some news for you son. The car's fucked.' We lost the game, my car was fucked and so was my night. I was glad to get rid of that car.

Thankfully, not everything was a disaster that season. We started off a bit slow and lost the first two, then drew a couple, but on 2 September 1978 we played at West Ham and beat them 1-0. That game was on *The Big Match* and I played against Trevor Brooking, Alan Devonshire, Billy Bonds (Bonzo) in midfield and up front was a player for them called Bryan 'Pop' Robson, who was a terrific goalscorer, but we kept him quiet. When we were coming down Green Street on the coach, we didn't get any stick or anything like that, but the whole place was heaving and the energy around the ground was on fire. I actually thought, 'I wouldn't mind playing for this club.' The West Ham fans were incredible that day and we were a little bit fortunate to hold on, but they still stuck by their team, and I thought, 'That don't happen much.'

One team however we did struggle against that season was Brighton, losing 3-0 away and 1-0 at home. Their old pitch at the Goldstone Ground no longer exists, which is a real shame as it was on the coast and you had seagulls constantly flying over. That was one of those lovely old-school picturesque grounds that had loads of history and was loved by the locals but has kind of been lost over time. Since then they've changed grounds twice and moved to the Withdean Stadium and then to a lovely ground down the road at the AMEX in Falmer. However, if you talk to Brighton fans, for those who remember, they'll always favour the Goldstone.

Funnily enough, Alan Mullery, who was at Fulham just prior to me coming, tried to sign me for Brighton because he wanted me to play alongside Mark Lawrenson. They wanted to sign me for £600,000 which was a lot of money at the time, but Fulham were demanding £800,000. Liverpool also tried to sign me, in a joint bid for myself and Richard Money for what was a great team at the time. Bobby Campbell got us both in the office and said, 'I'm selling you,' pointing to Richard, 'But I ain't selling you,' as he looked at me. I wasn't bothered at the time and I'd have backed myself if I'd have gone to either team, but now it's a case of what might have been. There was also a bit of international interest. At the time I used to read the papers every Sunday and Bobby told me that Bayer Leverkusen and a few other German clubs had been enquiring about me. I was young, so my answer would have been 'Nein danke' – no thanks. The thing is, my style of football probably suited the teams abroad more than it did in England, but we'll never know either way.

On 18 November 1978, we lost 5-3 at Burnley. That was always a horrible place for us to go and that's nothing against Burnley, but I don't think I've ever played there and it wasn't pissing down with rain. I do however remember travelling up in my first season and Mike Summerbee, one of Bobby Moore's best pals, was playing on the right wing for them and Bobby Campbell said to me, 'Watch that man's movement. Watch how good he is.' Mike Summerbee was a great forward who played about 400 games for Man City and was a massive influence in that team winning the League, FA and UEFA Cups between 1968-70, so I guess that was one positive to take from a Burnley trip.

Going into 1979, we played Man United in the FA Cup, but I was injured for the first game in January, which we drew at Craven Cottage. However, when we played at Old Trafford in February, we lost 1-0 from a deflection off my arse which gave Jimmy Greenhoff the goal. Not a great result, but being captain at 18 at Old Trafford was unbelievable. You can understand why they call it the Theatre of Dreams.

In the final 19 games, we only won three, lost eight and drew eight, which was a great learning curve for the young players who had just come into the team. At the beginning everyone was fresh, but that's when the going gets tough and the tough really do get going. We finished 10th again, but it was obvious that we couldn't sustain that level of losses and draws going into the new season.

We may not have finished as strong as we hoped in the league, but I had some great memories to take away that season off the pitch. At the time flares, sideburns and big haircuts were all in, while punk was also very popular. Towards the end of 1978, a couple of blokes who were big Fulham fans contacted us and asked us about doing a record up at a recording studio. Most teams do it if they get to a cup final like Fulham when they got to the '75 Cup final and did *Viva El Fulham*, but this was for no other reason than having a bit of a laugh.

We were called The Fulham Furies and we did a punk cover version of *These Boots Are Made For Walkin'*, which was originally by Nancy Sinatra. We all went to the recording studio in Soho near Ronnie Scott's and the producer Mike Berry said to us, 'The best way to do this lads, is to have a good drink and then fucking belt it out.' That's exactly what we did. There we were singing *These Boots Are Made For Walkin'* but shouting it out almost like we were on the terraces. I think the only people who actually enjoyed listening to that track was us.

These were good times and a nice change of scene, however, my football career was also about to go through a number of changes – most of which I didn't see coming.

Chapter 8

THE DROP

'Way down like a tidal wave
Way down where the fires blaze
Way down, down'
– Elvis Presley

THE FIRST game of the season was on 18 August 1979 at St Andrew's, Birmingham. It was a baking hot day and we were 3-0 down at half-time, but it could have easily been 6-0. There we were in the changing room and mugs of tea were flying up in the air as Bobby Campbell was reading us the riot act. 'You need to go out there and play for pride now. You're fucking rubbish, the lot of ya. You've all let me down, you've let your families down and I'll probably get the sack after this game.' Everything he could think of came out. The bell was going for us to come out for the second half and he's not even talked about tactical changes or any of that. It was as if it was the end of the game. Just before we went out, he shouts, 'There's two thousand people behind that goal supporting us. Come on. Just fucking go out there and win the second half.' Well, we came back and won the game 4-3 and Gordon Davies got a hat-trick. That's the most memorable first game of any season I've played in.

Bobby Campbell was more than just a manager, he was a mentor in life. At the age of 19 I was getting £60 a week, then when it quickly went up to £150, Bobby turned up at my mum and dad's and said, 'What's he doing with his money?' I said,

'I'm saving it, Bob.' He replies, 'Listen. You're buying a fucking house. I'm gonna take you to look for one today.' Off we went.

As we leave my parents flat he says, 'Where do you wanna live?' I said, 'I don't know. I've always lived in Pimlico.' He said, 'No, no. You're not living there, you've got to move out a bit.' At the time, all my uncles lived in Surrey on the Hurst Park estate in East Molesey and when I mentioned that he said, 'Right. We're buying a house there and we'll sort the mortgage out for you. We'll give you a loan for the deposit and you'll repay that through your wages. Then you'll sort the mortgage out and you stick your money away.' Job done. I bought my first house for £29,850 and I wasn't even living in it. I ended up renting it out to another player, who Bobby signed later on called Roger Brown.

My dad didn't see the point in buying a place as he was quite happy renting from the council. Then, shortly after I bought mine Margaret Thatcher introduced the 'Right to Buy' scheme. This basically let council tenants buy the properties they lived in for an unbelievable deal from the local council. My dad was a London taxi driver and I said, 'You should think about doing that.' He replied, 'No. I ain't buying a flat because it's Thatcher's scheme. I'm a Labour Party man. I pay me taxes,' and all that. I tried to explain to him that a mortgage would be cheaper than the rent he was paying, but he didn't want to know. So I said, 'I tell you what. I'll do this. I'll buy the flat and you pay me the rent.' I was blagging it though, because I couldn't afford to buy it. He said, 'You ain't buying me anything and I ain't paying you any fucking rent.' Shortly after he bought the flat for £12,000 and my mum's still living in it at the time of writing.

As a professional footballer, you had to watch how you behaved in public. It's not as bad as these days, where everyone has cameras on their phones, but you did need to be aware that journalists would often be out and about and looking for something to write about. For me personally, I had eyes on me all the time. Most of my family were taxi drivers and the ones that weren't, like my uncle Terry, worked at Covent Garden Market. This meant I had family all over London every day. My dad would say stuff like, 'What were you doing up in Oxford Street yesterday about 3pm?' and I'd say, 'How did you know I was there?' He'd say, 'I spoke to George at the cab shelter and he said you were walking up there with so and so.' You couldn't get away with anything. Big brother didn't exist, it was just eyes looking at you. That was old-school CCTV.

However, as a young man, there's no way I wasn't going to have a bit of fun and get out. When I was 17, the coach driver used to occasionally drop us off at the Golden Gloves on our way back from away games, which was down the Fulham Palace Road, at the Hammersmith end. The pub was owned by Terry Mancini, who was coming to the end of his playing career in football at this point. As 17-year-olds, we weren't supposed to be in there, but the senior players used to look after us and say, 'Just sit in the corner and behave yourselves.' Funnily enough, a few years down the line, Malcolm Macdonald brought Terry in alongside Ray Harford to be our third coach at Fulham. His nickname was Henry, after Henry Mancini, the music composer, and he was a great addition to the coaching staff. It was like another three amigos, who got on really well together.

Then there was a drinking club up in Tottenham Court Road which operated after hours and was owned by Ronnie Knight, who was married to Barbara Windsor at the time. Ray Evans, who was a top lad and one of our senior pros, knew Ronnie quite well and on this one occasion, Ray took me, Perry, Tony Mahoney and a couple of the pros to Ronnie's for a Christmas drink. There we were, three good looking lads in our late teens playing as young pros and Ray said to us, 'Sit yourself in the corner. Half a lager only and if any of these birds look at ya, don't look at 'em back.' In other words, you might get done. We hardly moved all night.

On Sundays, Andrew would come round and play cards with me and my parents, then after losing pretty much every hand we'd walk down the King's Road about 7pm or get the No.11 bus to the Bird's Nest pub, right next to Chelsea town hall and sometimes meet up with a few other mates, like Perry. The Bird's Nest had great live music and it was around that era of Rose Royce and Carwash. I can remember some of my friends doing choreographed dance moves picking handkerchiefs up off the floor with their mouth and all that game, to impress the ladies. As we started to go more regularly, the bouncers recognised me through football, got to know us and would let us in for nothing, which was very nice of them. The Bird's Nest used to close at 10.30pm on a Sunday and sometimes on the way home we'd go to a place called The Chelsea Kitchen, to have a spaghetti bolognese and half of lager. That became our routine on Sundays for about three or four years. Other places we used to drink included The Eight Bells pub by Putney Bridge, which was somewhere we'd go for a quick one after training and The Crabtree in Hammersmith.

People have often asked me if I ever got involved in the drug scene and the answer is no. I've never even touched a cigarette in my life. My dad was on and off with smoking, whereas my mum was always the smoker and normally you'd get your smoking habit from your parents, but thankfully I never did. I wished I had never touched a drink, but I do like a glass of wine and a vodka and tonic!

As I got older I realised some players were doing drugs, but the first time I came across it was outside of a football environment. I was out with one of my cousins having a drink and all of a sudden he's jumping around dancing. I thought, 'What's he been drinking?' but it wasn't that, he'd taken one of them ecstasy tablets. I said to him, 'Don't you ever put that shit near me.' I think the problem with a lot of people who do it to excess is admitting they have a problem. The best thing to do is attend those meetings and be open about it. It's the only way to get help. I feel sorry for the young-uns now because they've been born into this culture.

*****

BY 20 October 1979, we'd played 12 league games, two League Cup games and only won three of the 14. Things weren't going great. Our next game was on 23 October, but it was a friendly against Merthyr Tydfil. Here's how that game came about. When Gordon Davies signed for Fulham from Merthyr, part of his agreement was that Fulham would come down Merthyr's ground and have a game to raise money to pay for their floodlights. Bobby Campbell said, 'Fine. No problem.'

Gordon was already down in Merthyr in the changing rooms waiting for the Fulham coach to arrive. Everyone was out there looking for autographs as our coach pulled up, while Gordon was sitting there chatting to the Merthyr physio. As we started to come in, the physio says to Gordon, 'I'll leave you now. See you after the game.' As he's walking out, the first person he saw was me as I'm having some banter with Gordon. 'Bloody hell, Ivor. Did you used to play at this shithole?' He said, 'Cheers Galey! You've had a good journey down then?' The physio overheard that, but took it all very literally.

The physio went to the Merthyr changing room and said, 'You'll never guess what that big lump just said. He's just called this place a shithole.' The Merthyr captain, Doug Rosser, who was an ex-Swansea player, had four missing teeth at the front and used to take his teeth out before the game. He was a bit like

Joe Jordan but looked a lot fiercer. As he's coming down the line, he stopped next to me and smiled with the four teeth missing and he said, 'You think this place is a shithole? Just wait for the first tackle.' I think he was just trying to put the frighteners on, but it was hard to kick me because they never had the ball. Anyway, that night we won 4-2 and Gordon scored a hat-trick. Not sure how popular he was with his hometown after that, but over the years I ended up going back a few times for functions and got a great reception from them!

After many of my games, my dad would pick me up and it was like I'd get a second team briefing. There's one particular game at Luton on 16 February 1980 that comes to mind and Andrew Dickie was also there. In black cabs, there's the glass division between the driver and the passengers. In my dad's cab he used to remove the piece of wood so the glass partition would go all the way back and then he'd do an analysis of the game, of where I went wrong and where I could improve. It was like 'The Gospel According to Peter.' Considering my dad wasn't a professional player or coach, it was actually good feedback and he knew what he was talking about. We lost that game against Luton 4-0 and the only memorable thing was that it was Strongie's 300th appearance for Fulham.

It almost didn't make sense that season why we performed so badly, because we had some really good players and there was also a new addition to the team, a good mate of mine, Robert Wilson – you might remember his dad used to sort us out with train tickets at Putney train station. I'm a couple of years older than Rob and when he joined Fulham at 14 we played together in the youth team, while I was also playing in the first team. Rob was born in Fulham, went to school at St Edmund's, which was in the Hammersmith and Fulham Borough and was a Fulham fan through and through.

I went on to develop a personal friendship with Rob and his family and we were at each other's houses all the time. He signed as an apprentice in June '77, got into the first team at 18 and we ended up playing alongside each other for five seasons. He used to say that I had a bit of a turtle neck in terms of heading the ball, because I'd pull my neck in when the ball came my way. I would feint to head the ball a lot, but then I'd bring it down to my chest and play the ball out. That said, I headed the ball so many times during practice, especially when it was wet and the balls back then weighed a ton. They were nothing like the ones prior to us, the laced up leather ones and all that, but those balls on wet, muddy days were still like rocks.

Looking back, you can understand why there's so many players who have dementia as a result of heading balls, because heading is a very natural part of the game. One of the best headers of the ball I've played with attacking wise was Alan Shearer, who could shape his headers. If a ball was curling one way, he'd go against the spin, so he could get curl on them. He also had that lovely attribute, although he wasn't the biggest guy, that he could hang. He'd jump before you, then as you elevate, like a lineout in rugby he'd get the elevation from you.

Teddy Sheringham was also good at that. Defending-wise, Roger Brown at Fulham was great with his head at clearing, Colin Hendry at Blackburn and Alvin Martin at West Ham. Naturally aggressive footballers who could really attack a ball, although, as defenders we'd be more open to injuries through-out the season and back then, if you got a career-threaten-ing injury, your salary wasn't big enough to see you through the rest of your life. We all put money into pensions, which later on in life you think, 'I probably should have just bought a house,' or something like that, because pensions were really not that great in terms of insurance, unlike perhaps today. I saw quite a few players retire and then struggle financially through injuries, which was very sad.

I had a dodgy hamstring during that '79/80 season and I used to have cortisone injections, which I don't think are great for you. If you have an injury and you put a cortisone injection into play, then you can't feel the pain when you're playing, but after about 60 or 70 minutes it starts hurting again. So actually, you're doing more damage to that injury by playing on it. Having said that, in defence of the players back then, they were playing through small injuries and strains all the time.

Back to Robert Wilson. Rob made his debut at Blackburn on 8 January 1980 during an FA Cup game. Howard Kendall was player-manager at Blackburn and Bobby Campbell brought Rob in to man-mark Howard and stop him playing the ball. He was an 18-year-old kid making his debut, so before the game me, Gordon and Strongie told him, 'Don't be nervous. Get out there and enjoy yourself. Just don't fuck it up though!' Rob did well and we drew the game 1-1, but unfortunately we lost 1-0 to Blackburn at home the week after.

Another new addition to the team was Ray Lewington, who played his first game in March 1980. Ray was three years older than me and had played for Chelsea for four seasons, then a split season between the Vancouver Whitecaps and Wimbledon, before he came to Fulham. He was a solid midfielder who was just over five feet tall and was a brilliant addition to the team. Great player, really nice bloke and someone I would talk football with away from the team, just to bounce ideas off. You could already tell at that stage he was going to make a great coach and manager.

We nicknamed Ray 'Little Legs' and shortly after he joined, whenever we had our pre-match meals, especially at away matches, me and Strongie would go flying out the coach looking for a kids highchair to put around the dinner table. Then, when we got to our hotel rooms on a Friday, Ray Lew and Roger Brown, who was 6ft 4 and about a foot taller than him, would be sharing a room with Ray. I'd go to reception and ask them to take out one bed and put in a cot and the moment they got to the room, you'd hear Ray Lew shout, 'Gaaaaleey!' Even now, over 40 years later, we still look for a highchair at the place we meet and if they haven't got one, we ask them to put extra cushions on the seat.

Unfortunately, despite having some great banter with the players, on the football front, things were terrible. Being the captain of a team which finished 20th in the 1979/80 season, with only 29 points and got relegated into Division Three, wasn't great. There were a lot of problems that season with the chairman Ernie Clay and uncertainty about whether the club was going to be sold for redevelopments and things like that. You kind of felt that tension was building up behind the scenes on a number of fronts. Going into the 1980/81 season, all eyes were on Fulham's board, manager, players and myself especially.

Chapter 9

A SUPER KICK UP THE ARSE

'He had a big build and an ability that was sheer class, but with everything that had gone on prior to me being there, as young as he was, he seemed to have lost his way. He was a very intelligent lad, particularly footballing wise and I had to find a way to knock him out of this apathetic mood he was in. He wasn't doing it purposely, it was just a reflection of how the club was at the time.'

– Malcolm Macdonald

DIVISION THREE football was an eye opener. Everything from the shithole dressing rooms, through to there being a fans' favourite at each stadium. For example, at Exeter it was Tony Kellow, who was their greatest scorer and the fans went mad the second he touched the ball. Being in Division Three also helped me as a pundit years later when I was able to talk about every single ground over the four divisions, because I'd played at almost every one of them. Some of the teams would go down to the fourth division and as a result, we'd had the opportunity to experience their stadium. When I finished, I think there was only four stadiums I hadn't played at.

The first game of the season was at Rotherham on 16 August 1980. At the time we had a number of injuries, so Bobby thought I had the ability to turn my hand to playing up front and made me centre-forward, which added to my development curve. We managed to get a 1-1 draw and then, a couple of months later, I played up front again against Plymouth and had the shit kicked out of me by their two defenders. We lost that one 2-1.

Everyone thought that we'd bounce back quickly from relegation and get out of Division Three in one season, but unfortunately, it wasn't meant to be. In the first 10 games we won four, lost three and drew three, which was not a disaster, but we should have been doing better. Then we hit a really bad stretch of six losses on the bounce, including a 4-0 defeat against Oxford United at home on 19 October 1980. That's when the board decided to give Bobby Campbell the sack.

Bobby was a great manager and I'd have kept him on. What he achieved overall was brilliant, but in the short term we were struggling and that's where the board had to make that decision. This was my first experience of a changeover of managers in professional football and a new era for Fulham. Nobody knew what the future held.

* * * * *

MALCOLM 'SUPERMAC' Macdonald came to Fulham as a commercial manager when Bobby was there, but we kind of thought there was something in the air. The chairman, Ernie Clay, was always looking for an angle to develop the football ground. Unfortunately, it never quite happened when he was there, but I think it turned out well because they remained at the same ground and had some really good owners over the years. Anyway, Malcolm was a commercial man in the background and I'd kind of met him but didn't know him that well. He was born in Fulham and played in the first team when he was 18 for a year, before going to Luton for a couple of years and then making his name at Newcastle. In football, Malcolm was a superstar in his own right with what he'd achieved and probably would have played for a few more years if it wasn't for injuries. He was only 29 when he stopped playing football and the year after he was working at Fulham.

At the time there was a physiotherapist called Ron Woolnough and a former player called Ted Drake, who famously played at Arsenal for many years and managed Chelsea for nine seasons, and they were brought in temporarily before Malcolm Macdonald came into power. My form hadn't dipped and I wasn't left out of the team, but Ron decided to give the captaincy to an experienced player, Dave Clement, who was a great pro and was part of the best QPR team ever, not to mention also being capped for England. I didn't have any qualms about Dave doing it, but when he left after a couple of weeks and Malcolm decided to change the captaincy again, I thought I'd be back in my old position.

One of my best friends in football is Les Strong, who's seven years older than me and made about 430 appearances for Fulham from 1972 to 1983. These days, Les calls me Fatty and I call him Big Nose. As I've got older, I've developed a belly and every time we go out, Les will say, 'Can I sign that ball under your shirt?' and I'll say, 'Can I sign that thing on the end of your face?' It's all affectionate. Anyway, Malc approached Strongie to become captain and it put him in an awkward position. Les said, 'I couldn't possibly take the captaincy from Tony, because I know his mum and dad, his sister, we live close to each other and we go to training together every morning. I also think you're taking the captaincy off one of our best players. It's not right.' Malc replies. 'Les, I know Ron took the captaincy off Tony but I don't want to give it back to him, because I want him to play his football. We all know Galey's going to be a great player without a shadow of a doubt, but I think he's too young to be captain and

I don't want that to affect his confidence long term. I want you to be my captain.' Les didn't budge.

Malcolm then says, 'Listen, I want to make a change and if you don't take it, I'll give it to someone else.' Strongie replied, 'It's not a good idea. Leave it as it is. You're just disrupting things.' Malc then said, 'I'll give you an extra £100.' Strongie replied in a heartbeat, 'I'll have it!' So much for feeling awkward.

Getting that captaincy kept Strongie in the game for a while longer. He played left-back, I played left centre-back and Brian Greenaway, who was a year older than me, played in front of Strongie. Les would be directing us around and me and Greeners would be thinking, 'We're doing all the work here?' At the end of the season, Strongie went up to Greeners and said, 'Brian. You and Galey have been a revelation. You've added four years to my career.' Greeners turned around and went, 'Yeah, but you took six off mine though!'

Malcolm wasn't a coach, more of a man-manager, which he was very good at. When he first came to Fulham, we were fifth bottom of Division Three and he felt we were a team who were depressed and struggling to lift ourselves. His immediate plan was to get us to win points and pull us away from the relegation zone. One of the first things he did was getting a coach from Arsenal, Roger Thompson, who had a good sense of humour. Very serious football person but had a real funny side to him.

However, the turning point was when Roger Thompson left and Malcolm brought in Ray Harford as his assistant. Ray had vision that was unbelievable back then and was instrumental in introducing those ideas. We still had some very good senior pros like Peter O'Sullivan, Strongie, Ray Lewington and Roger Brown, but when he successfully combined them with all these youngsters like Gordon Davies, Dean Coney, Jeff Hopkins, Sean

O'Driscoll and Robert Wilson, that eventually turned out to be key to getting us promoted back up to Division Two.

As Ray Harford was training the team, Malcolm was moulding it. Ray was an informal pioneer of the diamond formation which certainly benefited Rob Wilson because he was an attacking midfield player who got in the box in literally every attack. Therefore, if you had the likes of Gordon Davies, Dean Coney getting in the box and then Robert, you had three in there with two midfield players outside. However, Malcolm also wanted to maximise the talent of the current players in the squad and that's when he decided to give me 'that' talk.

A couple of months after being dropped as captain, Malcolm calls me into his office. He said, 'I'm going to talk very bluntly with you.' After speaking for a while he put a list he'd written down in front of me. I said, 'What's this?' He said, 'That's the list of all the things you are not doing.' He told me I couldn't head the ball, I couldn't run, I ain't got a left foot and the list went on. I always had plenty to say for myself and said, 'I may as well retire now.' He said, 'I'm not saying you've got to start doing them, but you've got such wonderful attributes to become a top player, but you're not showing it. I'm going to leave you out of the side for the cup game against Charlton this Saturday and what I'd like you to do this weekend is go home and write down all of your strengths and weaknesses.'

I left that room shaking my head and was really disappointed about being left out of the side, but perhaps more embarrassed. It was the first time I'd been dropped for a game in my life. When I sat down I thought, 'You could lose a lot here,' because if that person who replaced me had a good game I might not get back in. Fortunately for me, they lost against Charlton at home and the geezer who replaced me didn't have a great game.

When I came in on the Monday, Malc asked, 'What happened

at the weekend?' I said, 'I've written you a list,' and passed it to him. He said, 'I think you're being fairly honest about yourself, which is a good thing and a good start.' He then said, 'I've also written a list.' I thought, 'Here we fucking go again,' but said, 'Oh yeah. What's that?' He gave me a list of five things and said, 'They are your strengths. You're a good passer of the ball, good positionally, you're brave on the ball, you read the game well and you're decent in the air. Make those stronger than anything else and you'll be a great player. You've got them within you, but you're faffing about with stuff you shouldn't get bothered with on the pitch and in training. Play to your strengths.' My first thoughts were, 'He's talking bollocks,' but it worked.

Malcolm put me straight back in the side next match and I had a great game. Between the coaching of Ray Harford and the man-management of Malcolm, when Roger Thompson visited back a few months after leaving, he watched a game and said to Malcolm, 'Fuck me. What have you done to Tony? He looks some player now.' Malc said, 'I just had him in the office and told him to take a good look at himself.' Roger came up to me and said, 'Malcolm was right. You had it, but just needed to get it back.' I was doing it but maybe had a six-month period where I took my foot off the gas. Malc's talk gave me a kick up the arse, which we all need now and again.

* * * * *

DESPITE LOSING the captaincy and being dropped from a game, we had some of the biggest laughs and best football under Malcolm, mainly because he gave us a bit more freedom compared to most managers at the time. In all fairness though, we did drive Malcolm and his management team round the bend with our pranks.

Malc and his assistant George Armstrong were always late for the team talk on a Friday and on one occasion, me and Strongie had a word with the team. 'When Malc and George walk in, we'll tell them we've done the team talk and then we'll all get up and walk out.' Malcolm's walked in and says, 'Sorry I'm late,' and me and Strongie have turned to the lads and said, 'OK boys, that's it for the day. See you tomorrow. Arrive at the ground at 2pm.' Malcolm said, 'What are you doing?' I've said, 'We couldn't wait any longer Malc, so we've done the team talk for you.' Malc's said, 'No, no,' as all the players got up and walked out of the changing room. Then 20 seconds later we've all walked back in as they're laughing and swearing at us.

Then when they finally did get the team talk up and running, we had the next one lined up. We used to have a magnetic board which Malcolm would show us the team formations and tactics. Me and Strongie used to peel off the magnetic bits at the back of these black and white discs, so every time he put one up, it fell on the floor. We said to the players beforehand, 'Every time one falls on the floor, we'll all shout, 'Hooray!'' After a couple, Malcolm looked our way and said, 'Strongie! Galey! I know it's you!' He didn't mind though, because everybody got a good laugh and that helped to relax the dressing room and made a good atmosphere.

Malcolm wasn't bad at dishing it back though. In fact, Malcolm and Roger worked quite a bit on piss-taking in those early weeks, just to get the spirits up. Here's an example. Up at the training ground in Roehampton we would have a five-a-side game in the session and the coaches would vote for who was the worst player. Then after the session we'd drive back to Craven Cottage and we would stop on the Putney side of Putney Bridge. The player who was voted the worst had to get out and run over the bridge in a yellow jersey with everybody hanging out the windows jeering, swearing and taking the piss.

My favourite wind-ups involved our coach driver, Alan Hooker, who was this lovely little geezer with an old private rickety coach who was also friends with Malcolm from his Arsenal days. One day he asked me and Strongie, 'Can I come to the team talk?' We said, 'Yeah, alright. Just sit at the back and keep quiet.' Malcolm's come in and he's started saying, 'Today we are playing,' then he's looked up and seen the coach driver. He's carried on taking the team talk and after he's said, 'Let's go to the coach downstairs. Galey, Strongie, stay behind.' He knew it was us two and said, 'What the fuck is the coach driver doing in our team talk?' I said, 'Well, he's a nice lad and just wanted to listen.' He's said, 'That's ridiculous. I don't want to see him in the talk again. That's very unprofessional.'

Next away match, Alan's asked us, 'Can I come to the team talk?' We've said, 'The problem is Al, Malcolm's got the right hump with it. I tell you what we'll do. How about if you take your shoes off and sit in the bath, pull the curtain and we'll leave the door open, so you can listen to it?' He's said, 'Alright.'

Alan takes his shoes off, goes in the bath, pulls the curtains and me and Strongie took his shoes and put them by the curtains, so his shoes were poking out the bottom. Malcolm's walked in and you could see him looking around to see if Alan was there. Once he was happy Alan wasn't in the room, he started the talk. As he gets going, me and Strongie were nodding our heads towards the pair of shoes. Malc's still talking away, so we keep nodding down to look at the shoes and he's spotted them. He's run over to us and said, 'This is ridiculous. Strongie, Galey, you're in trouble.' He's gone over to the curtains, whipped them back ready to give the coach driver a right mouthful and there was just the pair of shoes. All the players were falling about laughing.

That first year with Malcolm we got back to 13th after nearing relegation at Christmas, but the next season is when it all took off.

Chapter 10

RISING UP

'So many times it happens too fast
You change your passion for glory
Don't lose your grip on the dreams of the past
You must fight just to keep them alive'
– Survivor, Eye Of The Tiger

THE OPENING game of the 1981/82 season was at Brentford. They were a good team and had some good young players like Chris Kamara and Terry Hurlock but also some greats who were coming to the end of their career such as Ron 'Chopper' Harris and Stan Bowles. Chopper was a really good player who came with a hardman reputation but was one of my heroes from the 1970 Cup final. Whoever was up front with him had their hands full, because you could get away with a little bit then and Chopper got away with a lot. I'd played against him when he was at Chelsea in the late '70s and even at this point at Brentford he was still hard as nails, even though he was coming to the end of his career. He was about 15 years older than me and was very respectful on the pitch, and since retiring I've seen him around over the years and he's actually a really nice man.

From coming to terms with relegation the previous season, we were now having such a good run and winning a lot of games in Division Three. As a result we tended to be on *The Big Match* quite a lot. Brian Moore was on the programme and I remember thinking, 'He really does his research.' Brian used to come regularly to the grounds, as did Martin Tyler and they'd come to watch the players train on a Friday. What an absolutely lovely gentleman Brian was, but also a great commentator. He didn't say too much, didn't say too little and knew exactly when to let the game breathe on air.

Going into the last game of the season, we'd only lost 10 games in the league and won 22. The last game against Lincoln at home was a proper nail-biter. If they won, they got promoted, if we drew or won, we'd go up. The Lincoln game should have been played in January but got called off because of bad weather and that's why we didn't end up playing until 18 May, but nobody knew it would end up being a decider.

That night, it was packed and we had a few young players who struggled with the occasion. Lincoln went down to 10 men because defender Steve Thompson got a second yellow after fouling Dean Coney, then shortly after I took a well-rehearsed free-kick and Roger Brown scored with a great header even though he had a cut eye with blood streaming down his face. Lincoln threw everything they had at us and with 20 minutes to go, Dave Carr scored the equaliser. That gave us the fright of our lives, because, had they scored one more, they would have gone up and we would have remained in Division Three for another season. Thankfully we made it to the final whistle, at which point the Fulham fans went absolutely nuts. Roger was known for scoring goals from corners and free-kicks, but after that goal which got us up to Division Two, he ended up being a bit of a talisman and cult hero with Fulham fans for the rest of his career there. We needed a point to go up in third position and didn't play that well, but who cared. We were out of Division Three.

One week after the Lincoln game, Strongie had his testimonial match after 10 years of serving at Fulham. We played in front of 7,000 people, against an England representative side who were going away to the World Cup, which was virtually the full team. We ended up losing 3-0, with Paul Mariner scoring two and Bryan Robson the other, but it was such a great day and a very fitting testimonial for my big nose mate.

When you have a testimonial, it's not just a match, it's a whole year of events. As a result, you need to try and get auction and raffle prizes to generate a few extra quid. Les asked Malcolm if he had anything to auction and he said, 'I gave all my shirts away and you can't have my caps. Hold on though, I've got the boots I played with against Cyprus if that's any good?' Strongie said, 'Lovely! Cheers, Malc.'

The Cyprus game Malcolm was referring to was when England beat them in April 1975 and he scored all five goals. So there we are in some flash hotel up town in London and these boots went for about a grand, which was an absolute fortune at that time. About two weeks later on a Saturday, me and Strongie pulled up down some side street near Craven Cottage and then got out of the car to head to the game. Next thing we hear some geezer shout out, 'Strongie! Galey! I've got a bone to pick with you.' It turns out it was the same geezer that bought Malc's boots. Strongie's walked over and this bloke's gone, 'Them boots you gave me that Malcolm Macdonald scored all five goals against Cyprus with.' Strongie went, 'Yeah.' This guy's said, 'I've looked at the video and he scored all five goals with his head!' It was true. It was the only game someone had scored all five goals with their head. Les said, 'Well, I couldn't give you his fucking head, could I?' We all burst out laughing.

Topping off a great season, I got married to my childhood sweetheart Lyndsey in Westminster Cathedral, which is the Wembley of churches. Sounds a bit extravagant, but it was our local parish and it's also where both our parents got married, not to mention where our kids would also eventually get christened. It was a big local wedding with all our friends and family and my best man was my cousin, Steven Collins. We had the reception over at Nine Elms in Vauxhall, above the flower market where a lot of my family worked and even the priest, Father Pat Brown came along after the ceremony for a couple.

Nail-biting end to the season, married and promotion. Surely the next season would be a quiet one?

Chapter 11

DEMOLITION DERBY

'We were just one game away from maybe being in the top division and then suddenly all we saw was loads of people encroaching on the pitch. In today's football the game would have had to been replayed. We all started to leg it, and as I ran down the tunnel I got rammed by 'The Ram.' I was taken out by the Derby County mascot around my kneecaps.'

– Paul Parker

FROM WESTMINSTER Cathedral to Stormont Castle. The pre-season outing of 1982/83 was a little tour of Ireland, starting up north against Larne FC. We stayed at the Stormont Hotel, opposite Stormont Castle and they took us down on a tour of the Falls Road and the Shankill Road where there were bullet holes in pubs and cafés. Ian Paisley was staying in the same hotel as us because he was doing a conference there and we thought, 'Fucking hell, let's hope a bomb doesn't go off.' You have to remember, this was at the time of The Troubles, so there was a lot of military out there and wherever you went, you had to be really careful.

The night after the game we went to a nightclub and *God Save The Queen* came on and we didn't know we had to stand up. Next thing the bouncers came over shouting, 'Stand up or you'll

79

get chucked out.' It was quite frightening. We also played Cobh Ramblers in the Republic of Ireland and had to go through bandit country at the border. You could see the army laying in the trenches with their rifles by the side of the road and it's probably the best I've ever seen our team behaving on tour.

After two seasons in Division Three, everyone was kind of looking at us as if to say, 'They've made it back up to Division Two, but do they belong here?' Of course we bloody did. We took the season by storm.

We had some great young additions to the squad that year, like Geoff Hopkins, Peter Scott, John Marshall, and also Leroy Rosenior and Paul Parker who had come through Fulham's youth system. There was also Ray Houghton who was 20 and had come from West Ham on a free transfer. Incredibly, Ray was at West Ham for three seasons in the reserves and in his last season he scored 19 goals from midfield, and they released him! That was a tremendous kick up the arse for him, so when he came to Fulham, it was like, 'I will show you that you made a mistake.'

Ray was a sensation who played left-side midfield among a great young team, adding that sprinkling of experience. The first time I met Ray was when Malcolm brought him up to the Cottage to meet the players and he instantly fitted in. He had a great Scottish family who used to come to all his games, however, his mum was Irish which is why he went on to clock up over 70 caps for the Republic of Ireland. Honestly though, he could have played for England, Ireland and Scotland. He was a great player.

Funny fact about Ray. He didn't really drink before he came to Fulham and not long after joining us he came out with all the lads for a few beers. Me and Strongie were sort of in charge of things and we all got up the bar and were having a pint of lager and because he doesn't drink, he ordered a Malibu and pineapple. Who orders a Malibu and pineapple? He got absolutely caned. We said, 'Do you want a couple of umbrellas and some cherries in it?' and he laughed and said, 'No. Just some ice.' We came back from the bar and handed him his drink and he looked at it as if to say, 'What the fuck is this?' Instead of putting ice cubes, we put cheese cubes.

I first met Leroy when he was a 15 or 16-year-old kid and was doing trials to play for Fulham. Leroy was raw, game, put himself about and went in where people didn't want to go on the pitch. However, at the beginning, whenever I passed the ball to him in training, he kept miscontrolling it, whereas 'Dixie' Dean Coney was silky smooth. One session, I passed it to Dixie and he brought it down from his chest and did exactly what he wanted to and I gave Leroy a little wink as if to say, 'That's how you do it.' Leroy finished that session deflated, but he was a trier and you can't help but like anyone that wants to make themselves better. I went up to him and said, 'Look at Dixie and try to copy a little bit of what he does. When I'm on the ball, I'll find you, don't you worry. Just make sure you give me the eye contact and I can see in your eyes what you're going to do.' Technically he was a terrific player, who had a great ability to hang in the air and for me, as a defender passing to a striker, he was always a great target, because he always won it early. It was no surprise that he ended up winning Fulham Young Player of the Season that year.

Paul Parker was young, but you could already see he was going to be a terrific player, which he ended up being. He was small, but very quick and despite being a full-back, he was just as good in a centre-back position, especially when we started to play against the big boys.

The first game of the season was at Rotherham on 28 August

1982 and Emlyn Hughes was player-manager for them, which was a great memory, because he was one of my heroes as a central defender at Liverpool. He took himself off at half-time and then I ended up laying on the equalising goal for Kevin Lock to make it 1-1.

Three weeks later, on 18 September we played at Middlesbrough and won 4-1. Our goalie Gerry Peyton got one of the most horrific injuries I've ever seen. One of the strikers from Middlesbrough accidentally slid into him and his studs hit him on the side of his forehead. I went over to Gerry and he was holding his hand over where the boot had hit him. As he pulled his hand off, the skin flapped out and blood started pissing out like a fountain. He calmly pushed the flap back on, which stopped the blood and he still wanted to carry on, but there was no way he could. We didn't have goalies on the bench, so Kevin Lock had to go in goal.

They talk about goalkeepers being good with their feet now, well, Kevin Lock actually played the game in goal as a sweeper. We were passing it back to Locky and then he'd come dribbling out with the ball and pick out a spare man. Middlesbrough couldn't work it out. Towards the end of the game, Kevin was getting ready for an incoming corner and as he jumped, instead of shouting, 'Keeper's,' he shouted, 'I'm up, Cottagers,' taking the piss out of Middlesbrough. Well, he caught it and you should have seen the look of fury from the Middlesbrough players. That was one of the best games I've ever played in and was the closest I've seen to 'total' football. Their manager, Bobby Murdoch, got the sack straight after the game.

A week later we beat a strong Leeds side 3-2 at home, which had the likes of Frank Worthington, Arthur Graham, Frank and Eddie Gray. What made it better was that it was the main game on *The Big Match* on telly the next day. However, it was the game against Newcastle on 16 October which really got everyone talking about Fulham.

We went up to the hotel on the Friday and loads of Newcastle fans who were staying there, along with all the staff, kept saying, 'Can't wait to see what Kevin Keegan does to you lot tomorrow.' Their manager was Arthur Cox and Newcastle were riding on the crest of a wave.

We all used to meet in a room before the Saturday games and watch a bit of *Football Focus* on the telly together. There we were watching about midday and Malcolm pops up live at St James' Park. Malcolm was idolised up in Newcastle after playing a couple of hundred games there and scoring about 100 goals, but he also loved the attention. There was a lot of media buzz around Fulham's young team and he was asked how he felt being back in Newcastle and he said something like, 'Yeah, I'm really looking forward to the game and hope I get a good welcome.' We're all watching, rolling our eyes. The guy asking the questions said, 'You've only got a team of youngsters and you're playing against the likes of Kevin Keegan and Terry McDermott. How do you think you'll get on?' Malcolm says, 'That doesn't worry us. We'll definitely win the game. I've got every faith in my team.' The guy asks, 'How are you going to deal with Kevin Keegan?' Bearing in mind, I was marking Kevin with Roger Brown. He says, 'That's easy. We'll stop Kevin Keegan's supply line.' He's telling everyone on *Football Focus* our tactics and we're there with our heads in our hands saying, 'What's he doing?!' In Malcolm's defence though, he was getting great publicity for these young players, many who had gone under the radar in the media. It also gave Fulham great publicity, showing that the club was well and truly alive.

When we arrived at St James' Park, Malcolm went out early on the pitch and got a standing ovation from the whole stadium.

However, when we kicked off, all that went out the window. Marking Kevin Keegan was a privilege. He was like a little body-builder, twisting and turning and was kind of the superhero after Malcolm at Newcastle. He wasn't what you'd call a traditional centre-forward, but the way he played that day up front with Imre Varadi was poetry in motion. What an experience to play against one of the top strikers of all time. Admittedly, he was past his best at this point, but he certainly wasn't spent.

We played really well and won the game 4-1. Two of the goals which came from Ray Houghton and Gordon Davies were in the top three of 'Goal of the Season' that year on *Match Of The Day* and one of them won it. In all honesty, 4-1 didn't flatter us, because we could have scored a few more. That goal was extra special for Ray, because it was the first time he'd been in a televised game. What was also interesting was that we scored four goals in four away games in the space of two months. Middlesborough, Newcastle, Grimsby, which I scored at, then Wolves.

We played really well for the next five months, but then the last few games cost us promotion. We needed to invest in another centre-forward as cover for Dean Coney who was a very good player, but he was only a youngster and needed a bit of help. We'd had a player on loan called Andy Thomas, who we could have alternated, but the club neglected to buy him and that cost us dearly.

On 23 April we played Leicester at home with five games to go and they were our closest rivals. It really was between us and them. QPR were clear, then it was Wolves and then us and Leicester who were fighting for third. Unfortunately, we lost 1-0 to a long range shot from Ian Wilson.

After that game we went to Sheffield Wednesday and Robert Wilson scored to give us a 1-0 lead. However, they equalised and then we conceded in the last minute and lost 2-1. Next was QPR away on the bank holiday Monday and we lost 3-1, with Ray Lew getting sent off. Then we beat Carlisle at home and went to Derby for the last game of the season. If we won we would finish third and get promoted, whereas Derby were hovering over relegation. What could possibly go wrong?

As a club, we played a style of football that was on the floor and exciting. Pitches at the start of the season were good, then you got to Christmas and they started getting a bit shitty, but you still got through it. When it came to the end of the season the team started to play the ball a bit longer to eliminate the ball bobbling with the passes. Also, at the time Fulham had just set up Fulham Rugby League Football Club, now known as London Broncos, which obviously helped to fuck our pitch up even more. Going to Derby, we knew the pitch was going to be shit, but that all added to the drama in front of over 21,000 people.

Peter Taylor was the Derby manager and they had a team of experienced players like Kenny Burns and Archie Gemmill. We missed our chances in that game, whereas they scored from a rare opportunity. However, we were battling two teams that day. Derby County FC and their fans.

With about 10 minutes to go, the fans opened the gates round the side of the pitch and started to come over the fences. They were standing around the touchline and at one point, the keeper came out and caught the ball and one of the Derby fans from the crowd came and congratulated him and patted him on the back. It was madness.

Towards the end of the game, my pal Robert Wilson was running down the touchline, taking a Derby player on, when a fan ran out and whacked him in the leg. Robert went to retaliate and we all had to stop him, while this geezer went back into the crowd. The referee stood there helpless.

You could tell something was about to erupt and it didn't take long. In the 88th minute the referee blew the whistle for a free-kick. The crowd thought it was the end of the game and stormed the pitch. The police got involved, but they had no chance to get about 10,000 people off the pitch. We also now thought it was full-time and sprinted back to the changing rooms, with most of us taking a few blows on the way. One of our young players, Jeff Hopkins, was at the other end of the pitch getting a bit of a kicking. The rest of us managed to run off in time, but he didn't. We shut the door and thought we were all there and that's when we realised there was one missing. When Jeff walked in, he looked like something out of a zombie movie the way his shirt was hanging off his back. He was an emotional wreck.

The referee then comes into the changing room and says, 'That wasn't the final whistle. We need to clear the pitch.' Well, that never happened. It was then decided that it was the final whistle. We missed out on those two minutes and injury time, and yes it was highly unlikely we'd score two goals in that time, but it wasn't impossible. Who knows what could have happened, especially as our reward for winning was getting promoted to Division One.

Malcolm did his interview afterwards and said to us, 'Be careful of your holidays, because we might need to replay this game.' We didn't though. Fulham finished fourth, Leicester City finished third and absolutely nothing happened to Derby. Two appeals were lodged for a replay and both times the FA ruled against them.

It's not the result we wanted, but we proved a lot of people wrong. In two consecutive seasons in Division Three, I won the PFA player of the year award for my position and I won it again the next level up. After marking Kevin Keegan this season, I wondered who I'd be up against next.

Chapter 12

IRON WORKS

*'I say luck is when an opportunity comes along
and you're prepared for it.'*
– Denzel Washington

I PLAYED against some incredible strike partnerships in the lower leagues such as Alan Warboys and Bruce Bannister at Bristol Rovers, who were known as 'Smash and Grab.' Then as I went up the leagues I was up against Mark Hughes and Eric Cantona, Ian Wright and Alan Smith and loads more. They don't tend to do partnerships these days, which means if you're a centre-back you've got a dream ticket. One person up against you and you can't play one single forward ball and have the most touches in a game. That takes away a lot of the creativity from the back, which is a real shame.

For the 1983/84 season, the strike partnership I won't forget was Ian Rush and Kenny Dalglish. We took on Liverpool at home on 8 November 1983, at a time when Liverpool were in the top three sides in the country and one of the best in Europe. On paper we were going to get killed, but we had other plans.

Back then, Fulham weren't on the telly all the time, so people didn't always get to see our tactics, which meant we could get away with things time and time again. Without the likes of YouTube around, Malcolm used to go and see teams live, so he could get that first-hand information and work out his strategy. A couple of days before our game with Liverpool, Malc and Ray

Harford went up to Anfield to see Liverpool rip Everton apart, 3-0.

On the drive back, Ray asked Malc, 'How are we going to play this?' Malc replied, 'I'm really in the mood for taking the bull by the horns. We're playing well. Let's not forget that.' After chatting for a bit, Malc says, 'Let's focus on their front line. They've got Dalglish, who's a master on the ball and Rush is quick and sees things early and he's a great finisher. Liverpool are not going to kick crosses high in the air, which negates Roger Brown almost. It's vital that we find a way that our players can play to their absolute strengths, in a way that Liverpool can't attack their weaknesses.'

In the end, he dropped Brownie and played Paul Parker alongside me as a centre-back. We played a back four with Kevin Lock, Jeff Hopkins, me and Paul Parker, and the idea was that Paul picked up Rushie, because he could match his pace and was relentless and I picked up Kenny when he came into my zone, making it difficult for him to turn and get a shot in.

We took them to two 1-1 draws, one home, one away and then in the third game, it was 0-0 and Dalglish snuck into the box and nicked the goal. That was the only shot at goal that Liverpool had in all three games. We might have lost that game, but the achievement against Liverpool was massive and we got some great plaudits from some of the Division One teams that season. Even former Liverpool gaffer Bob Paisley said that we were too good to be playing that sort of football and be in Division Two.

Shortly after that game, my son Anthony was born on 1 December 1983. There was no problems with the birth and despite being hyperactive as a young-un, he was a great kid.

* * * * *

IRON WORKS

WE SPENT a lot of time in the 1983/84 season around mid-table, which kind of flattened us. Back then there wasn't playoff positions or anything like that, so, sometimes it was easy to drift a bit when you're in the middle of the league and that's what we did as we started to slide downwards. We won the last five games, but those wins were cheap wins which got us to finish in 11th place. Based on the rest of the season we actually needed to do a lot more work.

My contract with Fulham ran out at the end of the season and they desperately wanted to sell me, because they needed the money and I was probably the most valuable player on their books. The rule was that if you re-signed a player you had to improve their wages. Fulham realised they had to offer me a new improved contract otherwise I would be a free transfer and they'd get nothing. In the end, they offered me a new contract, which was a good one.

The problem was we weren't buying any experienced players, just getting younger players coming through and with my contract running out I thought it would be interesting to see what would happen when other clubs found out. I never had an agent and around that time a rule had come out that allowed you to negotiate your own contracts, so I kept saying, 'I'll wait, I'll wait.'

Well, West Ham and Chelsea came in on the same day to try and buy me. There was a phone call and it was John Lyall from West Ham. 'We're half an hour away. Are you in?' They'd obviously checked I was in and obviously knew where I lived! I said, 'Yeah, I'm in.'

John Lyall and Eddie Baily pulled up and knocked on my door. John was a proper charmer and a natural man-manager who reminded me of Bobby Campbell and Alec Stock. They were proper blokes who genuinely cared about everything. Not just the football side of things, but your family. Some fell out with Bobby because he was a little bit more abrasive, but over the next 10 years I never saw anyone falling out with John.

Eddie Baily was his lieutenant, who did a lot of scouting for John and he had also played for the great Spurs 'Push and Run' side in the '40s and '50s. Eddie was a little harsher than John, but I think it was a bit of an act between them. John would ask something like, 'What's your weight?' and I'd say whatever it was and Eddie would say, 'I did notice a couple of times you looked a bit lumpy, son. You'll have to keep your weight down if you sign here.' Then John would say, 'That's a bit harsh Eddie.'

John and Eddie stayed for about 45 minutes, gave me their sales pitch and said, 'We'll be back in an hour. You're coming to West Ham.' Shortly after, Ian McNeill turned up from Chelsea. Well, Chelsea was my team as a kid and I was living in Surrey, so that would have been a lot closer, but you can imagine how much better John Lyall sold West Ham to me, taking into account I'd have to do all that extra travelling every day.

Kevin Lock had gone from West Ham to Fulham about 1978 and I went to him and said, 'West Ham have weighed in with Chelsea. What's West Ham like?' Locky was Bobby Moore's replacement when he was at West Ham and played in the 1975 Cup final against Fulham, when Bobby Moore played for Fulham. Locky couldn't speak highly enough of West Ham. 'You're moving to a better team and a bigger club, and John Lyall is a brilliant manager.' I also spoke with Ray Houghton who gave me the lowdown about what the club was about and he said the same as Kev. After I'd weighed up the two offers, there was only one place I was going. Upton Park.

My fee had to go to an independent tribunal, where Fulham were demanding £1million and West Ham were offering £200,000. They gauged what wages you are on, what wages

Fulham, West Ham and Chelsea were going to offer me and they took into account my age in terms of what was a decent offer. West Ham bought me for £200,000 and paid me £600 per week, which was a steal for them.

However, I was getting a five per cent signing on fee of £10,000, which didn't work out too well for me. As I was leaving Fulham, they turned around and said, 'You owe us five grand from the loan of your house when you were 19.' I ended up walking away with five grand when I went to West Ham. Was it worth it, though?

Chapter 13

HAMMER TIME

'He was not just a good defender, he was one of the best in one-on-ones against strikers I've seen. If you looked at Bobby Moore, there's similarities. Bobby Moore wasn't quick but he could understand the game and read the game. I didn't play with Bobby Moore, but I did play with Tony Gale and he was an outstanding defender.'

– Ray Stewart

ON MY first day at West Ham, captain Billy Bonds came up to me and said, 'Hello, son. How are ya? If you have any problems here, don't hesitate to ask me. I'll be your confidant. Any questions at all, just ask. Welcome to the club.' You have to remember that Bonzo was in his late thirties and John Lyall had brought me in to replace him, so it was almost a bit strange for me having this legend come up to me and be so nice. As it goes, Bill reverted to midfield and played on for a good few years until he was nearly 42.

There were some great characters at West Ham. After playing at Fulham for seven seasons, I think I got a bit cocooned into thinking, 'There's no life after Fulham,' but then all of a sudden, coming into a West Ham team with the likes of Ray Stewart, Bonzo, Dave Swindlehurst and Stevie Whitton, I was now part of another family.

I became room partners with Alvin Martin and played

alongside him for almost my full 10 years at West Ham, but as people, we were like chalk and cheese. Alvin liked to go to bed early, wake up early, go down for breakfast and then have a pre-match meal about midday, whereas I preferred to watch the telly until the last programme and then have a lay in, miss breakfast and just go in for the pre-match. Before he was going to kip, he'd let me know and I'd turn down the sound on the telly. He'd then get up quietly and do his best to not wake me in the morning.

One occasion he comes back from breakfast and I said, 'Good breakfast, Alv?' and he's said, 'Yeah. You just woken up you lazy bastard?' I said 'That's right mate.' He's then said, 'I didn't have any toothpaste, but I used yours. It's funny the brand you use mate.' I said, 'What do you mean?' He goes, 'It's got this applicator at the end of it and I couldn't get a lather from it.' That's when the penny dropped and I said, 'You've used my pile cream. That applicator has been stuck up my arse!'

Ernie Gregory was the goalkeeping coach and had played for West Ham in goal from the late 1930s for about 20 years. Ernie was a real character and he said to me early on, 'You're going to love it down here, son. You won't be half as good as what I was, but you'll be good down here.' He was the sort of character you needed around the place. If you made a mistake in a game, he'd say something like, 'That was a bad mistake, Galey. I had one of them once, but only once, son.'

The first dozen games of the 1984/85 season went well, but we had quite a few injuries at the time. Our first London derby was at Chelsea, which we lost 3-0, but it was the next one against Arsenal at home on 27 October 1984 that stuck in my mind. Bonzo was super hyped up before the game, doing block tackles up against the wall with a ball and throwing water in his hair, getting ready for battle. He also used to have one tiny swig of brandy before the game. Our physio Rob Jenkins was a real character and he used to say to Bonzo, 'Second shelf down, Bill,' and there was a little brandy flask. He'd have a swig, followed by a little shiver and he was good to go. We won that game 3-1.

I'd like to mention a couple of players who I connected with really quickly that season and who became very good friends of mine. When West Ham signed Phil Parkes from QPR in 1979 they broke the world record by paying £565,000, making him the most expensive goalkeeper on the planet. I'd played against Parkesy when I was at Fulham, but never really knew him at that point. By this time he was 34 and was simply brilliant. He was a natural goalkeeper who had hands twice the size of any normal human being and was 6ft 4 inches tall, with a gigantic wingspan. He'd pull off save after save and bearing in mind the size of him, he made them look easy. With just one England cap, I certainly don't think he got the recognition he deserved at national level.

The other player I'd like to mention is Alan Devonshire. Dev was West Ham's best player but he suffered a horrible cruciate ligament injury in the FA Cup against Wigan Athletic in January 1984 and played just twice during my first season of 84/85. I ended up taking his No.6 shirt until he was able to return, then when he was nearing fitness again he said, 'Galey. I've always worn the No.6 and you've got it.' I said, 'Mate. Of course you can have it back. It's your number.' That's when I started to play No.4.

Everybody was telling me what a great player he was, which I already knew, because I'd played against Dev before, but I struck up an immediate friendship with him because we were from the west side of London and used to travel together. I was already giving him lifts here, there and everywhere because he didn't drive and I'm sure he still doesn't drive to this day. He must owe me 20 grand in petrol money.

Here's the routine I had. Say we had to be at training for 10am at Chadwell Heath, if I'd left too late from Surrey to drive into London, I would have hit rush hour, so instead I used to go up to my mum's in Pimlico every morning nice and early and there she was waiting. 'Do you want a cup of tea?' Now and again I'd stay up there, but most of the time I'd just go to bed for a few hours, unless the cricket was on live from abroad from the likes of Australia or the West Indies, then I'd listen to a bit of that on the radio. After a kip my mum would wake me up and say, 'Get out of bed. You need to pick Phil up.'

Parkesy lived in Woking and used to get the train to Waterloo and then hitch a lift with me. I'd jump in my Ford Orion, drive to Waterloo station, where I'd park on the yellow line to pick him up at this little café outside the station. When he came off the train from Woking he'd have his routine down to a tee. Have a cup of tea, then as soon as he saw me pulling up, he'd order us a couple of bacon rolls and came running out, with his roll usually hanging out of his mouth. Those rides are how me and Parkesy ended up becoming good mates.

Once Parkesy was in the car we'd drive under the railway bridge, where the great train robber Buster Edwards had a flower stand and every morning Parkesy would shout, 'Bustaaaa!,' and wave to him. Funnily enough, Buster used to order all his flowers from my uncle at Covent Garden.

After leaving Waterloo we'd then travel on to Dev and pick him up at Barking station, where he'd be in the Wimpy inside the station having something like a burger and chips or a full fry-up. Dev was so fit and naturally gifted, he could eat anything back then, which made him the envy of me and Phil. When we pulled up to Barking station, I'd toot the car horn and Dev would come running out and then we'd drive for about 15 minutes up the road to the training ground at Chadwell Heath.

People ask me what education we got on nutrition when I was playing football. The answer is, we didn't really. When I got to West Ham there was a canteen, run by Shirley, who still works for the club to this very day. Our Friday meal after training was ham, egg, chips, beans and a couple of slices of bread, with apple crumble, custard and ice cream for dessert. I always used to look forward to the Friday session just for the food after. Then you'd get home and have your dinner later, which was all wrong.

Everyone had their own routines before a game at West Ham. One thing I always liked was a new pair of socks and whichever club I went to I always had to chat up the kitman to get a new pair for each game. The other thing that became a bit of a habit was my pre-match vomit. When you broke into the first team, they asked you what you wanted for your pre-match meal and you either had baked beans on toast, poached eggs on toast, fried eggs or scrambled eggs. That was basically it. I always had poached eggs. I didn't throw up before every game, but most matches I'd stick my fingers down my throat and get it out. Not in the sink though as I didn't want to block it up. I just liked to have the empty feeling when going on the pitch. Tony Cottee (TC)'s routine was going to the toilet about six times before the game for a piss. He didn't need to go, but he'd just stand there and by doing that he knew it would relax him. We made for a very odd couple. He'd be going for a piss in one cubicle, without pissing, and I'd be next door throwing up.

During that first season I picked up a few injuries, but I still went to all the games. On Saturday 9 March 1985, Man United were playing against West Ham in the sixth round of the FA Cup and I decided to go up with my mum, dad and auntie Joyce and we also brought my young cousin, Terry, who was about 14 or 15 at the time.

We pulled up at Old Trafford, got out our tickets, sat in the section where the comps were allocated, which unfortunately meant we were also with Man United fans. This game was on *Match of The Day* and Mark Hughes scored the first goal for Man United, then shortly after they scored an own goal. Just before half-time, Norman Whiteside scored, making it 2-1 for Man United. The fans didn't recognise me because I'd only just joined West Ham, so I wasn't an instantly recognisable person, but either way we started receiving a little bit of abuse, maybe because they saw we weren't cheering Man United, or they recognised our London accents. With five minutes to go it was 3-2 to Man United and they started pelting coins at us, spitting and whatever else. I said to everyone, 'It's getting a bit lively here. Let's hop off.' As we're walking out, Norman Whiteside scored another to get his hat-trick, making it 4-2 to Man United.

We got out and started walking back to the car, which was over the bridge next to Old Trafford, when next thing we see about 500 West Ham fans, who had done the same thing as us and got out early. We hung back because I didn't want to put my family at risk in case anything happened and we might be stuck in the thick of it. We're about 100 metres behind them when next thing we hear chants of 'United, United.' I've turned around and there were about two thousand Man United fans running towards the West Ham fans. Instead of the West Ham fans running away, they turned round and hurled into Man United, and just like the film *Green Street*, the fans started shouting, 'Stand your ground.' Me and my dad had our coats over my mum, auntie and little cousin as things were flying over our heads. Thankfully, nobody touched us, but that was one massive ruck.

It died down and they started to walk away from each other for about a minute and then it all kicked off again. I said to my family, 'We've got to get back to the car, right now.' Thankfully, we managed to make a break for it, got back in the car and headed out of Manchester quickly. There was a documentary that came out later that year called *Hooligan*, and there's me and my dad on the bridge with our coats over our family, shielding them from the crowds.

Six days after the riot at Old Trafford, we were playing Man United at home and that also ended up being an eventful one. I wasn't playing that day, I was sat behind the dugout and after the match, John said to me, 'What happened to Peter?' I said, 'What do you mean?' He said, 'He's been kicked out the ground.' I said, 'You sure? My dad wouldn't cause any trouble.' I went outside and managed to get him back in and that's when he told me what happened.

A big group of my friends and family were at Upton Park watching the game, when this crowd of Man United fans started throwing sweets at my uncle Terry, my mum and my aunt Joyce. My dad got up and said, 'Leave it alone.' He told them once, told them twice and then the geezer below him who was among three Man United supporters, got up and told my dad to fuck off. Without hesitation, my dad chins this bloke and he went flying back a couple of seats down. Then a few more Man United fans came over, at which point all my uncles came running down to the stand and it all kicked off. It all got broken up by the stewards, while the West Ham fans were all singing 'ICF, ICF,' which was the Inter City Firm, whilst it was actually just my dad and uncles. Then the next day in the paper there was an article talking about crowd trouble at West Ham and some geezer kicking it all off after punching a Man United fan. Good old Pete.

Fanbase wise, Fulham's was a nicer crowd, whereas West Ham were far more vocal to say the least, especially on the Chicken Run side, because all it took was a little nudge and you'd be right in it. I'd seen players going flying in there and taking a couple of smacks before climbing back out and I don't think I ever saw a winger who intentionally hugged the touchline at West Ham.

The Chicken Run was where you either lived or died. It was only about two yards away from the touchline to the terrace, which meant you could hear everything that was being said. Whoever was playing wide or full-back for the opposition, or if someone had their jersey tugged in front of them, they used to get a lot of stick. But they also used to give our players stick if we weren't having a good game. If you gave 100 per cent they were behind you, but they suffered no fools when it came to their football. Mind you, neither did the fans from the other clubs, QPR being one of them.

On 8 April 1985 we played QPR at Loftus Road on their plastic pitch and lost 4-2. Our goalie Tom McAllister got injured after falling on the hard surface and landed on his elbow, which broke two of his ribs and punctured a lung. Ray Stewart, who was a prolific penalty taker, went in goal and maybe thought he could make history by saving a penalty against Terry Fenwick. Well, Fenwick scored and to show their appreciation of Ray, the QPR fans started throwing coins at him. Most people would have sprinted off as the coins were flying his way, but Tonka picked up all the coins and reckons he bagged about £8.50, which was a lot of money back then. He was never one for missing a commercial opportunity.

I love Tonka. He was called that because he used to love to smash a ball. He's one of the best penalty takers I've seen and when he used to step up, you'd see goalies looking in fear, because he hardly ever missed. During his time at West Ham he converted 76 out of the 86 spot-kicks he took. Ray was also very astute off the pitch. I always thought he would have made a great agent.

Anyway, I can't think of many positive experiences on those

plastic pitches back then. We wore the pimple football shoes, which was like a boot-cum-trainer which Adidas had made at the time. It was like playing a big five-a-side game. Another time at QPR in the FA Cup fourth round in January 1988, all the police came on to defuse some crowd trouble with their horses and of course, they shit everywhere. It's different with grass, but on the Omni-turf, it's a solid surface and it just sat there and stunk.

Our penultimate game that season was on 17 May 1985 at Ipswich. It was one of the few games I missed that season because I was ill and we ended up winning 1-0, which turned out to be the game that secured safety.

Our last game was Liverpool at home and what was significant about that one was that it was Frank Lampard Sr's farewell to West Ham after 18 years and 670 appearances. Frank hadn't played the whole season, but John gave him the opportunity to have a great send-off in the last game and then I came on for him midway through the second half. We lost 3-0, finished 16th that season and only survived relegation by two points. John always had a positive outlook and he'd been there and done it so many times with West Ham, so you just felt he'd always have a way to figure it out.

Unfortunately, May 1985 left the football world with some horrible memories that put our relegation issues into perspective. On 11 May, a gigantic fire broke out at Bradford City's stadium when they were playing against Lincoln and 56 people died, with hundreds injured. We couldn't believe what had happened, but when you've grown up on wooden terraces watching games, it was frightening to think just how close you were from a disaster.

Then, on 29 May, the Heysel disaster happened and another 39 people were killed after a wall collapsed on Juventus fans.

It's very sad that it takes a disaster to make improvements, but Heysel, Hillsborough and Bradford have led to better and safer stadiums, with more entrances and exits. I can remember as a kid trying to get in at the Shed End of Stamford Bridge and you were instantly into the sway of the crowd. Now, thank God, there are more turnstiles and the overall health and safety is so much better.

Unless I'm a paid spectator, I've always preferred standing up at football, especially when I do my commentating. I'm glad that safe standing areas are slowly getting introduced again, but this time with better safety in mind, because standing is part of a long tradition in football.

*****

A FEW days after our last league game we flew out to Japan for two weeks to take part in the 1985 Kirin Cup against Brazil's Santos FC, Yomiuri, the Malaysian Tigers and the Japanese and Uruguayan national teams. We slept on the flight and within hours of landing played against Santos and lost 2-1 on 26 May in Shimizu. However, all was not lost as I did manage to nick one of the Santos shirts that one of the players left on the side. I would have exchanged a West Ham top, but we only had two each.

That Santos shirt wasn't all that went missing though. We were all saying, 'We need to get some souvenirs and presents for our families.' We stayed in the top hotels during this trip and I was in the room with Alvin for one stop and I said, 'Look at all this gear. This looks nice.' There were these kimonos, so we bagged one each, then I said, 'Look at all this stuff in the bathroom,' and it carried on like that.

Two days later we had to go from this hotel to Okayama, where we were playing. John got us all on the bus as he went to settle up the bill. He's chatting to the general manager of the hotel, who was a little Japanese fella, and me and Alvin can hear the conversation, because we were sitting up the front of the bus. This guy's said, 'Mr Lyall. Many things go missing from the hotel.' John's going, 'You accusing my players of being thieves?'

John's got on the microphone in the coach and said, 'Look lads. If anyone's taken anything out of the hotel rooms, just get off the bus now, undo your bags and put it inside the hotel. I'm going away and when I come back, I don't want to know who it is, but just leave the stuff behind.' I'm thinking, 'Fucking hell.' I've nudged Alv and said, 'We've been rumbled.' Just as John gets off the bus, everyone stood up and headed to their bags. They'd all done the same as us! When John came back, there was a mountain of dressing gowns. You should have seen his face.

We drew 2-2 against Japan in Okayama, before heading off on a bullet train to Tokyo to take on the Malaysian Tigers. John had said to Phil Parkes, 'Parkesy, take a break from the game, because you've had a hard season.' Phil said, 'OK,' and totally relaxed on the three-and-a-half-hour train ride over to Tokyo. Well actually, he over-relaxed on the booze.

It was stifling heat in Tokyo and because Parkesy wasn't playing he decided to have a drink in his room. John had told us we had three hours' kip and then had to come down for a pre-match meal before the game, which was going to be live on Japanese telly.

We came down for the pre-match meal and Phil was nowhere to be seen. John said, 'Where's Phil?' We said, 'He's not going to bother coming to the game because he's having a rest now.' John replied, 'No. He is coming. Everyone's coming to the game. Also John Vaughan (our reserve goalie) has got the shits, which means Phil's now playing.' We ran upstairs after the meal and

Phil was sparko. We woke him up, but he had a raging hangover. We explained he was playing and as you can imagine, he was hardly over the moon.

Phil still stunk of booze, but we managed to smuggle him past John and into the stadium, even though it's not easy to smuggle a 6ft 4inch goalie anywhere. Phil goes over to the shade to warm up in the stifling humidity and the sweat was pouring off him. I thought, 'I hope this team is no good, because one shot from them and we'll be losing.'

Thankfully, they weren't that good and we were 4-0 heading into the break, when this geezer came at us and we let him shoot from about 35 yards, because we knew Phil could handle anything like that. Well, the ball was clearly going straight down the middle of the goal, but Phil's done a full-stretch dive to the right. The ball's continued straight down the middle and they've pulled a goal back.

As we're walking off the pitch, the cameraman has zoomed in on Phil and we all walked to the changing room. Everyone was asking, 'What happened, mate?' 'Parkesy?' 'Phil. How did you let that one in?'

Phil's in the changing room with a towel over the top of his head. He pulls it up and says, 'I saw four balls. I had to go for one!' Thankfully we won the game 9-2 and David Swindlehurst scored four. We then drew 0-0 to Yomiuri in Sapporo on 2 June, followed by 1-1 against Uruguay two days later in Nagoya. We came third overall, behind Santos and Uruguay, in what was a brilliant trip.

My first season at West Ham had certainly been fun-filled, but finishing just above relegation was not what I was hoping for. At the back of your mind, you did wonder where we would end up next season.

Chapter 14

THE BOYS OF '86

'I played 38 games that season, whereas Parkesy, Galey and Wardy played every single match. By playing every week with the same team, we got to know each other inside out. When you have confidence in your team-mates and everyone understands one another, it's not telepathy, but you know what to expect from one another. That season, it all came together nicely.'

– Alan Devonshire

GOING INTO the 1985/86 season West Ham signed Mark Ward from Oldham and Frank McAvennie from St Mirren. One was from Glasgow, one was from Liverpool, both were quick and aggressive and they didn't give a fuck about anything other than winning for the team.

Wardy never used to bottle anything. He was a five-and-a-half-foot winger who was as hard as centre-backs, not maybe in the air because of his size, but he could take a challenge. I think Frank was the surprise package. We didn't know who he was or how he played, but he endeared himself to the team straight away because he ran his bollocks off. He was deceptively quick, had a very awkward running style and as the season progressed, whoever we played against they doubled up on him.

One revelation about Frank that we didn't realise straight away was that he was ginger. When he turned up, he had this massive blond hairdo and we only found out he was ginger when we dug out an old Panini sticker book. The deciding evidence was when he got in the shower and we saw his downstairs area. That's when we shouted, 'You forgot to dye them, didn't ya!'

Frank quickly became the party animal in the team and our wives soon found out what he was like on a night out and would be asking us, 'Is Frank going out tonight?' and we'd all have our answer rehearsed. Say something like, 'Frank coming out tonight? Nah. He's going back to Scotland for a couple of days.' Then an hour later he'd meet us at some pub or club.

That season was almost as if we had another two new signings because Alan Devonshire came back from two years of injury and he was by far our best player in the team. Then there was Parkesy. Phil wasn't even sure if he was going to be playing in the first team because he'd missed the season before with an arm injury and was now 35. He'd managed to get back to fitness and was playing in the reserves, but in the meantime Tom McAlister played so well they could have easily left Parkesy out. Phil didn't know he was playing until right before the start of the season, then he got the nod. He ended up being one of three who played all 52 games that season, along with myself and Wardy.

Our final pre-season friendly didn't exactly set the tone for the season, but it went down in West Ham folklore. We lost 3-1 to Orient, who were in the lowest division, Division Four and obviously, being the game before the season started, loads of West Ham fans turned up and we got booed off the pitch.

We're sat there in the dressing room all shaking our heads in disbelief, when John came in and didn't know what to say. He just stood there in silence. We knew he was about to go into one, when suddenly the dressing room door banged open and some geezer walks in with Doc Martens, jeans, tank top, covered in tattoos. He pushes John out of the way and starts to do the team talk. 'What the fuck do you think that was? Ray Stewart – best penalty taker around, but you're shit at the moment. Tony Gale – paid 200 grand for ya and you're fucking hopeless.' We're all sitting there shitting ourselves and John lets him carry on. He then went on to Georgie Parris and says, 'You're too slow. Stevie Walford – you're a fucking has-been. Frank McAvennie – I've never even heard of ya.' He then goes into midfield and slaughters Neil Orr.

Next thing, the Old Bill come in and drag him out of the dressing room and you can still hear him shouting abuse as they're dragging him all the way out the tunnel at Brisbane Road. By now he's screaming at the young players, 'Stevie Potts – you'll never make it. Don't bother,' until finally he faded out into the distance. John composed himself as we're sitting there trying to work out what just happened and then turns to us and says, 'He's right though. Ain't he?'

Our first league game of the season was on 17 August 1985 at Birmingham City and we lost 1-0. John played me, Ray Stewart, Steve Walford and Alvin Martin in the back line and up front he put Frank behind Tony Cottee and Paul Goddard in a diamond formation, which didn't particularly work. Unfortunately, Paul dislocated his shoulder in that match and was pretty much out for the season. Frank liked running in behind and looked a little bit lost in the diamond system, so, out of adversity came another way of playing. John reverted to putting Frank up front, which acted as a little bit of a catalyst for him and TC to hit it off.

Three days later we beat QPR 3-1 at home, and then shortly after lost 1-0 at home to Luton. Next up was Man United away, on 26 August. When the likes of Wardy and Frank got signed that season, I started to hear, 'He's on this salary and he's on that,' and thought, 'It's time for me to see John Lyall and ask for a rise.' I wanted to pick my time right and thought the Friday before we travelled up to play Man United on the Saturday would be ideal, in order to give him time to think about it. Well, I couldn't have picked a worse time.

I went in his office and he goes, 'I can't believe you're bothering me before a game. What's the matter?' I've said, 'Well, John. You said to come to you when I thought I'd been established at the club to maybe get a rise. I've also been hearing about other boys and what they're on.' He replied, 'Not now son. Never on a Friday before a game. Let's get the game out of the way and we'll talk about it on Monday.'

We played Man United and I gave a goal away to Gordon Strachan and Mark Hughes nicked one. We lost 2-0 and when I came back to John on the Monday, I knocked on the door and as I've walked in, John's said, 'Don't tell me. Let me guess. You want to take a wage cut!' I laughed and said, 'Alright John, I'll wait.'

In our sixth game we played Southampton away and Greg Campbell, Bobby's son, came on in place of TC after he'd asked to be left out for the game. Whenever Bobby had the chance, he'd come over and watch some of the games at West Ham. He was always so happy to see me and he'd come in the players bar after the game and see my mum and dad, my sister and did what he did best, which was being Bob.

We drew that game at Southampton 1-1, which meant we'd only won one in seven games. TC hadn't scored in any of the games so far and when he asked to be left out of the squad for the Southampton game we knew something had to be done. TC didn't need a break, he just needed to get back to scoring goals. That's when we all had *that* chat with him.

Me, Alvin, Ray Stewart, Parkesy and Dev went to John Lyall and said we wanted a meeting. John Lyall said, 'If you want to have a meeting, have one, but I'm not coming into it and neither are any of the coaches. If you've got any problems, sort it out among yourselves.' You can't imagine that happening nowadays.

I always say that defence is your first line of attack. The under-lying message from managers I've worked under was always, 'Play, but don't give it away', which is all well and good, but you had to be brave enough to play, especially when you had brilliant strikers from all round the country closing you down. I never went for the soft option of whacking one down the channel as a panic play. Also, intercepting is very important.

You hear people talking about crashing through players, but if you crash through anyone, you are very rarely going to come out with the ball. If you intercept, you'll come out with the ball the other side, which puts you and your team on the front foot. I used to love watching people like Bobby Moore, Franz Beck-enbauer, Rudi Krol, who all had the ability to play the ball. I wasn't as good as them, but that's what I wanted to do. In the same breath, as a striker, there's more to just goal-hanging and nicking goals, and that's what we had to explain to TC.

I'd nicknamed him Harry, because there used to be a guy at the training ground, who was West Ham through and through and I can't remember his surname, but we knew him as 'Old Harry'. He used to walk around with a fag in his mouth and John gave him a job doing various bits around the ground like keeping the baths and showers clean, just to give him something to do. However, Harry would do everything to hide, like run to the broom cupboard or the gym, just to have a fag. Basically, Harry did fuck all and that's what we jokingly called TC before we had this talk.

We had to explain to TC what we wanted him to do and be firm, but obviously we didn't want to go in heavy-handed, because he was only 20 years old. We said, 'You're a great player and you score goals, but when we're defending, you're doing fuck all. We need you to win the ball back now and again. Why don't you try and get between the full-back and the centre-half, so that if the goalkeeper tries to throw it out, or if they try and play it out, if you win the ball higher up the field, then you've got less yardage to run to get to the goal.' As John Lyall used to say, 'Let's win the ball in the last third, because the nearer we are to the goal, the better chance we have to score.'

TC's initial reaction was going off the handle and saying, 'How we going to get goals like that?' and I replied, 'You will get goals, when a team builds them for you and Frank to score. Also, if you get to this position when defending, not only are you helping us, but you'll get the ball more on the regain.' He took to it like a duck to water and we flew. Maybe, possibly, almost 40 years later, he might even admit it made sense! If TC got on the wrong side of you, there was no chance of catching him and stopping him scoring. After that meeting, TC scored in the next game against Sheffield Wednesday and we went the next 16 games unbeaten.

On 26 October we beat Ipswich 1-0, with Tony scoring the only goal. We ended up playing Ipswich five times that season, which included three FA Cup ties, but this was one of those games where we weren't at our best and the team had to rely heavily on our defence. In brief, the back four did all the work at the back and TC got the winner and all the accolades.

Three days later we were up against Man United in the Milk Cup at Old Trafford and lost 1-0 after Wardy's goal was disallowed from a free-kick because he shot direct, whereas it should have been indirect. It was going in the top corner and keeper Gary Bailey went full length to his right hand side and tipped the ball into the goal. It was a clear touch, which now made it indirect, but the referee disallowed it.

On 30 November we played West Brom at home, which came with a pre-game mini drama for myself. I used to drive to Pimlico, leave my car there and then jump in my dad's cab and he'd drive us there. On this day we head off and we're about a mile away but couldn't move in traffic because there was a burst water main and there was no Google Maps or any of that to tell you an alternative route. I got out, found a telephone box and rang John. He was like, 'Don't worry. We've got your name on the team sheet.'

Normally we'd get there two-and-a-half hours before a game, but there I was with less than an hour to go now. We got to the end of Green Street at the Forest Gate end and I said to my dad, 'I'm not going to get there.' I jumped out with my suit, tie and smart shoes on and ran down Green Street for about 10 minutes as people were going, 'Alright Tony,' and I'm being polite, smiling, giving them the thumbs up and running as fast as I can, going 'Alright mate!'

I managed to get to the ground half an hour before kick-off and there's loads of fans there queuing up. As I'm trying to squeeze through they're all saying hello and can you sign this and that, while I'm saying, 'Hello, 'scuse me, 'scuse me, alright mate, 'scuse me, yes, I also hope we win, 'scuse me.' Then typical, just as I head into the ground my dad pulls up in the cab because the traffic had thinned out!

I ran straight into the changing room and John said, 'Calm down. Everything is alright.' I said, 'Am I still playing?' He said, 'Yeah. At least you've warmed up! We knew you'd get here.' I was thinking, 'Yeah? I didn't think I would.' I certainly went the extra mile that day. We ended up winning that game 4-0, with TC, Neil Orr, Georgie Parris and Dev scoring. That put us third in the league.

Our next game was on 7 December against QPR, at Loftus Road, but Frank had to go to Australia to play for Scotland in a 1986 World Cup qualifier, which meant there was little chance of him playing at QPR. Or so we thought.

He goes to Melbourne and drew 0-0 which meant Scotland

were going to the World Cup because they'd beat Australia 2-0 at Hampden Park. Frank has a couple of glasses of wine after the game and then falls asleep on the plane home. He gets to Heathrow and decides he wants to play and calls John Lyall.

'John. I want to play. Have you got my boots ready?'

John said, 'You've been travelling all night.'

Frank replied, 'John, staying up all night has never been my problem!'

John wanted to see what state Frank was in and said, 'Come and have a chat with me.' Frank goes over, John took a good look at him and said, 'Okay. No problem.'

Frank arrives at the hotel where we were eating before the game and then shortly after we went to Loftus Road. In all honesty, Frank didn't have the best of games, but you wouldn't really after stepping off a 24-hour flight. We had a lot of pressure in that game because QPR were really good on their plastic pitch and it didn't help when I managed to get a cut eye and Alvin also suffered an injury. Just as we were thinking we'd be happy with a draw, the goalkeeper parried a shot and old sneaky bollocks Frank scores the only goal to give us 1-0 and gets all the headlines. Winning that game on that pitch was a brilliant three points.

Spurs on Boxing Day was always the big game. We used to take massive support to White Hart Lane and were particularly gutted to lose that one. We played well, but Steve Perryman scored with five minutes to go and that loss ended our unbeaten run of 18 games.

* * * * *

ONE BIG factor that made the 1985/86 squad work so well was our ability to have fun. The banter in the changing room came as standard, but we also made the most of our time on the coach trips, mainly playing cards. We'd play three card brag with Frank, Wardy, Georgie Parris and a few others. It got a bit silly sometimes because if you had a big hand, there would be a few quid there and John didn't like that. Once, he came past and picked the lot up and said, 'If you can afford to play cards with that sort of money, I'm taking the lot and putting it in the Christmas fund,' and he walked off. We had no comebacks for that. On reflection it was wrong, because if you lost money on the way up there, it could play on someone's mind and they had the pressure to win it on the way back, not to mention we had a game of football in between!

Frank was shit at cards. He didn't have a great attention span, his poker face was crap and he got bored quickly. He may as well have just left £200 on the table and walked off. He used to dread going to places like Sunderland and Newcastle because he'd lose a packet on the six-and-a-half hour coach journey. In the end he found it was a lot cheaper to get a flight home from Newcastle.

We kicked off 1986 by beating Charlton 1-0 in the FA Cup, then beat Leicester in the league 1-0 away on 11 January, before losing to Liverpool 3-1 a week later. We gave a penalty away to Paul Walsh that should have never been awarded, then Ray Stewart got sent off for disputing that penalty. I remember Dev, who had a great footballing brain saying, 'Whenever we play Liverpool, we never get hold of the ball, but this time I can't believe how much possession we've had in this game, but we've unfortunately lost.'

From 25 January to 6 February we played Ipswich three times in the FA Cup. The first two games were draws, then we beat them 1-0 on a snow-covered pitch with a bright orange ball, because you couldn't see a blade of grass at Portman Road. It wasn't icy, which meant we could move the ball, but it was thick snow. Either way, we won.

Our next two games in the FA Cup were against Man United. On 5 March we played them at home and drew 1-1, and Ron Atkinson was shouting, 'You flash Londoners. Wait til you come up to Old Trafford.' We played them four days later and beat them 2-0, with Geoff Pike scoring from a long range bullet header from outside the area. They said it was a well rehearsed routine, but actually, Mark Ward was trying to hit it in on the near post and pulled it out to the edge of the area where Geoff scored that famous curling header.

To add insult to injury, just before we played them in the Cup we also beat them 2-1 at home, with Wardy and TC scoring. That was our first league game back on telly after the ban of televised football was lifted and I vividly remember David Pleat was commentating and he said it was 'end to end, like a fight where two sluggers are going at it.' Balls going across the area, challenges going in, people getting knocked in the balls and getting up. No arguments on the pitch, just battles to get possession of the ball and nobody got the hump. Good old hungry football.

On 12 March we lost against Sheffield Wednesday 2-1 in the sixth round of the FA Cup, which was our second year running of missing out at the quarter-final stage. Sheff Wednesday were a good team at the time and Nigel Worthington scored the first, then Carl Shutt shortly after. Despite TC pulling one back, we were out of the Cup.

From here on until the end of the season, the next 16 games were rapid fire, come hell, water, wind, snow or sun. Three days after Sheffield we lost at Arsenal 1-0, even though we played well. I remember Alvin having a fight with David O'Leary on the pitch, because they were the opposite centre-halves and were marking each other at set pieces. The tension was building up throughout the game between them and then it hit boiling point and fisticuffs happened. That's not one you wanted to get in the middle of, but I would have backed Alvin, who for his sins got sent off.

By 22 March we were in seventh place. Our next two matches over the Easter weekend were against Chelsea away on 29 March and two days later against Spurs at home. Those two games were significant because they were the only two games that Alvin missed in the season, because he was suspended. Paul Hilton came in and he hadn't played all season and now had to play alongside me, but I must say, he played ever so well. We ended up beating Chelsea 4-0 on the Saturday and Spurs 2-1 on the Easter Monday, which could have easily been 7-1. They were stand-out performances.

We won two out of our next three and lost against Chelsea 2-1 at home on 15 April, in a game that was originally supposed to be earlier in the year, but got postponed due to the big freeze. That game I had to come off at half-time with a dead leg. I got a kick in the first half and ended up with a massive haematoma in my thigh and just couldn't run. They had to re-shuffle the defence and Neil Orr came on and went into the back four after not having played there all season. We got a little bit dishevelled in that second half and that's why we lost 2-1. After the game my leg was throbbing and badly bruised, and with the next game being four days later on Saturday against Watford away, there was no way I was going to be able to play.

I went in the next day for treatment with Rob Jenkins and for once he actually worked on the correct leg. By now the thigh had really come up and he explained that the bleeding had to go down and we'd have to see how it went for Saturday. I didn't train for the next couple of days and on the Friday I couldn't move my leg. John Lyall called me in and said, 'How are you for tomorrow?' and I've said, 'I can't move.' He said, 'Come in early in the morning and have another bath, do some ice and then see how it is.' I was thinking, 'You must be mad. I can hardly walk.' I said, 'Okay. I'll get in early before we travel to Watford.'

There I was on the Saturday morning sitting in the bath and John comes over and says, 'How is it?' I said, 'Feels a little bit better, but not great.' He said, 'You're playing.' I started to say, 'John, it's...' and before I could finish the sentence he said, 'You're playing. I'd rather have a 50 per cent fit you and get back to the shape we were in, than having to shuffle everyone around again, where we come unstuck.'

I ended up playing and leant heavily on Alvin, who had a really good game and we won 2-0. I managed to put myself in a position throughout the game where I wasn't going to get involved with long chases and physically do myself in. I played alright and that's the psychology of football sometimes. When you feel 100 per cent and don't have a cough or anything, you might have a shit game. Then another day you have a chill, an injury or the shits the day before and you won't be looking forward to it, then you have a great game. Football has no rhyme or reason and there are so many people and factors that can influence that game around you. The players, the subs, the referee, the crowd, but on this occasion it was the manager who gave me that push and the gamble worked out just fine.

We had to play our last 13 games across 38 days and our final six matches in 15 days. We were in fifth place and were starting to think, 'We can win the league?' However, we also knew that Liverpool were on a fantastic run and Everton were right up there, too. I suppose we were the underdog and every other fan wanted us to win because Liverpool and Everton had won it a number of times before and we never had.

Two days after the Watford win we played Newcastle at home on the Monday evening. I went in for treatment on Sunday, came in early Monday for more treatment and by now my leg was feeling a bit better and mentally I was a little bit happier because I'd got through the last game at Vicarage Road.

We ended up beating Newcastle 8-1 and it could have been many more against a good team with the likes of Neil McDonald and Peter Beardsley. Alvin scored a hat-trick, which went down in the record books because he scored each goal against a different goalie in the same game. Two of the goals were against Martin Thomas and Chris Hedworth, who both then had to go off with injuries, but the more memorable one was against Beardo.

Then Paul Goddard came on as sub and scored and got a standing ovation from the whole ground, given that he'd been on the periphery the whole season due to injury. Even the players applauded him when he scored, we were that happy for him. Glenn Roeder scored an own goal for Newcastle, Neil Orr, Frank and Ray Stewart also bagged one each, which put us in third place with just five games to play. At that point in the season it was all getting tight, so the goal difference was definitely needed. A few years later, Glenn became the manager at West Ham and Neil McDonald became assistant to Sam Allardyce. After that game, whenever I saw Glenn and Neil I'd say, 'How the fuck did they appoint you after getting beaten 8-1 down here?'

Our penultimate game of the season was against West Brom and we won that 3-2 at The Hawthorns. If Liverpool had lost or got a draw in their last game at Chelsea, that meant ourselves or Everton could have won the league on the Monday at that point. Of course, we were also banking on Liverpool not winning.

Towards the end of the second half at West Brom it was going around that Liverpool were losing and we thought, 'We've got Everton on Monday and we could win the league', but it was all a hoax by the crowd. We were on such a high and then when we got back into the changing room, John Lyall told us, 'We've lost it lads. Liverpool have won.' Kenny Dalglish scored against Chelsea at Stamford Bridge as player-manager and got the only goal of the game to win Liverpool the title. How ironic that later on in my career Kenny would be my manager and lead that team to success, but he took great pleasure in constantly reminding me about that goal.

Back in the changing room, I've never seen so many grown men crying after that West Brom game. The dream had slipped away from us by the tightest of margins. The whole weight of the season, the highs throughout and now this. It was heart-breaking. None of us felt like playing on Monday, but we knew we had to. The journey to go up to Goodison Park was horrible.

As we got off the bus on 5 May 1986 at Everton, Howard Kendall, a proper nice bloke, shook all our hands and said, 'Great season lads,' and I think it was as if both Everton and West Ham had already acknowledged it was the end of their season without even playing the game. The game was a total anti-climax. If Chelsea had beaten Liverpool, that game on Monday night would have been for the title and that would have been some game. Everybody would have been up for it and you would have seen the best from Everton and West Ham, but that wasn't the case. We lost 3-1 and finished just one point behind Everton, which was a shame, because coming third is still the highest position West Ham have ever had.

The Boys of '86 squad was probably the best West Ham team of all time, but because of the restrictions after Heysel, we were banned from taking part in the UEFA Cup. I think our team was perfectly suited to European football in terms of the way we played at the back, the way we played through the middle third and the strikers we had. John Lyall would have also loved it because he had history of being in Europe. Unfortunately, it wasn't meant to be.

* * * * *

A LOT of people praised TC and Frank because they scored 56 league and cup goals between them, and rightly so, but if you look back there were a lot of defensive records broken too that season. For example, we only lost 10 league games, two of which were at home, we only conceded 24 goals and Parkesy went 559 minutes without conceding a goal. These days you hear about teams needing a big squad, but the '85/86 season showed how well it worked with a small squad, although we were incredibly lucky with injuries.

For those of us who weren't playing in the World Cup, at the end of the season a few of us went to The Phoenix Apollo restaurant in Stratford run by a really nice man called Gil Panayiotou, who I'm still mates with to this day.

That place was phenomenal and it was always full of stars. They had a fire there in early 1985 and when they reopened it in September 1985, Trevor Brooking did the lunch opening with Leyton Orient manager Frank Clark, then in the evening Samantha Fox did the grand opening, which had the likes of Ray Winstone, Jamie Foreman and Glen Murphy in attendance. We had 10 successive testimonial seasons, so you can imagine how many functions were held there. Stag nights, ladies nights, whatever nights.

That season we were winning loads of games, so as a result we ended up at the Phoenix a lot. People would literally beg to come to these parties as you'd spot the likes of the cast from *EastEnders*, *London's Burning*, Telly Savalas, every one of the Page 3 girls at the time, loads of top boxers like Marvin Hagler, Roberto Duran and Nigel Benn, politicians, you name it.

Tottenham and Arsenal players also came in, but it was more or less everyone and anyone who was in and around East London.

The papers once said it was 'The West End that came to the East End,' which I agreed with. Drink is drink, but they had the best food, the best waiters who were all fun guys and it was just totally relaxing. Me and my dad would plod in, particularly after the evening matches because I always used to struggle sleeping after games, so it was good to go in there and have something to eat. It was only 10 minutes from the ground and it was open late. By the time we got out of the ground about 11pm, we'd get there about 11.30pm and unwind.

And if it was on a Saturday after the game, Gil used to let us go upstairs to their flats where they lived and watch *Match of the Day* with his mum. There wasn't all these smartphones and social media back then, you just worked on trust and we trusted Gil and his family. It was a much better world to live in. I pity some of the kids growing up now who can't move because your life is like being on Big Brother. Mind you, after that season, all eyes were on us to go one better and win the league.

Chapter 15

INJURY TIME

'I joined a West Ham team who were doing very well the year before, looking possibly to get the club and players to different places on that success. However, they weren't doing so well when I joined them in March '87. They were struggling towards the bottom of the table, had quite a few injuries and quite a few unsettled players.'

– Liam Brady

PRE-SEASON GAMES are a standard part of professional football, but few beat the beginning of the 1986/87 season.

On 12 August 1986 we played a friendly against FC Den Haag in Holland. I had a bit of a niggle and John said to rest it up. During the game we're playing poorly and went 1-0 down, so he said, 'Come on. Get out there in midfield. It will be good for your fitness. Remind them that we've got to pass the ball.' I came on for about half an hour and ended up equalising with a header from Wardy's free-kick. The final score was 1-1.

After the game John said, 'Go on, have a couple of hours out, but I want you back by 11pm, because we're flying home in the morning.' We got in bang on 11pm and John was sitting there in the hotel with all the coaching staff counting us back in. TC got back with Frank and Wardy, and Frank said, 'I don't go to bed at 11pm, I go out at that time.' The three of them go down the fire escape out the back but coming behind them with the same idea was me, Alvin and Stevie Walford. We were all like, 'What you doing here?' We all go down the escape, through the kitchen and got to the nightclub thinking we were the only ones out, but everyone had slipped out in their little threes and fours. There we were in the club on the dancefloor doing the rowing boat song, *Oops Upside Your Head*, and there must have been a West Ham fan there or someone who knew us, who decided to grass us up, because we got rumbled.

In the morning, we came down for breakfast and John came into the room, looking mainly at Wardy, TC and Frank, then shouts, 'I know some of you were out last night. Whoever was, you're fined 50 quid each,' which was a lot of money back then. As John's still fixed on those three, we're all looking at each other, thinking, 'He doesn't know.' He then said, 'I'm going to get out of the room now and when I come back in, I'm going to pick up whatever money has been left on the table.' I think he thought it was going to be 150 quid, but when he came back, there was about a grand on the table. Pretty much everyone had gone out including some of the coaching staff. He wasn't overly impressed.

The first game of the season was on 23 August at home against Coventry, which was a tough first game. Cyrille Regis played up front with Keith Houchen and it was a baking hot day. Cyrille was a top player who was really good in the air, good with his feet and scored a good few 30 yarders, but the main asset he had over a lot of centre-forwards was that he was very good at running with the ball and holding you off.

Our reputation from the previous season of scoring goals was preceding us, which meant they would not come out of their own half. This made it very difficult for us to break down until I took an opportunity in the second half from a free-kick outside the penalty box and curled one in the top corner past Steve

Ogrizovic to give us three points. That was the first time I won man of the match and that was my first ever goal for West Ham, which came in my 93rd game.

Most people won a flash telly, a nice stereo and stuff like that for man of the match, but instead they gave me a bottle of champagne. Typical. I went up to the lounge and Nick Berry, who was a big West Ham fan and had just started off in *East-Enders*, presented me with the award.

For whatever reason, all seven of my goals for West Ham were either free-kicks or headers, which is funny because everyone says I've never headed a ball in my life. I had loads of strengths and weaknesses to my game, both of which I had to accept. My main strengths were passing, striking the ball and being calm in possession. Weaknesses were slight lack of pace and sometimes not being as aggressive as I should have been for a centre-back. As far as the free-kicks are concerned, I used to love striking a ball and used to get in early at Chadwell Heath to practise. I loved taking free-kicks and hated it when we got one on a matchday and everyone crowded around saying, 'Who's taking it?' I'd be like, 'You know who's fucking taking it. We've rehearsed it all week and now you all want to get on the ball?' It was usually TC or McAvennie, who were shit at free-kicks.

Four weeks later we played Luton at home and I scored again, along with Georgie Parris, although I'll admit I scored with a lucky header. Normally, if I was attacking corners, my role was to be on the near post flicking them on. This was a secondary header that came back and I headed it in. Whichever club I was at, near-post headers were very much in vogue and I don't understand why they don't do it nowadays. They just tend to whip a ball in with pace, because these balls are a lot lighter and quicker. The more movement there is in a corner, the more you can move defenders around and the better chance you have of scoring a goal.

Butter wouldn't melt:
An early picture with
Mum and (right) putting
pen to paper as I start my
football career

*Photo (right): Courtesy of
Ken 'Mr Fulham' Coton*

Big day: Signing professional for Fulham in 1976. I'm welcomed to the club by the Cottagers' former England midfielder Alan Mullery – and it's smiles all round from youth team coach Ken Craggs (far left), my parents Peter and Valerie and my sister, Joanne
                                                                    Photo: Ken 'Mr Fulham' Coton

Star man: Accepting the KPM Trophy for Fulham's Player of the Year in 1977 from former Fulham player and England boss Ron Greenwood

Photo: Ken 'Mr Fulham' Coton

Seeya later: Giving the slip to Notts County's Brian Stubbs

Photo: Ken 'Mr Fulham' Coton

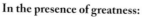

Head master: Rising to get a header on goal at Craven Cottage (above) and battling against Liverpool's Alan Hansen under the floodlights (left)

Photo (top): Ken 'Mr Fulham' Coton

In the presence of greatness: Les Strong alongside me at the back, Alan Slough in front of me and a front line of Bestie, John Evanson and Bobby Moore – I learned from the legends!

Roker raid: Rising high against Sunderland

Photo: Ken 'Mr Fulham' Coton

Goal buzz: It was always a delight to score at Craven Cottage

Photo: Ken 'Mr Fulham' Coton

Classy finish: Chipping Tony Burns to score the winner against Crystal Palace at Selhurst Park, October 1977

Photo: Ken 'Mr Fulham' Coton

Best of times: I met Bing Crosby in an aiport in Gran Canaria and two days later I was playing alongside George Best for Fulham against Luton away. You couldn't make it up!

Photo: Ken 'Mr Fulham' Coton

Young Lion: Here I am, 17 years old and captaining England Under-18s during the 1977/78 season, along with (left to right) Mark Lovell, Perry Digweed, Tony Mahoney

Photo: Ken 'Mr Fulham' Coton

Gale force: Slide tackling Everton's talented hitman Gary Lineker in front of the Chicken Run

Roles reversed: On the attack against Watford as the great John Barnes attempts to block my shot

Tough opponents: Contesting a high ball with Arsenal's Alan Smith. I came up against some lethal strike partnerships and his double act with Ian Wright was one of the best

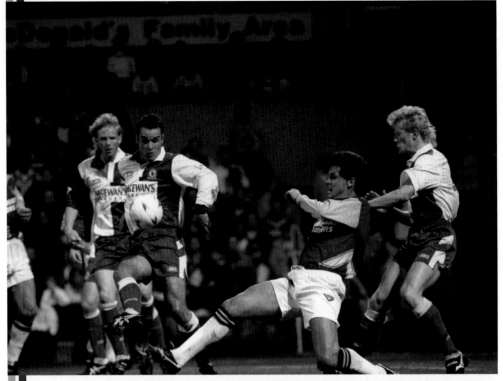

Future team-mates: In years to come I'd be lining up alongside Colin Hendry but here I am in the thick of the action against Blackburn Rovers at Upton Park

Seeing red: FA Cup semi-final at Villa Park against Nottingham Forest in 1991. Holding my head in my hands as I am sent off by referee Keith Hackett in the 20th minute

INJURY TIME

Towards the end of November, we'd played 16 games and only lost three. Bearing in mind we'd lost three out of our first four games the season before and finished third, yes, we were feeling confident going into the game against Newcastle away on 30 November, especially as they were hovering around relegation at the time. Well, we got smashed 4-0.

At this point in the season we had a number of injuries in the team, which gave way to a number of academy players being pushed up to the first team. Players like Stevie Potts and Paul Ince were all good hungry players coming through and Incey made his league debut in this game, coming on as sub for Alan Dickens and you could tell from the off that he was a quality player. People would call him flash, but I saw another side to him, almost like an arrogance that he was going to be a top player, which is exactly what he was.

On 9 February 1987 we played against Sheffield United in the fourth round of the FA Cup and we beat them 4-0. Frank scored two and me and Stewart Robson scored one each. Robbo had only been signed a few weeks before, to play alongside Alan Dickens, but taking the place of Geoff Orr or Neil Pike, who I thought were very good players. Sometimes, when those players are missing you don't realise how good they were in the first place until someone else comes in. Robbo came in as a big money signing from Arsenal, with quite a big reputation from there, and no disrespect to Robbo, but I think bringing him in at the time kind of broke the team spirit a bit for the rest of the season and in my opinion he didn't fit our style of play. What I mean by that is, statistically we won far more games when we were together with a consistent team, than when we were not, or experimenting, albeit injuries for the team also curtailed us that season.

However, one player who slotted in immediately was Liam Brady when we signed him from Ascoli, Italy in March. John

Lyall wanted us to pass the ball out from the back and that was the way Liam was brought up to play, which meant I complemented him nicely. I'd break into midfield and we would do combination play together. If I wanted to come out with the ball, he'd make himself available and I'd pass it to his feet.

Liam was a legend who was coming to the end of his career and when he arrived, unfortunately, a few of the players got transferred and a number were injured, including myself with an Achilles. What he brought to the table was experience and the fact that we were in the presence of a legend. I used to see things in training and think, 'He's a great player now, imagine what he was like in Italy and at Arsenal...'

Coming off a record breaking season, this one was certainly an anti-climax when we finished 15th. Injuries played their part, but I also think that money caused some issues, especially after the previous season. Some of the boys started to look at what the players at Liverpool and Man United were on, or hear what the players in international circles were pulling in and all of a sudden, from having that mentality of thinking we were going to be there for evermore, many moved onto the carrot being dangled. It worked for a few, but not for most.

As far as myself goes, my last game of the season was against Aston Villa on 25 April 1987 and I didn't play again until New Year's Day 1988, due to rupturing my Achilles. One positive though was that Bonzo was voted Hammer of the Year, which he thoroughly deserved as he missed the Boys of '86 season and was gutted. He'd come to games and watch from the line and it was such a shame he couldn't play that season, because he deserved to be part of that team. Bonzo being Bonzo, he would watch the game and say afterwards, 'This is some of the best football I've ever seen here.' There was no ego or animosity with him, he was always just pleased for the team.

INJURY TIME

Think about it though, how can someone not start a game for 21 months and then come back at 40 years old and still be one of our best players? When he came back into the gym and we started playing one or two touch football, he'd say, 'This is a bit too fast for me, I might need to retire,' but he soon got back into it and absolutely loved it. Despite his enthusiasm and John's positive outlook on everything, the next season turned out to be a tough one on a few fronts.

*****

OUR FIRST game of the 1987/88 season was a 0-3 defeat at home against QPR and Dev snapped his Achilles after 15 minutes. Both Dev and Ray Stewart were replaced by Dicko and Gary Strodder, which was the first time two subs were allowed in a game.

I was in the middle of doing rehab for my Achilles and it helped that Dev was in the same boat so we could do it together. Dev's rehab took longer because they didn't realise at first that he'd snapped it. They thought he'd just pulled it and put him in plaster for three weeks instead of operating straight away. That put Dev out for over a year. I felt particularly sad for him because he'd spent two years out with a cruciate knee ligament injury and then he came back and ruptured his Achilles. It takes great strength of mind to bounce back twice like that, especially as he was at his peak just before the injuries. That said, even after the injuries he was still our best player, which shows how good he really was.

We still went to Upton Park to watch games, but sometimes we had to do rehab at home, which meant we'd miss out on games. We had a trampette to jump on which helped to strengthen the tendon and had various exercises that we had to repeat daily, but getting back into training after an Achilles problem ain't that easy.

If you lose two key players it certainly hurts the status quo of the whole team. In the meantime, with me out, John changed it to a back three system, with Incey sometimes in midfield and others playing as sweeper.

In 1985/86 everything worked like clockwork and was in our favour, but it was starting to become the opposite in 1987/88. In the first 10 games we only won once, against Norwich. Robson, Brady, Tommy McQueen, Strodder, Potts, Ince had all come in, while Frank left early October 1987 and TC would leave at the end of the season. Things have to change, that's inevitable, but it takes time and doesn't always work. This was one of those occasions.

One game we did do well in was against Newcastle at home on 19 December 1987. I wasn't playing because of my Achilles, and Paul Ince and Stewart Robson both scored against a good Newcastle squad which included a young Paul Gascoigne. I played against him when he was at Newcastle and Spurs over the years and he was an incredible talent, who was always chirping on the pitch and winding people up. This game Billy Bonds marked him and Bill was 41 years of age and I remember him coming off saying, 'That kid's going to be some player.' I tell you what though, Bonzo gave as good as he got against a 20-year-old Gazza. Bonzo wouldn't have roughed him up because he was always totally fair, but he was hard as nails. If Gazza could play against Bonzo and hold his own, it was obvious at that point that he was going to be fine with any Italian man-marker at that time.

Off the pitch, there was something else that was memorable that season. We were invited to go on the Christmas edition of the television show *Whose Baby?* and on the panel guessing were Nanette Newman and Henry Cooper. The host was Bernie Winters, who had this gigantic St Bernard dog with him called

Schnorbitz and there was about six or seven of us players on there with our kids and my son Anthony was running riot.

I had to be on my own for a little while I was being told what to do by the TV people and Parkesy's son Scott, who was older than Anthony, volunteered to look after him. Anthony was wearing this all-in-one outfit which had a cross belt on it and when they eventually got on the stage Scott was being led by Anthony holding onto this cross belt like a pair of reins. I said to Scott, 'You alright looking after him?' and he said 'Yeah, no problem,' as Anthony started shaking the Christmas tree as if he wanted to take it down. Thankfully he didn't try anything on with Schnorbitz, because he might have eaten Ant. As we were walking out a couple of old girls walked over and said, 'We just came to see you.' I said, 'Ahh. Very nice to meet you.' They quickly said, 'Not you. Your son! He's hilarious.'

Signing Leroy Rosenior in March 1988 was a good move. John was very good at making signings to light the place up a little bit, which was definitely what we needed at the time. After Frank had left and TC was on his way out, we needed centre-forwards and John asked me about players who I thought were appropriate. I mentioned Leroy and John said, 'Is he good enough. Are you sure?' I said, 'Yeah. I'm sure, I'm sure.' John didn't hang around and here's how quickly he got Leroy in.

That particular week in March, Leroy had already agreed to sign for Watford. He went to Vicarage Road, spoke with the manager Steve Harrison and Elton John and as he was walking out the door Steve said to him, 'You have to live within 12 miles of Watford.' Leroy had a really young family in South London and there was no way he could pack up shop and live up there, so the deal fell through.

He went back to Fulham and in the morning John Lyall turned up at the training ground. The guys at Fulham said, 'John Lyall wants to see you. West Ham have agreed a fee.' He had a chat with John, sorted a deal and agreed to play a game the next day, which funnily enough was at home against Watford on 19 March.

We were in the relegation zone at that time. On the morning of the game, Leroy walks straight into Upton Park dressing room to meet the lads. As he walked in, I made him feel at home by doing what I do best, taking the piss out of him and cracking a few jokes. The best part was the game itself. We won 1-0 and I passed the ball to Leroy and he scored the winner. He came off exhausted at the end of 90 minutes after the most incredible introduction to Upton Park, but to a standing ovation. That's the way to introduce yourself as a new striker.

There's only one positive I could draw from the games that season and that was our performance in evening games was better than our Saturday matches. In fact, during the 10 years I was there, evening games were always good at the Boleyn Ground. If every game had been played in the evening, we would have won the league three years on the trot! The atmosphere was better and the pitches were quicker because there was an evening dew on the surface and we were a passing team that liked to move the ball around quickly, instead of playing on a dry pitch on a Saturday. As far as the fans were concerned, everyone went to work during the day, left work about 1pm, had a drink, something to eat and then headed to the game. It was an earthy atmosphere and I reckon there's more West Ham supporters up the City of London than any other team. Their commitment to the weekday matches was unparalleled.

On 30 April 1988 Bonzo played his last game of football as we lost 2-0 against Southampton at home. He was 41 years and 226 days old and I said to him, 'I think you can play on Bill.' He said, 'I've had enough Galey. I'm looking forward to retirement.' Thankfully, that wasn't the last we saw of him.

INJURY TIME

We finished 16th that season, which was a place lower than the season before, but you just kind of got the feeling something bad was on the horizon.

Chapter 16

HAMMERED

'We should have never been in that position. I think we proved that in the cup competitions beating some of the big boys. We could do it on the day, but we weren't consistent.'

– Liam Brady

WITH TC leaving in the summer and Frank McAvennie having left the previous season, it was like starting all over again. We signed a lad called David Kelly from Walsall and immediately, the pressure was on him to perform. He didn't hit the ground running and the crowd had a go at him. Another guy called Allen McKnight came in as keeper and he didn't hit the ground running either. Both David and Alan had big shoes to fill and they were really unfairly treated by the crowd, who could make or break you.

One player who did start well was Julian Dicks. Dicksy came to West Ham towards the end of the previous season and I nicknamed him Norm, because he looked like the geezer at the end of the bar from the television programme *Cheers*, because he was a little bit plump when he turned up. Fair play to him he trained like mad and got his weight down really quickly, but we still called him Norm anyway. When he walked into the changing room, we'd all say, 'Nooooorm!' Dicksy was a good lad and if it wasn't for the sending offs he had, he would have definitely played for England many more times, but those cards preceded him, which is a real shame, because they disguised just how good a player he was. Great striker of the ball and a great penalty taker.

The opening game of the 1988/89 season was at Southampton and it was one-way traffic. I had to come off at half-time because of a calf injury and we were already 2-0 down. Not a great start to the season for me as it took me out until early October. Paul Hilton came on for me in the Southampton game and Stuart Slater was replaced by Alan Dickens. Stu had just come into the team and was a terrific young player. He emerged just after Kevin Keen, Stevie Potts and Paul Ince as the next new kid on the block. Stuart's nickname was 'Chopper,' because he couldn't tackle. He used to get chopped down by everyone because he was a great runner with the ball. Anyway, we lost 4-0 against Southampton, which was obviously not the start we were hoping for.

Our first home game was against Charlton on 3 September 1988 and we lost 3-1. The most memorable part of the day was when Bonzo got presented an award for his retirement after making a club-record of 799 appearances for West Ham. Four players he'd played with over the years – Geoff Hurst, Frank Lampard, Brian Kinsey and Patsy Holland – presented him with a frame showing various highlights of his career. A few months earlier he had been awarded an MBE and I started bowing to him and calling him 'My Lord.' He was like, 'Cut it out Galey!' Sir Trevor Brooking, Billy's best pal, often says, 'If it was services to football on the pitch, he should have received a knighthood,' and I couldn't agree more. Both Bonzo and Trev are two really humble blokes, and I'd say, after Hurst, Peters and Moore, it's Bonzo, Brooking and Dev who are up there with them.

On 10 September we beat Wimbledon away, then drew with Aston Villa at home the week after, but then it started going very wrong. If you would have said to me at the beginning of the season that a team which had Alan Devonshire on the right and Liam Brady on the left would get relegated, I'd think you were crazy. Sadly, it was like we were in a relegation battle from the beginning. It was another season riddled with injuries and anyone who could have got injured, did. In the first eight games we lost six, won one and drew one and started to get that feeling of 'we're going down.' However, for whatever reasons, we did alright in the cup games.

In the League Cup, we beat Sunderland 3-0 away on 27 September, then 2-1 at home a couple of weeks later, followed by a massive 5-0 thrashing over Derby on 1 November. The fourth round of the cup was against Liverpool at home on 30 November, which everyone thought we'd get slaughtered in because they were flying high at the time, winning all the competitions.

We were second from bottom and they were in fourth spot, but we had a great night beating them 4-1. Paul Ince scored two, I scored from the free-kick and Steve Staunton scored an own goal. West Ham hadn't beaten Liverpool since October 1982 and our next win over them wasn't until May 1995. It wasn't the best free-kick I'd scored, but to have done it against Liverpool in a cup game, that was maybe my most memorable goal for West Ham. We all went down to the Phoenix Apollo straight after the game and The Stylistics were playing live, singing *You Make Me Feel Brand New* and all that.

In my opinion, that game is what really launched Incey into the public eye and it was no surprise that he won Hammer of the Year that season. Three days after the Liverpool game he scored the only goal against Millwall away, to give us a badly needed three points in the league, so I guess, in a shit season, that was a great week.

Back to the League Cup. In January we beat Villa 2-1 in the

quarter-finals before coming up against a good Luton side on 12 February, which had the likes of Steve Foster, Mick Harford, Ricky Hill and Roy Wegerle. We lost 3-0 at home to them, which was a case of our strategy going wrong.

As a team, we knew we would be playing the second leg on their plastic pitch, so we went for it and left ourselves exposed. Allen McKnight didn't have the best of games and the crowd really turned on him. Then we played at Kenilworth Road for the second leg on 1 March and we got beaten 2-0. Luton played well and reached the final, but lost 3-1 to Nottingham Forest. At the same time, we'd been doing well in the FA Cup, beating Arsenal, Swindon and Charlton, but unfortunately we lost against Norwich 3-1 in the sixth round replay on 22 March. On the league front, we'd only won five, lost 15 and drawn seven by the end of March.

Shortly after the loss to Norwich, Frank McAvennie came back to West Ham after less than two seasons at Celtic and played in the last nine games. Frank could have gone to Arsenal at the time, who went on to win the league, so you can imagine why people thought he was crazy coming back to West Ham. The truth is, he loved the club and loved John Lyall. John said to him, 'We're getting relegated, but I want you to bring us back up.' Frank said, 'Yeah, no problem.' It was great to have him back on board and those last games kind of showed that, as he played with Leroy up front. Although he didn't score any goals, he certainly helped Leroy and his presence in the changing room was always priceless.

Unfortunately, 15 April 1989 was a day many would never forget for other reasons. A total of 97 fans would eventually lose their lives following a crush during an FA Cup game between Liverpool and Nottingham Forest at Hillsborough. We didn't see clips of it on telly until we got home, all we were hearing after the game was what was on the radio and you just couldn't believe it. When I got home and saw on the telly the bodies laid out on the pitch, that was horrible and my heart went out to the families.

Back to the league. We had only won five games the whole season, then in the last seven we won another five. There was no logic behind it. The ability was there, but John didn't quite solve the goalkeeping problem when Parksey was more often on the sidelines than not and key players kept getting injured. That was a lot for John to contend with.

One week after Hillsborough we played Millwall at home and won 3-0, then won the next three, lost against Everton, then beat Forest 2-1, with Leroy scoring both goals. It was surreal with Leroy, because he'd play, get his knee drained, rest and play again. He wasn't training with the team, just playing. He had a great career, but he could have done so much more if it wasn't for his injuries.

On 9 May we played at Hillsborough, which was the first home match at the stadium since the tragedy, less than four weeks before. There was a really eerie feeling at the ground, with the Leppings Lane end covered with tarpaulin. We won 2-0, but I came off early in the second half after a clash of heads with Steve Whitton and ended up being carted off to the hospital with concussion.

There was a lot riding on our final game against Liverpool on 23 May. A win would have kept us up, whereas a loss would see us relegated. At the other end of the league, Arsenal needed us to either win, draw or keep Liverpool's goals down to a minimum, so they could win on goal difference.

Although Leroy equalised John Aldridge's opener, we ended up losing 5-1 and it was his goal that helped Arsenal win the title. As soon as that final whistle went at Anfield, Leroy went straight to hospital to have his knee done. We stayed up in Liverpool that night, but as a team we certainly weren't celebrating.

We went from having the best season in West Ham's history in 1985/86, to 15th, 16th and now relegated in 19th place. My immediate thoughts were, 'We've got them in this trouble, so we need to get them out and back up straight away,' but you could sense some of the other players were thinking, 'I need to stay in the top flight and get away from West Ham.' Let's just say the next season came with a lot of changes.

Chapter 17

END OF AN ERA

'We were THE family club, but once John went we just became like all the others.'
– Eddie Gillam, West Ham kit manager

ON MONDAY 5 June 1989, I was on a golf course and someone ran out to tell me I had an important phone call I needed to take in the club house. I thought someone had passed away and in all honesty, it turned out to be a mourning process of sorts.

John Lyall had been sacked. I couldn't believe it. The previous season, we suffered a lot of injuries and struggled to find our form as we went down, but John's parting words were, 'I've been down with West Ham before and we'll bounce straight back.' We got relegated and he had already organised the tour for the pre-season, but he was sacked in that summer before we got back. Alvin Martin, Liam Brady, Dev and a few others were all first team regulars and missed a large chunk of the previous season due to injuries, which is another reason why I think it was bang out of order giving John the sack, because he didn't have his players at hand to play.

John had been at West Ham Football Club for 34 years and never ever did anyone think he was going to leave. I still don't think the club has been the same since that man left. What he created was unique. Similar to what Sir Alex Ferguson created at Manchester United, with that whole family environment. John knew every player's name, every wife and child's name, your parents and he sorted out Christmas parties for the lads and the families, making sure all the little-uns got presents. And we all got a turkey from the local butchers! When my family came up on matchday, he'd come right across the foyer and if he saw my dad he'd say, 'Alright Peter. How's it going? How's the cabs?' If any player was sick or injured in hospital, he'd be the first person there to support them. But let's not forget, first and foremost, he was a wonderfully skilled and respected coach. We'd have the likes of Sven-Göran Eriksson at Chadwell Heath looking and learning off him and he always made sure he had time for any of the attending coaches.

John should have been made director of football or something like that and West Ham legends Bonzo and Trevor Brooking should have been appointed joint managers in the meantime. With those two being such good friends and totally different personalities, they would have been a great blend. Talk about getting the crowd onside. It was the dream team that never happened and instead they appointed Lou Macari, which was like appointing chalk after cheese. I'm not having a go at Lou, because what he achieved as a player was incredible, but the contrast of management styles with him and John was so different, it came as a culture shock to the team.

You had John's lovely footballing philosophy of playing out from the back and then you had Lou's philosophy of turning teams around, fighting for second balls, playing long balls and basically playing in a totally alien way to how we'd been playing all those years previously. Consequently, Lou had a bit of a senior players revolt on his hands.

That year, I'd mis-booked my holiday, but John had okayed it without any bother. I flew back a day later than everyone else because I knew I couldn't get the money back on my holiday and on arrival I found out that Lou had organised a pre-season friendly. Nobody had trained the whole pre-season and we came back and were playing Bordeaux on 15 July, who had the likes of Manny Kaltz, Klaus Allofs and Jesper Olsen playing for them. Lou says to us, 'We're off to Bordeaux tomorrow. Make sure you bring your gear and passports.' We were all looking at each other in bemusement and I said, 'We haven't been training. We're not ready for this. We need a couple of weeks behind us first.' He says, 'No. You're alright.' We got beaten 2-1 and it turned out to be a great running session, because they kept the ball for 90 minutes.

The opening game of the season was on 19 August at Stoke City. We drew 1-1, but the lasting memory was Frank McAvennie's injuries after Chris Kamara went in for a tackle on the hour-mark. Frank never attached any blame to Kammy because it's one of those tackles you both go into. Frank was on the turn, on one leg and that's when Chris tackled him. It was just one of those unfortunate things that happened, because Kammy was never like that as a person or a player. He was a good, athletic, aggressive player, but he never had that streak in him to actively want to hurt anyone. Unfortunately for Frank, he broke his leg and ankle, and also snapped his ligaments. Kammy felt awful and straight after the game was calling round the hospitals trying to find out where he was and how he was.

Frank was put into a taxi with Ray Stewart and sent to Stoke hospital, which was a crazy thing to have happened. The first guy Frank spoke to at the hospital was in Accident and Emergency and wasn't a specialist. He told Frank, 'You'll never walk properly again, never mind play football.' Frank said, 'Who the fuck are you?' and he said, 'I'm the surgeon.' Frank replied, 'Bollocks to you.'

Frank got on the coach with us lot and sat at the back in agony with this big balloon thing strapped to his leg. He ended up

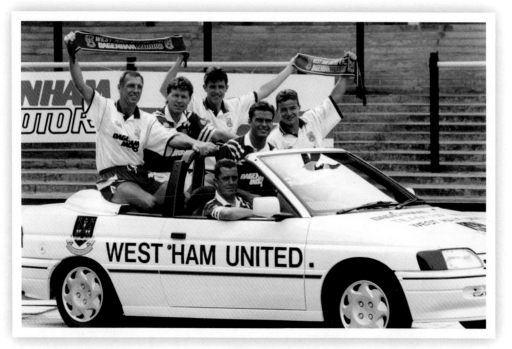

Getting in gear: Julian Dicks takes the driving seat as we announce Dagenham Motors as our new kit sponsors in 1992. Behind Julian are (left to right) Alvin Martin, Clive Allen, me, Steve Potts and Stuart Slater

Proud occasion: I was awarded a testimonial for 10 years' loyal service – but shortly before the game at Upton Park, I was told I was being released

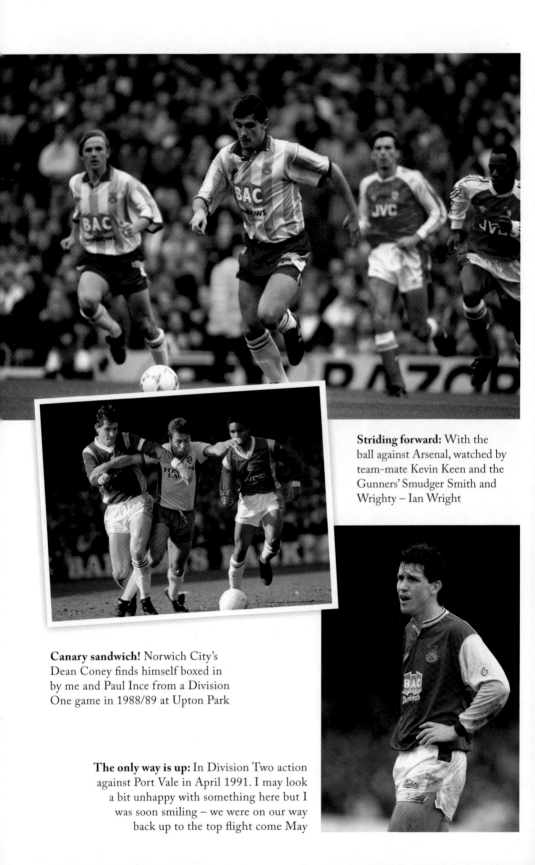

Striding forward: With the ball against Arsenal, watched by team-mate Kevin Keen and the Gunners' Smudger Smith and Wrighty – Ian Wright

Canary sandwich! Norwich City's Dean Coney finds himself boxed in by me and Paul Ince from a Division One game in 1988/89 at Upton Park

The only way is up: In Division Two action against Port Vale in April 1991. I may look a bit unhappy with something here but I was soon smiling – we were on our way back up to the top flight come May

Kenny comes calling: August 1994 and I find myself in Kenny Dalglish's Blackburn Rovers team

Fowler the prowler: Up against Liverpool's brilliant new striker Robbie Fowler

Sparks fly: Up against Sparky – aka Manchester United's Mark Hughes – as Colin Hendry looks on

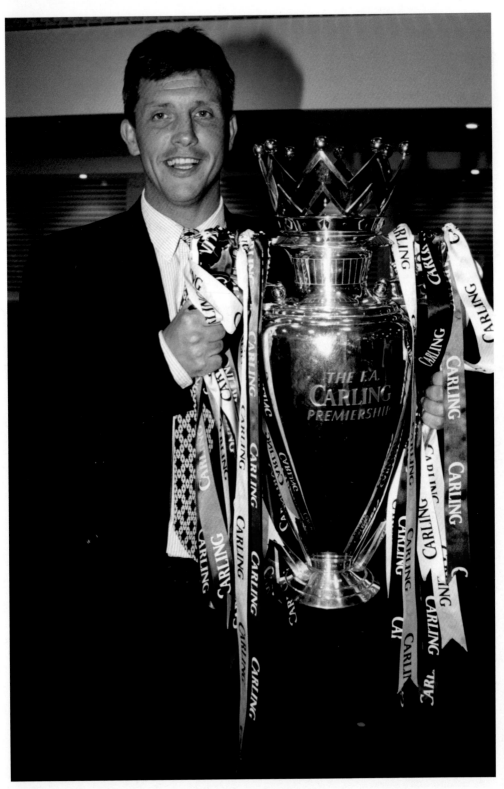

Campione: That season with Blackburn was a fairytale – from non-league football to Wembley and then a Premier League champion. I had to pinch myself when I held the trophy in May 1995

Smile for the camera: Being filmed in the dressing room with Alvin Martin as the 'old boys' from West Ham 1986 were reunited

Behind the mic: A career change which suited me just fine, reporting live for Sky Sports. This is me imparting some pearls of wisdom on the Carling Cup fourth round game between Luton and Everton in 2007

The next generation... With Walton Casuals college students at West Ham, explaining how the media works

Forever blowing bubbles: With my daughter Alex at the last game West Ham played at Upton Park in May 2016 and (right) with my son Anthony as the Hammers take on Manchester United in a Premier League game at the London Stadium

Picture (left) courtesy of Richard Pelham

Strange times: I become a cardboard cut-out in the stands at Ewood Park alongside Alan Shearer, Kevin Gallacher and Chris Sutton as Covid hits. The club were trying to create a sense of atmosphere as games resumed behind closed doors in July 2020

Surprise trip: Celebrating my 60th in New York with my partner Dee

Gone fishin': With my mate Stewart Lawson, Frank McAvennie, Paul Walsh and Paul Parker filming a six-part BT Sport series called Angling Outlaws

FULHAM FOOTBALL CLUB

Back at the Cottage: With former Fulham player Simon Morgan and one of my best friends in football, Les Strong (centre)

Looking forward: I've been a player, pundit, commentator, mentor and chairman in football – but the most important things to me these days are health, happiness and family

Photo: Tony Woolliscroft

seeing a surgeon at 2am in London who said, 'Yeah. I'll fix that.' He was out for the season, but thankfully did make a return.

Another early departure in 1989/90 was Paul Ince, who left after the opening game. Incey had rang me and Dev for advice long before the start of the season. 'Man United are interested. What do you think?' Me and Dev said something along the lines of, 'You could probably do with another season here.' That wasn't us being selfish, we just thought, with him being guaranteed a place in the first team, he could learn a lot and increase his profile that much more to prepare for a big move down the road.

Incey's agent at the time was Ambrose Mendy, who also used to manage the boxer Nigel Benn and a lot of footballers at the time like Ricky Hill and the Stein brothers. Well, he made the move and it turned out he was right and we were wrong. He was transferred to Man United for a million quid and was absolutely brilliant up there.

Lou was a fitness fanatic and his training was focused that way, with running and stamina. He was that kind of player himself and he brought it to his management style and that really wasn't what West Ham was about. If Lou had introduced his systems gradually, it might have been okay, but at the speed everything happened, it just didn't work. I remember travelling up to Hull in our fourth game of the season and we took some trainers which we thought we were going to use for a walk in the evening. We travelled up there, five hours on a coach and normally Friday was a light session, but instead he had us running round the docks of Hull and said, 'If you can't do a cross country run the day before a game, you're not a fit player.' Liam Brady got injured running on the concrete – he was 33 at the time – and a lot of players were stiff to say the least after. We did well to get a 1-1 draw the next day.

Lou did however make some good signings in the coming months, with experienced pros like Colin Foster, Martin Allen, Jimmy Quinn, Tim Breacker and Luděk Mikloško arriving, as Parksey played out his last season. I was very lucky to have played with two top keepers at West Ham with Ludo and Parkesy and there was not much between them really. Phil probably shades it for me, but Ludo was excellent. He was super fit and used to do all the running with us and was usually leading up the front.

Ian Bishop also joined in December 1989 in a swap deal alongside Trevor Morley, for Mark Ward, who went to Man City. Bish was one of the few that could have competed for a position in the Boys of '86 team. He could play with both feet, had good vision and was a real good fella.

As far as I go, Lou tried to sell me that season. He said, 'Luton have come in for you.' My old mate Ray Harford was manager there and had made the approach, but I said, 'I don't particularly want to go there.' He said, 'They want to do a deal, a player exchange, I can't tell you who. You ring Luton up and sort the deal yourself.' I said, 'What? If you want to sell me, you've got to do that side of things.' It was the strangest conversation and nothing came of it.

At the start of the new year, we played Torquay in the third round of the FA Cup and at the time, Georgie Parris had a bad ankle and Leroy had a bad knee. It was freezing and at about 10pm Lou asked Leroy and George to go with him into the sea in Devon, and had them standing in it for about 45 minutes. I understand the logic in that, because it's cold water, but I don't know why they just didn't put an ice pack on in front of the telly in the hotel. Either way, we got beaten 1-0 the day after in a big cup shock.

On 14 February, we played Oldham in the first leg of the semis of the League Cup. How's your luck when you draw two different teams in two successive seasons in the semi-finals of the League Cup that have plastic pitches? There was always battles between us and Oldham and they were a really good team, led by Joe Royle. He used to call his midfielders 'Dogs of War,' with the likes of Andy Ritchie, Mike Milligan, Rick Holden, Ian Marshall and Paul Warhurst in the line-up.

Lou took us up there the night before to train on the pitch to get used to it and he also announced we were going to play a back five against an attacking side who knew their pitch inside out. We all looked at each other and said, 'We ain't played a back five all season. How are we going to suddenly transfer into a back five? If we play a back five, we'll just get pinned in by Oldham who will put five up front against us. We won't get out of our own half.' He wasn't budging.

We lost 6-0 and we were lucky to get the nil. It was pissing down with icy rain and all of the West Ham fans were doing the conga when Oldham scored their sixth goal. They could see the farcical side of it. We can't completely blame tactics though, because we played shit. We couldn't get out of our own half and played with no plan whatsoever. This also happened to be Dev and Parksey's last ever games for West Ham. What a pair of legends.

Ludo's first game was at Swindon on 18 February 1990. Bill was like Lou's unofficial right hand man travelling with us everywhere and helping the team on all fronts. Bonzo says to me on the Friday before the game, 'I want you to room with him.' I said, 'Why?' He replies, 'You talk a lot and it will help him integrate.' I said, 'He doesn't understand a fucking word of English. How am I supposed to talk to him?'

Although Ludo couldn't speak English, you could tell he was a really nice guy just by his mannerisms. He's made me tea in the room and there he was with his pocket dictionary laying on the bed going through his pronouns, adjectives and God knows what. I said, 'Throw that book away. This is the best way to learn English,' and popped the telly on. I was trying to explain things with my own form of sign language. He says, 'Tomorrow,' and kind of shrugs. There I am on a Friday night standing there in my underpants trying to explain, 'As a goalkeeper, you only need to know two words. When the ball comes over and you go for a catch, shout 'KEEPER'S,' as I'm jumping up for an imaginary ball in my underpants. He understands that one. Then I try and lighten it up a bit and said, 'When you make a mistake, or fumble it in the goal, you say, 'Fucking hell.'' Ludo nodded.

Next day we played Swindon away and he concedes a goal which slipped through his grasp. He throws the ball out of the back of the net and says, 'Fucking hell.' I didn't know whether to laugh or cry. We drew that game 2-2. The West Ham fans loved him and it didn't take them long to create a song about him. *'My name is Ludo Miklosko I come from near Moscow, I play in goal for West Ham, West Ham! When I walk down the street, Everybody I meet says, Oi big boy, What's your name, My name is Ludo Miklosko I come from near Moscow, I play in goal for West Ham, West Ham!'*

A few years ago, I said to him, they still sing that song about you, even though you left West Ham in 1998. He said, 'It's very heartwarming, but the only thing I don't understand is that I didn't come from Moscow. I come from Prague.' I said, 'Yeah, but Prague doesn't fucking rhyme with Mikloško!'

* * * * *

LOU MACARI resigned on 18 February 1990. It was a short stay and he made a lot of good signings, but his style of football was never for me. I just want to say, I never had cross words with Lou and since he retired from football, he's done an incredible amount of charity work for homeless people, which he's been rightly recognised for. Well done, mate.

Ronnie Boyce took over in the interim just for a few days, then one day came in and said, 'I want to introduce you to your new manager.' We were all looking around thinking, 'Who's it going to be this time?' In walks Bonzo and we all started clapping and said, 'Thank fuck for that.'

Bill was appointed manager on 23 February and the day after we were playing against Blackburn at home. He inherited a team from Lou which had some good signings, but he had to mould it into his own squad now. In his first team talk I had a guess at how many 'fucks' he'd throw in. We had a little sweep in the dressing room beforehand and I was in my normal corner of the changing room getting changed. There was Ian Bishop and a few others and I said to them, 'I'll go for 15 fucks in the team talk.' Just to clarify, Bill was a different animal on and off the pitch. He was a quiet and mild-mannered man off the pitch who hardly swore, but when it came to football, he went into battle mode.

The talk starts something like this. 'We're playing fucking Blackburn today. They've travelled a long fucking way.' I'm standing there counting on my fingers, one, two, then when I got past 10, I started laughing and he says, 'Galey. What you fucking laughing at?' I said, 'I'm really sorry Bill, but we guessed how many 'fucks' you'd have in the team talk!' Everyone burst out laughing, including him. After everyone got their breath, he says, 'Let's get fucking serious,' which sent us off laughing again. It was a joy to work under Bonzo.

Bill's third game in charge was the return leg of the League Cup semi-final against Oldham on 7 March and we beat them 3-0 at home, but it could have easily been 10-0 that night. Eleven days later, on 18 March 1990 my daughter Alexandra was born. Despite arriving three weeks early, the birth itself went well, however, she required a blood transfusion, which was obviously a very worrying time for us as a family. After spending two weeks in special care Alexandra soon gained her strength, returned home and thankfully grew up to be incredibly healthy.

Our last game of the season on 5 May was at home against Wolves and it was a memorable one. Liam Brady had already told Bill at the turn of the year that he was going to call it a day, but those last few seasons weren't as good a send-off as they should have been for him due to bad injuries. However, his last game was the perfect goodbye.

Bonzo asked him, 'Do you want to play?', but because there was nothing in the match as we couldn't get into a promotion position and neither could Wolves, Liam said, 'No Bill. Put one of the kids in. Give them a chance.' That was typical Liam, putting the team first.

Kevin Keen played up to 52 minutes, then Liam came on and subbed him as we were 3-0 up. In the dying seconds of the game, Liam takes the ball from the halfway line and runs with it, before striking it with his left foot from outside the penalty box and swerving it across the goalkeeper into the bottom right hand corner of the net. Stunning strike. That was his last kick in football and then the referee blew the whistle. I went up to him and said, 'What a way to go!' We signed the football after and he's still got that in his trophy cabinet to this day.

What a great end to the season. We had a fantastic run with Bill from February and finished seventh, only two points off the play-offs. The question now was whether we could go one better next season?

Chapter 18

REFS, RED CARDS AND REVELATIONS

'The greatest glory in living lies not in never failing, but in rising every time we fall.'

– Nelson Mandela

THE 1990/91 season was Bonzo's first full one in charge and it was as if he gave us our old West Ham back. Bill was always a leader of men, but also a man of few words. He simply made decisions, honestly and correctly. Some people didn't appreciate that honesty, but I did, instead of a manager kidding you on and then talking behind your back and trying to move you out. I genuinely believe, because he loved the playing side so much, he underestimated what a good manager he was and perhaps never realised just how much we looked up to him.

We started that season in great form and went the first 21 games unbeaten in the league. The most significant game in that run was beating Hull 7-1 at home on 6 October, not for the result, but because Steve Potts scored his one and only goal of his professional career, which for the record was over 500 games. Stevie, like Paul Parker was a great man-marker, but most importantly, what a nice man.

Although we got knocked out of the League Cup early doors, we started well in the FA Cup. After a 0-0 draw against Aldershot, we had the replay on 16 January 1991 at home and beat them

6-1. They were a fourth tier team and switched the opening tie to Upton Park because their ground only held about 5,000 people and they could generate more money holding it at our ground. Ian Bishop came on as an early sub for Stewart Robson and I was captain. On this day, me and Bish were playing one-twos while moving forward, before he ended up going through and around the keeper and scoring.

Our team that season was a top flight set of players playing in the Second Division. It was just a question of us having our attitude in the right place and we knew we could go up. By the end of January we'd only lost once in 27 games and were flying, but then we started to go up and down in form.

One game that I won't forget in a hurry at that time was at home against Millwall on 24 February, which we won 3-1. I've had my nose broken four times in football and the one that stands out was against Teddy Sheringham during that game, when I jumped up and got into Teddy's elbow. It was all accidental and Teddy was the first one to check on me. I broke my nose on a Sunday and went to hospital the day after to have it reset. I came back on the Tuesday and had a plaster cast on my face. It was when they removed the cast that I realised I was allergic to plaster, as I had this massive red mark across my face like I'd missed a patch with the suncream. After the op the doc said, 'No physical contact at all for about 10 days, just to make sure it sets properly.' When I went in on the Thursday, Bonzo asked, 'You okay to play Saturday against West Brom?' I explained what the doc said and he replied, 'Can you do me a favour Galey? We haven't got a centre-half.' I said, 'Okay Bill.' That day I was up against Gary Bannister and was heading the ball with the side of my face the whole time. Banno says to me during the game, 'I'm surprised you're playing today, Tone. I heard you broke your nose in two places on Sunday.' I went, 'Nah. That was a misprint,' and got away with it.

Between February to mid-March we only won one in six, then on 20 March I scored the only goal at home against Bristol City, to win 1-0. At the time, me and Parksey had started a little company with the entertainer Richard Digance, which didn't last very long, but one Sunday in March 1991 we had a small function and Trevor Morley and Ian Bishop came along. After the function, Trev and Bish went on to have another drink, then Trev and his missus had an argument later that night. At the end of the evening, Trev got stabbed. By who? Let's just say I blame whoever had the knife in their hand.

After the Bristol City game we only lost one in the next eight, but it wasn't the league games that made the headlines in those weeks. The Denial of Goal Scoring Opportunity rule had just come out on the Wednesday and on Sunday 14 April 1991 we played in the semi-final of the FA Cup against Nottingham Forest. That morning, Spurs had beaten Arsenal in the other semi-final. Gazza got a great goal against David Seaman and they played at Wembley and we played at Villa Park. If we won the Forest game, we were playing Spurs at Wembley. That was a big London rivalry and although we were in the second tier, we really fancied our chances if we played Spurs.

We had a midweek game against Brighton which I missed, because I wasn't quite fit due to a calf strain. Bonzo said to me, 'Rest it and see how you are for the game on Sunday.' I had a fitness test in the morning with Rob Jenkins and I said to him, 'Rob, I ain't missing this. I don't even need a fitness test. I'm playing.' He said, 'Sorry mate. You have to do it.' I replied, 'Okay,' but I knew I was going to play, even if I had to play with one leg, because I didn't want to lose the chance of playing in my only FA Cup semi-final, but also due to the prospect of playing in the final if we won. I went through a few sprints and thankfully I got the green light.

We started the game and we were quite comfortable. It was a

shitty, sandy pitch at Villa Park, which was hard to get the ball moving on, but we knew that going out, because most pitches were in a state towards the end of the season. Gary Crosby was playing up front with Nigel Clough and on 27 minutes, the ball gets played wide at an angle and me and Gary both try to get in front by putting our arms in front of each other. I'm about six inches taller than Gary and my arm has come a little bit higher than him and we've got in a tangle and both hit the deck. I fell awkwardly and thought I'd put my shoulder out, but as I've got up and wiped sand off myself, I thought, 'I wonder which way that free-kick is going.' Next thing Keith Hackett, who was a bit of an overweight referee, amazingly sprinted over, looked at me and pulled out the red card. He didn't say a word to tell me what I'd been sent off for, or even make eye contact with me.

I shouted a load of expletives at him and then said, 'You're joking. I didn't even know which way that foul was going to go.' Gary Crosby couldn't believe it either. Next thing Stuart Pearce comes over from Nottingham Forest and says, 'You've got to go off mate,' and I've said, 'Pearcy, fuck off. It's got nothing to do with you.' I got ushered away to the tunnel with Tony Carr, who was one of the youth team coaches at the time. Bill says to Tony, 'Escort him up the stairs.' From the moment of my sending off until the end of the game, and all through half-time, the fans relentlessly sung, 'Billy Bonds' claret and blue army, Billy Bonds' claret and blue army.'

We go up the stairs and there was no key to get in the dressing room. I said to Tony halfway up the stairs, 'Leave me on my own.' I was walking up and down the corridor in my studs and I've asked, 'Has anyone got a key around here?' While I'm shouting and hollering I see one of the BBC analysts who had a screen and he's said, 'Terrible decision, Tony. Is there a few words you'd like to say for the BBC?' I said, 'Yeah. Fuck off.'

I got into the changing room after about five minutes and shortly after I heard the crowd cheering, as Georgie Parris had hit the post. Anyway, it's 0-0 at half-time and at this stage the team are coming back and I'm pacing up and down in my shitty shellsuit.

As they walked in I sat down and they all ruffled my hair as they went past, as I had my head down. Bonzo came in and didn't look at me and I thought, 'Oh no.' He's looking around, doing the team talk, rearranging the formation with 10 players, then before they went back out he went into a Churchillian one. 'Lads, that's one of the worst fucking decisions I've ever seen in my life. If you don't do it for yourselves out there, or your families, or the 40,000 fans out there and all those people watching on telly, you do it for your mate there. You do it for him.' They went out and lost 4-0!

I walked out with them for the second half and a suit from the FA comes up and goes, 'Really sorry son. I know you've been sent off and you're upset, but you can't go out onto the field of play.' Billy said, 'He fucking is. Ain't you done enough to us? Leave it alone,' then we walked to the dugout. If the incident had happened a week before, I wouldn't have even got a yellow card, never mind a red.

Roll the clock forward to 2014 and I hadn't spoken to the referee for 23 years and never received an apology or anything. There was a programme called *YouAreTheRef.com* and an agent rung me and said, 'We want to do an interview with you in a pilot show to launch it. It will be up at Hillsborough.' I thought it was one of my mates winding me up. He carries on and says, 'It will be you and Keith Hackett.' I said, 'What? You're having a laugh. Twenty three years and I haven't had so much as an apology. You want me to come up and do this show? Are you crazy? Hackett killed that match and our chances of winning the FA Cup.' I've gone on and on, and this geezer says, 'We'll give you two grand to come on the show.' I said, 'What time do you want me up there?'

I went up there, met him and off air he said, 'We need to shake hands on the show' and I said, 'I can't do that. Not in front of the fans.' Hackett reckoned he had to do it at the time and the FA said what a great decision it was, but I'm not so sure. Let's just say we're not on each other's Christmas card lists, but I don't wish anyone any evil or harm.

That sending off had an impact that not only cost us the FA Cup, but also winning the league. I couldn't play in those last three games because there was a two week lead-in before the ban kicked in. We finished second that season, but we could have definitely won Division Two, simply because we only won once in the last five games. I'm not the reason that happened, but it left us without a recognised centre-half. Stevie Potts had to play in there and played well, but there was little time to get used to the new set-up.

On a positive note, from a defensive perspective West Ham conceded fewer goals than any team in Division Two, letting in only 34. Middlesbrough were the next closest, conceding 47. Consequently, Ludo was Hammer of the Year.

Division One awaited us. Here we go again.

Chapter 19

UPS, DOWNS AND THE PASSING OF A LEGEND

'If you never concede a goal, you're going to win more games than you lose.'

– Bobby Moore

THE 1991/92 season was the total opposite of the previous one. It's like we couldn't get off this rollercoaster. In the first 13 games we won two, drew six and lost five. Injuries once again were widespread with myself, Trevor Morley and Julian Dicks down for most of the season, but Bonzo was as good as gold and said, 'It can't be helped. We need to get on with it.'

There were also a few players who were getting transferred or thinking of moving, like Stuart Slater. Stu came to me one day asking my advice on a transfer and it was like déjà vu with Paul Ince. Liam Brady was now manager at Celtic and Stu says, 'Liam's asking me to sign for Celtic.' I said, 'Mate. This happened to Incey. You should give it a go.' But this time I was wrong, again! Sadly, it didn't work out for him up there and he ended up moving on to Ipswich.

The truth is, we were good enough to get ourselves out of Division Two but staying in the top flight wasn't as easy. That said, we did beat Spurs 2-1 at home on 26 October, then the week after beat Arsenal away 1-0, followed by a draw at home against Liverpool. The problem was our consistency levels weren't where they should have been.

The most memorable game of the season for the fans was probably on 29 February, when we played Everton at home and lost 2-0. The game wasn't remembered for the result but for the bond scheme pitch invasion. West Ham needed to raise over £15 million for construction works to turn the Boleyn Ground into a 25,000 capacity all-seater stadium by 1994 and decided to approach the fans for the funds. The only way the supporters could vent their frustrations was on matchday by invading the pitch shouting, 'Sack the board,' which also meant they weren't fully behind us as a team.

We'd played Farnborough a few weeks before in the FA Cup and just like the Aldershot tie the previous season, the non-leaguers surrendered home advantage to play at a bigger stadium. The frustration from the fans was boiling over, to the extent they were cheering Farnborough when they were going for goal. That's how bad it got. The first leg was 0-0 and you would have put your money on them winning the replay, but thankfully Trevor Morley scored in the last couple of minutes to win the game for us.

I'd mentioned about the Chicken Run before, but this was the only season I got any shit off them, which was maybe a taster of the next season. We were playing QPR on 21 March and we were coming towards the end of the game and I slid into the boards right in front of the Chicken Run. Three geezers shouted out some obscenities about my mum and anyone else they could think of and I turned and gave them the finger. Unfortunately, the whole of the Chicken Run thought I was giving them the finger. They then started singing, 'Tony Gale is a wanker.'

When I got into the dressing room, Bonzo said, 'What the fucking hell have you done over there?' I said, 'Three geezers were giving me gyp and I gave them the finger.' He said, 'You silly git. You need to apologise to them publicly.' I ended up doing it in my 'Galey's Gossip' column in the *Newham Recorder*, with the piece entitled 'Gesture of Peace.' It took the Chicken Run a couple of games to get it out of their system, but even to this day, someone will always say, 'You gave the finger to the Chicken Run,' and every time I have to explain myself.

We only won nine games the whole season and two of those were in the last three games, which were actually decent wins at home against Man United and Nottingham Forest. The United game was three away from the end of the season and we were all but relegated at that point. I was captain for that game and Steve Bruce was captain for Man United. I remember going in and exchanging the team sheets with Brucey and he said, 'Can't believe you've gone down, with the players you've got. We need this game tonight though.' I said, 'You might need it, but there's going to be a full house out there and they're going to be roaring for your blood.'

Paul Ince couldn't attend the game, I'm not sure if it was through illness or injury, but we beat them 1-0. Kenny Brown scored from a clearance onto his shin from about 18 yards and it flew past Peter Schmeichel into the goal. It was a full house and I remember the crowd getting behind us, mainly because they didn't like Man United. That goal from Kenny Brown stopped Man United winning the league as they were in a battle with Leeds to get top spot.

The next day we woke up to the headlines from Fergie saying, 'West Ham's effort was obscene. If that effort had been put in throughout the season, they wouldn't have gone down.' I still wound him up years later about that win.

The last game of the season was against Forest on 2 May 1992 and Bonzo asked Frank McAvennie if he wanted to go on the bench. Franks says, 'Cheers. That's very kind of you.' The boys are doing the warm-up and Mitchell Thomas comes over and asks Frank, 'The gaffer's not putting you on?' and he said, 'No.' Mitchell said, 'Get ready at half-time, I'm going to pull a hamstring.' None of us knew about this, but suddenly Mitchell pulled this mysterious hamstring for Frank to come on. Bill came into the changing room at half-time and said, 'Frank, you're coming on. Hurry up and get changed.' Frank went, 'Why? What's the matter with Mitchell?' Bonzo's said, 'How the fuck do you know Mitchell's injured?' Frank's come on, scored a hat-trick and we beat Forest 3-0.

* * * * *

AUGUST 1992, new season and we're back in Division Two, which was now Division One, because Division One was now the Premier League. It was a new title, but the same division, but I don't think people realised just how much it was going to take off, with more games on telly and also how the wages would explode. Unfortunately, I wasn't around long enough to really benefit from that wage explosion which happened over the next few years, but you could already sense the gloss and the glamour of the advertising that was making the Premier League that much bigger.

However, fundamentally it was still the same game and that's what frustrates me when you see all these records they talk about in the Premier League. No, it's still the same league but with a different title. Tony Cottee got about 300 goals in his career, but you hardly hear that mentioned when they talk about top goal-scorers in the Premier League. And what about Ian Rush or Ian Wright? Those records in Division One should be mentioned in the same breath as Premier League all the time. It's as if when they started the Premier League they restarted the record books again and that's very annoying.

When Bill took over from Lou, I couldn't have been happier. For that season and a half I loved my football under Bill. Then when Harry Redknapp came in, that changed. Harry came in as Bill's No.2 at the start of the 1992/93 season and from the moment he arrived, I never got on with him.

Our opening game of the season was at Barnsley, which was a tough start as we went down to 10 men after Mike Small got sent off. Thankfully Clive Allen had joined us and scored a goal on the break to give us a 1-0 win. We also had his cousin Martin in midfield and the two were like chalk and cheese. Martin was called 'Mad Dog,' by the fans, but we used to call him 'Scatty,' because you never knew what he was going to do next. Also, he was so easy to wind up. Years later we were on a television panel at Sky and he said 'I hate anybody calling me Mad Dog. My name is Martin Allen. I'm a respected manager now.' But every time I referred to him I'd be like, 'So, Mad Dog, what do you think about that tackle?' and you'd see him getting agitated. A few minutes later, 'What a great goal, Mad Dog. Surely they've got this in the bag now?' You could see him ready to snarl, but laughing at the same time. Let's not forget though, Martin was a bloody good player.

Clive's striking partner that season was Trevor Morley, which basically meant Trev did all the work and Clive poached the goals, similar to the way TC was with Frank McAvennie. Clive wasn't a quick player, but positionally he was brilliant. If anything dropped he could hit it. A volley, half volley, side-foot, curler, drive, chip, any sort of goal Clive could deliver on. There were a lot of great strikers around at the time and I don't think Clive got the credit he deserved. He was a super goalscorer and definitely what we needed that year.

On 30 January 1993 I scored alongside Mark Robson to beat Leicester 2-1, which was when I got reintroduced into the side after being on the sidelines for ages. That turned out to be my last goal for West Ham. My mum and dad were at the game sitting in the front row at the opposite end of the pitch and when I scored I went running over and gave them a big cuddle. I had a really good game, but I'd been left wondering, 'Why have I been put on the sidelines in the first place so many times this season and why was I on the transfer list?' The Sunday papers the day after helped answer that question. One headline said, 'Gale looks a bargain.' The papers were saying that West Ham were looking to sell me to help reduce the wage bill, which was news to me.

When Bonzo took over as manager in 1990, I signed a contract which intentionally took me right through to the end of my testimonial season. However, at the time, certain individuals didn't want me in the side without a doubt and let's just say I don't think it was Bonzo. When I came in on the Monday, Billy and Harry called me in the office. I thought, 'Here we go,' but they just wanted to say well done. My gut feeling though was telling me I was on borrowed time.

*****

ON 24 February 1993, we got the news that Bobby Moore died at 51 from cancer, which was no age at all. I saw him on 3 November 1992 when we played Grimsby on a freezing cold night and he was doing commentary with Jonathan Pearce. He called me over after the game and for a minute I thought, 'Who's that?' When I recognised it was Bobby Moore, I then thought, 'Bloody hell, he don't look well.' He never told anyone he was ill because he didn't want any sympathy and it was probably only his wife Stephanie and a few others that had any idea of how sick he was.

UPS, DOWNS AND THE PASSING OF A LEGEND

The whole football community mourned, but he was also one of the few people who touched everyone's hearts in the UK and beyond. So many people had so many memories of Mooro and he was the greatest captain England's ever had.

The first game after Bobby's death was at Sunderland on 27 February. Ian Bishop was No.6 at the time and Bonzo came up to me and said, 'Do you want to wear the No.6 shirt today because you followed in Bobby's footsteps at Fulham and West Ham.' It was very nice of Billy to offer, because he remembered what Bobby had meant to me, but I said, 'No,' because I didn't want to take the shirt just to be photographed in it. I didn't want to seen to be making the most out of what happened. Ian Bishop continued in the No.6 shirt and don't get me wrong, Bish didn't make the most out of what happened either, but he was already wearing the shirt, so it was right that he should continue to wear that. The No.6 shirt at West Ham was eventually retired in August 2008.

From the moment we were relegated the season before, there was an air of expectancy on us, which kind of positively changed the atmosphere in the club. Then there was a strong confidence among us that we were going to be one of the top sides the following season. We got off to a good start and there was a real belief about the squad. We had a nice mix of players and I always felt we could comfortably make promotion come the end of the season. We won our last four games, but it was the final game against Cambridge at home which counted, because a win guaranteed West Ham automatic promotion behind Newcastle United instead of fighting in the playoffs.

Cambridge were a difficult side to play against, were notorious for their long ball games and had a good striker in Steve Claridge. David Speedie, who was on loan for us, got a little bit of stick from the crowds previous to that because he'd come from Chelsea, but when he scored against Cambridge on a shitty pitch after working his bollocks off, he got a standing ovation as he was running back to the kick off again. Speedo was a thorn in my side for many years when I was playing football, probably because he was everything I wasn't. He was an aggressive little terrier and whenever I played him he'd always be at it with late tackles, elbows and everything like that. When he turned up I shook my head and thought, 'Not you,' but he turned out to be one of my best pals for his short stay at West Ham and a good mate for life.

Back to the Cambridge game. There was a pitch invasion when Clive Allen scored in the 90th minute to all but secure promotion on goals scored over Portsmouth. When the final whistle went, it was absolute chaos afterwards, followed by great celebrations that went on long into the night for the players and all the fans. We stayed at the ground late into the evening at the players' lounge as the champagne flowed, before some dispersed and others went off to clubs and pubs.

In three seasons we'd gone from being second in Division Two, to 22nd in the top flight and back to second in Division Two. Nobody knew what to expect next season in the Premier League, especially myself.

Chapter 20

WRITING'S ON THE WALL

'West Ham were under fire today for telling Tony Gale he is no longer wanted – just hours before a testimonial to mark his 10 years loyal service. The 34-year-old was upset when the club confirmed, shortly before his benefit game at Upton Park on Sunday, that he was being released.'

– Ken Dyer, Evening Standard football correspondent, May 1994

AFTER OUR first six games of the 1993/94 season, we were in 19th place having lost four, drawn once and won once against Sheffield Wednesday 2-0 at home, with Clive scoring both goals. Both were very typical Clive Allen poacher-type goals with nice finishes from tight angles. That was three points badly needed because we didn't have a very good start. Unfortunately for Clive, those were his first and last Premier League goals, because shortly after he got injured and only made one more appearance that season. Unfortunately for me, my calf injury flared up again which also plagued me on and off for the rest of the season.

We knew it was going to be a tough start going back up into that top-tier league and were unsure if we could make it with the big boys. Also, Dicksy was sold to get new players in to restructure the team, which saw Lee Chapman, David Burrows and Mike Marsh come in, which was smart business. David was a really good left-back albeit not quite as good as Dicksy, while Lee Chapman was your archetypal big centre-forward that we needed and Marshy was a great operator in midfield. Things started to take off then and we started to get a few results.

After a 0-0 draw against Swindon on 11 September, Chappy, Marshy and Bugsy Burrows made their debuts as we beat Blackburn Rovers 2-0 away. Guess who refereed that game? You got it, Keith Hackett. The only game that I played in that he refereed after the Nottingham Forest semi-final game in '91. He wasn't allowed to referee us at home because he had death threats and hate mail in the post, which is bang out of order and I'm not condoning any of that shit, but here we are playing Blackburn away and I'm marking Alan Shearer. I must have fouled him four times on the trot and Hackett did not give a single foul against me. Shearer was obviously angry about it and must have been thinking, 'What the fuck do I have to do to get a foul my way here?' Hackett looked to me and said, 'No hard feelings, big fella?' I said, 'Don't even go there.' In terms of Blackburn, I thought this was a very good team in transition who had come out of the league below and were going to go places. Getting a result against them in the early stages was really good.

A week later we lost 2-0 at Newcastle then we beat Chelsea 1-0 before coming away with two goalless draws against Villa and Norwich. Then on 1 November we beat Man City 3-1 and by the end of November, we were in tenth position. Yes, we were anxious and aware that we'd been favourites for relegation at the beginning of the season, but we proved we were better than that. I'd been promoted and relegated twice at West Ham and I didn't want to go through another relegation.

December was a proper mixed bag. We beat Coventry City 3-2 at home on 11 December, then the following Saturday we played at Hillsborough against Sheffield Wednesday. Chris

Waddle was playing right-wing as a left footer for Wednesday and David Burrows was playing left-back. We called David Burrows 'Bugsy,' because Bugs Bunny was a rabbit who lived in a burrow. Either way, on that day Bugsy got turned inside out by Waddle. He wasn't the first one and he certainly wasn't going be the last. To be honest, as a team we should have helped him more because when you got left one-on-one with Chris Waddle you had no chance.

We lost 5-0 at Sheffield Wednesday that day – Waddle scored one and was involved in setting up the others. We came back to the dressing room after and everybody was throwing their kit on the floor. The ground was emptying and in the changing room they had the sash windows which meant we could see the crowd going past exiting Hillsborough. Bonzo and Harry Redknapp gave us the post-match talk and everybody knew Bugsy was distraught. You have to remember that he was a very good player who had won the League and FA Cup at Liverpool and we were telling him, 'Bugsy, don't worry. It can happen to anyone. Just forget it.'

We had our showers, the team talks had been done and were just sitting there in our tracksuits ready to go. Next thing a load of Sheffield Wednesday fans, who must have been listening to the talk from Harry and Bill, stuck their head through the sash windows and shouted, 'Burrows, you've been Waddled, Burrows you've been Waddled, la,la,la…la,la,la!' We all start pissing ourselves laughing, including Bugsy. That light-hearted moment instantly snapped us out of our misery.

On 7 March 1994 we had the Bobby Moore memorial match to mark the official opening of the Bobby Moore Stand. The game also raised money for The Bobby Moore Fund for Imperial Cancer Research and Bobby's family trust, and there wasn't a dry eye in the place. It was a West Ham team against a mixed team of players from the Premier League. Of course, TC, who was playing for Everton at the time scored for the Prem team which actually got him cheers instead of boos, but Clive Allen equalised and then Jeroen Boere scored the winner for us. What an honour to be involved in that.

We had a good run in the FA Cup and by mid-March had reached the quarter-finals and played at Luton. We had a 0-0 draw at home and I travelled with the team for the rematch at Kenilworth Road, but I didn't even make the bench. They had named the team and the subs already and then someone fell sick and I had to be sub. I remember rolling my eyes, thinking, 'This is what I get after 10 years at West Ham'. Harry Redknapp said, 'Did you see his face Bill? Did you see the way he reacted to that? Are you doing us a favour by sitting on the bench?' I replied, 'My face is fine and I'm really happy to be sub, but you're bang out of order.'

I must admit, it got to a point where I didn't like going into training and I have no problems in saying it was one of the lowest points in my footballing career. I'd been at West Ham for 10 years and was doing my testimonial tour and all the functions that come with it, but I was lacking enthusiasm. At the time I'd been writing my Galey's Gossip column for six years for the *Newham Recorder*, which gave me something to do as I wasn't playing every week. When we beat Man City 3-1 and Spurs 4-1, I wrote great reports, but when things were going badly, like say when we lost 4-0 to QPR or 5-0 at Sheffield Wednesday, then of course I would say something about that. Well, Bill sheepishly called me into the office one day and said, 'You're gonna have to stop this. We've seen you're doing a local column saying we're playing poorly.' I replied, 'But we did play poorly. We just lost 5-0. What do you want me to write?' Just like that, I had to stop doing the column and Peter Butler took over.

I had to bite the bullet with a number of similar things that season, because I had a lot of functions going on with my whole testimonial year and a lot of good people helping to organise these functions on my behalf, for which I'll always be grateful. My testimonial committee consisted of Alan Devonshire, Richard Quartly, Peter Stewart, Wally Morris and Sue Crowley. Small committee, but very good. I also had some help from Mike Osman and Richard Digance, who helped me write my speeches.

Within that year we had a number of functions, including a golf day in Brentwood and a dinner at the Royal Lancaster Hotel. For the golf day we arranged to be picked up in Pimlico by the West Ham coach, which had tellies on it and tables, so we could all play cards and have a laugh. My dad and my uncles all came and we met at the Pimlico Brasserie, round the back of Sloane Square, which Richard Quartly owned. We then got driven to Essex and all played in a fantastic golf day where I basically went round on a buggy saying hello to everyone. Ex-players were playing with my mates and people would pay to be on a team.

The whole day had been filmed by Andrew Dickie's brother Paul, and he captured some great moments. One particular episode does come to mind, when my uncle Terry Gale was in a bunker and Paul said to him, 'Right then, Tel. I want you to play out of this bunker. It doesn't matter if you mess the shot up, just follow through with your swing and the sand will come out and we'll throw the ball onto the green. Even if it ain't a good shot, it will look like a good one.' Terry's hit the ball and it's hit the lip of the bunker and come back and hit him in the bollocks. We played that clip back for years.

After the game, the lads had an idea, 'Let's go to Secrets nightclub.' All my uncles were knackered, but still came. Paul was rolling the camera all day and it naturally ran out of battery.

So, we went to Secrets in Romford with my dad and my mates and Paul gets the camera out and it's got this big light on it, but no film in it, because of the battery. However, nobody in the club knew that and all the girls were dancing in front of it like it was an audition.

* * * * *

I WAS only booked seven times in my career and 4 April 1994 was one of them. I was given a yellow card for dissent for disputing a penalty after Trevor Morley tripped up Gary Mabbutt. I guess seven bookings in over 700 games is not too bad though.

The last two games were against QPR away on 3 May, which was 0-0 and then four days later we drew 3-3 against Southampton at home in front of just under 27,000 fans, with Matt Le Tissier scoring a great free-kick for the Saints. We finished 13th, but unfortunately, that wasn't my lasting memory of the season.

West Ham had promised me a two-year contract which I'd agreed with the chairman Terry Brown and the managing director, Peter Storrie. All I had to do was negotiate the wages. Early in the season, my intention was to have my testimonial against Celtic, as Liam Brady was manager. Unfortunately, neither plan panned out the way I'd hoped. Liam moved on to Brighton and Lou Macari took over at Celtic.

My testimonial game ended up being against the Republic of Ireland and was the day after the Southampton game, which was ridiculous, because how many people were going to turn up so soon after for that on a Sunday? Thankfully I knew most of the Irish team very well and was able to get them to help drum up sales with very short notice. To this day I'm eternally grateful to the 8,000 diehard fans who turned up that day.

Shortly before kick-off, Harry Redknapp called me to the manager's office. Bonzo was also there and you could tell he felt really awkward. Bill says, 'We've decided not to give you a contract.' Although Bill had to tell me the news, I bear no grudges with him because in my eyes he was just the messenger. In one of Harry's recent books he says, 'It was Bill who wanted him out of the club,' which I think is nonsense. And as for how well things worked out for me afterwards, that was certainly nothing to do with Harry. When they told me my contract wasn't being renewed that close to the end of the season, I was fucked.

I'd had offers weeks before to go to Japan and America, but thought West Ham would deliver on the contract renewal they promised verbally, so why did I need to accept any other offers? To have my contract taken away from me on my testimonial day was the biggest insult that could have been thrown my way. If John Lyall had been there it would never have happened. All that cobblers about trying to sell me to generate money for the club and help try to reduce the wage bill and then they let me go on a free transfer without a club to move to.

I'd seen this happen to other players before and felt sorry for them when they had been left out in the cold and that's what I'd felt now. Our livelihoods were at stake and it's not like we were being paid £50,000 a week. In fact, I was on about £1,600 a week. Can you believe I even got charged for the sandwiches in the boardroom after my testimonial match!

That last season left a bad taste in my mouth, but I'll always look back at my decade with West Ham with pride and a smile on my face, and to this day I still love the club and its fans. At the time of writing, I'm one of only nine players in league football to have played over 275 league games for two clubs and over 300 matches, including cup games. All that said, I was only a few months away from turning 35 and thought, 'This could be it. Your career is about to finish in professional football.'

Chapter 21

OFF THE SCRAPHEAP

"For his age, he wasn't someone who was going to be playing every single game, but he was much more than that. His experience was a big help and the positive impact he made in the dressing room was excellent. Tony made his contribution to us winning the league, same as everybody on that team."

– Sir Kenny Dalglish, MBE

MY OLD mate from Fulham, Terry Bullivant was assistant manager and coach of Barnet Football Club alongside Ray Clemence and shortly after being released by West Ham I gave him a call. 'Tel. I ain't got a club. Can I come in and train with ya?' They had some good players at Barnet, but they weren't being paid a lot of money and he was straight with that. I said, 'I just want to train and try and keep fit.'

I had to travel to Edgware from Surrey and Bulli would ask every day, 'Anything?' referring to any interest from any clubs. The answer was always 'No, Tel. Fuck all.' Then two weeks before the start of the new season I received a call from my old coach, Ray Harford. 'Tony. Can you get to Hampden Park tomorrow night?' I said, 'How come?' He said, 'We're playing Celtic in a friendly. Me and Kenny have decided we need someone experienced to run around with the boys here at Blackburn and we'd like to take a look at you. Are you fit?' I replied, 'Yeah. Course I'm fit,' but I wasn't really.

Little did I know, Blackburn played at Aberdeen before playing Celtic and they were so short of players that one of the coaching staff had to play. They were struggling to get a team together because they had picked up so many injuries in the pre-season and that's when Kenny Dalglish asked Ray Harford, 'Do you know of any centre-backs you think would fit in well?' and he replied, 'Tony Gale. He was at West Ham and did well for them there.' Kenny said, 'Ray. It's your shout. I'll go along with you.' I'll always be grateful to Ray for that.

I called up Terry to let him know the news. 'Bulli. I had a phone call. Ray Harford's asked if I can play for Blackburn against Celtic tomorrow night.' He was over the moon for me. Terry helped me out when West Ham turned their back on me and things weren't great. He was getting close to offering me a contract when that call came through and I probably would have accepted it. I'll never forget Bulli's support and friendship during that time.

The Celtic game was on 8 August 1994 and my dad came up with me and even joined me and the lads for the pre-match meal with the likes of Alan Shearer, Tim Flowers, Chris Sutton, Dalglish and all that lot. I've introduced him to everyone and said, 'This is me dad, Peter,' and they've all said hello and started asking him, 'What do you do Peter?,' and he replied, 'I'm a black cab driver.' They loved him.

Although we lost 1-0, it was a great experience playing in this young side with a number of emerging superstars. Immediately after the Celtic game Ray and Kenny said, 'Have a couple of days off then come back to Blackburn and sign your contract for the year. Also, there's a game on Saturday which we want you to play in.' I asked, 'What's the game?' They said, 'We're playing Man United in the Charity Shield at Wembley.' I replied, 'Yeah, of course', as if it was nothing big. I'd knocked at the door three times in semi-finals with West Ham but never got to Wembley and here I am within four days of signing for Blackburn heading to the holy grail of football. I remember telling my son the news. 'Ant, Blackburn have offered me a contract. Also, I'm playing in the Charity Shield against Man United!' I don't know who was more excited, him or me.

On 14 August we took on Man United in front of over 60,000 people. United had a full team out, but Kenny rested Alan Shearer and Chris Sutton for the next week, because I think they may have had a couple of niggles, so we had a kind of makeshift pairing up front with Ian Pearce and Peter Thorne. Man United had a good team, with the likes of Gary Pallister, Eric Cantona, Mark Hughes, Ryan Giggs, Andrei Kanchelskis, Lee Sharpe and Roy Keane. I remember thinking in that game, 'We've got a good team here and that's even without Sutton and Shearer playing'. I said to the chairman, 'I think will win the league this year', and he said, 'You really think so? We got close last season.'

Unfortunately, we lost 2-0 with Cantona scoring from a penalty in the first half and Paul Ince scoring with about 10 minutes to go. After the game I went up to Incey and congratulated him on the goal and he said he was really happy for me being in the Blackburn squad.

It's hard to believe that within a week I went from being out of contract and playing at non-league Barnet, to representing Blackburn at Wembley and signing a contract with them in the Premiership. At the time, the owner Jack Walker had all the money in the world and could buy any player he wanted, but he listened to Ray and Kenny and took me on a free transfer. I'm sure a lot of fans and people in the media were thinking, 'Why?'

Well, they took a gamble on me and there was no way I was letting them down.

Chapter 22

CAMPIONE

"You look over the years at players in the Premier League who were great passers of the outside of their right foot, Tony's up there with any of them. He had wonderful distribution, really good presence and read the game beautifully. I don't want to give him too much credit, but suffice to say, without his influence it's debatable if we would have got over the line in the end."
– Chris Sutton

THERE I was thrust into a squad of young superstars – Sutton, Shearer, Sherwood, Flowers, Le Saux, you name it – however, I was the experienced one. Kevin Moran had retired the season before and the next oldest after me was probably Colin Hendry and he was six years younger than I was. This was a bunch of proper steely-minded players who were very driven, but who welcomed me to the team as one of their own and without any bullshit.

After a number of seasons at West Ham with injuries, I started at Blackburn in good shape. Going to Rovers gave me a new lease of life, in new surroundings, with people that genuinely wanted me to be part of the team. Because it all happened so quickly, I needed to sort out what was going to happen with the family, because I didn't want to uproot them from Walton-on-Thames for a one-year contract. As a result, it made sense for me to just stay up there for the season and I booked into the Dunkenhalgh House Hotel.

First game of the season was on 20 August away at South-ampton. It was a really hot day and Nicky Banger scored after 15 minutes after a great ball from Le Tiss, which went over Le Saux's head and I just couldn't get there in time to stop him getting his shot in. They took the lead, but we equalised in the second half with a Shearer goal. I remember the gaffer thinking that was a decent draw because they were a tough side to play away.

In September we played Swedish team Trelleborgs at home. When I was at West Ham we'd qualified for the UEFA Cup, but we were banned because of the Heysel disaster, so this was my first taster of the competition. Unfortunately, we lost that game 1-0, but two weeks later we headed over to Sweden. I played in the first half of the replay but had to come off due to a twinge in my calf. Ian Pearce subbed me and we were 2-1 up, which meant we'd go through on the away goals. Then Colin Hendry was running back towards his own goal and he booted the ball out of play for a throw, but he kicked it out the ground, which was impressive due to the size of the stadium.

Colin did the sensible thing, which meant Trelleborgs couldn't get a quick throw. Kenny in the meantime was going mad on the touchline. 'What the fuck did you do that for?' I was obviously protective of my fellow centre-back and said to Kenny, 'Gaffer. He doesn't want them to take a quick throw in.' He says, 'No. You don't understand. If you kick the ball out of the ground, it's bad luck.' I've said, 'Ah, come on gaffer. Don't have a pop at him because of that,' then I sat down. Well, Trelleborgs threw the ball in and not long after equalised! The game finished 2-2 and we were out of the UEFA Cup.

We got knocked out of the FA Cup by Newcastle early doors and Liverpool beat us 3-1 in the fourth round of the League Cup, but we were smashing it in the league. By Christmas we'd only lost two games, drawn four and won 15. The focus from the team and the overall quality was something else. Even the way they took a loss showed. After the Trelleborgs replay, our first game was against Norwich away, but I couldn't play because of my calf strain. We lost 2-1, with Chris Sutton scoring for us and I remember sitting in the dressing room after and nobody said anything for about 10 minutes. Total silence. I turned round to Tim Flowers and said, 'Anybody going to say anything?' He said, 'What do you mean?' I said, 'What do you normally do when you lose?' He said, 'We don't normally lose.' That was the first loss of the season after eight games.

Sutton and Shearer were prolific goalscorers and that season they were given the nickname SAS (Sutton and Shearer). Shearer's the best striker of a ball I've ever played with and you could see the fear in defenders' faces when they were playing against him. I also have to give credit to Chris Sutton, who was 23 and had been signed by Norwich for a record signing that season. He was a great athlete and excellent at holding the ball up.

Chris was a really lovely fella, had a good family and was an old-school, proper professional. His dad Mike was a very good player in his day, which is probably where he got his athleticism from. Chris and I roomed at the Dunkenhalgh House Hotel for about three or four months and he was dating a lovely girl called Samantha. At the time Chris was staying up at the hotel and we were always at training, so she was getting lumbered on her own for quite some time and was bouncing off the walls. They'd have these blazing arguments and I used to be like the agony uncle calming the pair of them down. I obviously did alright in my counselling role because they're now married and have five kids.

As a defender, the best attribute of my game was my passing

and I can honestly say that dropping balls into Shearer and Sutton was a dream. They could control the ball on their chest, head or feet and would make your good balls look brilliant, your not-so-good balls look good – and your bad balls still look decent. If you were drilling the ball into a target man like Alan or Chris, you had a big margin of error. You could hit it two yards off and they'd still get on to it.

There's quite a few people that could have easily been captain within that team, but Tim Sherwood was the man wearing the armband. Tim was always lively and positively infectious in the dressing room. I love those sorts of people around a team and as a player, he was excellent and vastly underrated. He was good in the air and was a great screen in front of the back four, but most importantly he was a natural leader who deserved to be captain that year without a doubt. He certainly demonstrated those leadership qualities as he went on to manage Spurs and Aston Villa later on.

I'd known Ray Harford since he became Malcolm Macdonald's assistant at Fulham and had always kept in touch with him and always thought he was one of the finest brains in English football and was very underrated. Ray was the coach at Blackburn and did everything on the training pitch, was great with the players and tactically very astute. He was the perfect foil to Kenny and everyone knew that Ray's input that season was astronomical.

Then of course, there was the gaffer, King Kenny, who was a softly spoken Glaswegian. Half the time I never understood a fucking word he was saying in the team meetings, but he had the credibility, and when he spoke, everyone shut up. Kenny was still very fit and used to train with us, mainly on a Friday in the five-a-sides and even though he was in his 40s, he was still a quality player. He was similar to John Lyall, in so much as he knew everyone's name and wanted to know his team, but also possessed that track record which informally said, 'I know my stuff.'

Kenny was putting me in the squad and then pulling me out. He also had Ian Pearce and Paul Warhurst, and Kenny juggled the squad around for what he thought best for each game. However, he also realised at my age I couldn't play Wednesday and Saturday week in week out and quite often in training he'd say to me, 'Get your feet up. Come off, you've done enough.' He was doing the same with others, trying to keep us fresh, which worked very well and nobody questioned Kenny's decisions.

* * * * *

ON 2 November 1994, Barcelona beat Man United 4-0 in the Champions League, then the day after we were being told we'd be playing them in a friendly on 8 November. We beat Spurs 2-0 on 5 November, then shortly after we were off to Almeria in south east Spain which turned out to be a shit journey.

We were up at the crack of dawn on the Monday to get an early morning flight from Manchester, but there were no direct flights, so we had to go via Heathrow to Madrid, and then got a coach to Almeria. We didn't arrive until late evening and if that wasn't enough, 12 kitbags had gone missing in transit.

Barca had a really good team, with the likes of Romario, Jordi Cruyff and Ronald Koeman all playing. They also had Pep Guardiola, Gheorghe Hagi and Hristo Stoichkov, not to mention Johan Cruyff as manager, but none of them were here for this game, which wasn't a bad thing.

Colin Hendry couldn't play for Blackburn because he had to rest for the Saturday, so Ian Pearce played alongside me. Pearcey was rooming with me and said, 'Do you think Romario will be playing?' I said, 'Could be, but don't worry about it. It's a friendly and I doubt there will be many there anyway.'

The match was on Tuesday evening, so after breakfast we all headed down in the coach to the Estadio Municipal Juan Rojas for a training session. After about an hour, the coach stopped because it couldn't get down this narrow road and we were told we'd be walking the last couple of miles. Everyone was saying, 'You having a fucking laugh?' When we did get there, the pitch was so shit, we couldn't even train on it. It looked like it had been abandoned for about five years, so we ended up going back to the hotel.

We had a pre-match meal and the police turned up to escort our coach to the ground with all their lights flashing. The streets were loaded with people and when we turned up at the stadium, about 25,000 were in there all singing the Barca song, jumping up and down. At this point we knew they were taking this friendly seriously.

To add a little bit more drama to this trip, someone had broken into our changing room and nicked some of our gear. Thankfully we had doubles of everything, but you did start to wonder if someone was trying to give Barca an advantage. This friendly got very competitive, very quickly as I blocked a shot from Romario not long after kick-off, as did Tim Flowers.

At half-time they subbed Romario for Koeman, but by this point, we were 2-0 up from a Shearer goal and an own goal from Barca. They struggled to get back into the game and Shearer scored again, making it 3-0. Despite Xavier Escaich nicking one back for them towards the end, we beat one of Europe's best squads and now had that lovely 14-hour journey home again. My son remembers the game very well, mainly because I brought him back a Jordi Cruyff shirt.

I played two games in December. The first was against Leicester away, which we drew 0-0 and the other was against Man City away on Boxing Day, which Ray had to take charge of because

Kenny was ill. The game was live on the TV and they had Niall Quinn and Uwe Rösler up front who were a force, but the way we played that day, nothing was going to worry us. Shearer scored after nine minutes, then Mark Atkins a few minutes later. Although Quinn nicked one back for them, Graeme Le Saux scored a lovely goal from a free-kick and we won 3-1. We played well that night and we had this feeling, even at this point that we were going to get close to winning the league.

The first game of 1995 was against West Ham at home. Before the game the West Ham lads came and had a chat with me. Ian Bishop said, 'We're so happy for you, mate. The second result we look for on match day is yours.' However, they also said they weren't going to do us any favours on the day.

Shearer was doubtful before the game, because he had a bit of a cold. When I came in early to sort my tickets out, I saw him in the bath, trying to sweat it out. He was going to have a fitness test and I said, 'Are you alright?' He said, 'I feel a bit under the weather.' I said, 'Mate you've gotta play today, it's against my old team.' He said, 'I'll see how I am.' He went out and had a mini fitness test and decided to play. He didn't play for me, he played for himself and the team and we were so glad he did.

We start the game and go 1-0 up after Shearer scores a penalty and I thought, 'That's handy', then West Ham went 2-1 up at the break after TC and Julian Dicks scored. When TC scored I think I slipped, but he'd already got away from me and I've said before, once TC gets on the wrong side of you, you're done. It was a great take and goal from him.

We get back to the changing room for half-time and Kenny gives us a proper bollocking and goes bananas. Then in the second half, Graeme Le Saux equalised and Alan scored another two, to complete his hat-trick which won the game for us 4-2. TC always likes reminding me, 'I turned you inside out in that game, put you on your backside and scored past you,' and my standard response is always, 'But you didn't win the game though!'

When the final whistle blew I went over to the West Ham fans to say thank you. Even though they travelled all that distance and lost, I got a nice round of applause and a little song. All the West Ham players came up to the bar afterwards before getting on the coach to head home, which was lovely as my dad was also there and he was chatting with the other players' parents at West Ham. It was like a reunion of sorts.

If the gaffer thought it was going to be my last game and for Ian Pearce to take over, then that was a great way to go out, especially as Harry Redknapp was manager and it was really good to put one over on him. I was fit and the lads were asking, 'Why aren't you playing?' But I didn't want to rock the boat. This was like an Indian summer for me and there was no way I was ever gonna knock on Kenny's door and say, 'Why am I not playing?' I was loving life with Blackburn and Kenny had a way, even if you weren't playing, to make you feel part of it. I travelled to every game with the team, stayed in every hotel, was in every squad and was asked to play in the reserves in the midweeks to try and help some of the kids out. Tony Parkes used to take the reserves and some of those younger lads coming through included Shay Given and Marlon Broome. I really enjoyed the role and I genuinely couldn't have asked for more.

A couple of days after the West Ham game, Ray Harford came up to me and said, 'There's been an enquiry from Middlesbrough for you,' who had Bryan Robson as player-manager at the time. Ray said, 'We'd love you to stay for the second half of the season, but I wouldn't want to stop you to get more money for a move to Middlesbrough.' I said, 'No. I want to stay.' which turned out to be the right decision.

CAMPIONE

BY 14 January, Blackburn had played 23 league games, only lost two, drawn four and won 17. Everything was looking great until the last six games of the season where you could see a nervousness and edginess in our play, scrambling with 1-0 wins, 1-1 draws and losing by the odd goal.

We drew against Leeds away on 15 April, then two days later lost 3-2 against Man City at home. After beating Crystal Palace 2-1 at home, we played West Ham away on 30 April. I'd travelled with the team down to London and spent a night at the hotel, but I wasn't playing. I went to the game and spoke to the West Ham lads before and they were good as gold with me. In fact, they actually wanted us to win the league.

I sat in the dugout which was really strange being in the opposite dugout to the West Ham team and watched them beat us 2-0. I thought that loss might have cost us the title to Man United, because there was only two games left now, but Kenny never said anything to us that implied we were not going to do anything but win the league.

Before the game Kenny said to me, 'After the game you can go home and see your missus and come back on the Monday.' After we got beaten I spoke with Ray Harford and said, 'Is it alright for me to shoot off with the family?' He replied, 'You better come back on the coach, mate. When we lose, we've all got to go back together.' I had to go back to Blackburn, but I totally understood why Ray had said that and it was a good decision. Imagine, all the lads on the coach taking in the loss and I've fucked off home? That was a good footballing decision.

On 8 May we beat Newcastle United 1-0 and our final game of the season was at Anfield against Liverpool on 14 May. Man United meanwhile were away at West Ham. We were two points ahead, so they needed to win and hope we slipped up. I was sitting in the dugout and there was a Sky Sports floor manager nearby called John Smart. He had a monitor and I'm watching the West Ham v Man United game while watching Blackburn live and when we went one up I thought, 'Happy days, I don't even need to watch the telly now.' It then went 1-1, then 2-1 to Liverpool and now I'm shitting myself. I was watching the West Ham game, which was also 1-1, and Ludo was making save after save, while the defenders were throwing themselves across the ball. Man United just need to score to win the league. It was like a siege on the West Ham box. Ray can hear me oohhhing and ahhhing and looked at me as if to say, 'Shut your noise. We've got enough to be looking at here without you doing all that.'

The whistle went full-time at West Ham and I said, 'We've fucking done it!' Ray's looked at me and said, 'You sure?' I said, 'I'm sure, I'm sure!' Then the message got out to the players on the pitch and it was surreal for about two minutes while we were playing. The fans around the pitch were going mad and even the Liverpool fans were cheering for us. Man United were first the year before, so it was a role reversal. If we weren't going to win it at home, then the best place for Kenny would be at Anfield.

The drinks started in the changing room straight after, but when we got on the coach after the game, we were like, 'Fucking hell. We've won the league! What we going to do? Where we going?' Then Kenny got on the coach and said, 'Don't worry. I've booked the Bistro French. Ring all your partners and tell them to meet us down there.' He had someone book it straight after the final whistle because he didn't want to book it before the result to tempt fate.

Preston's not that far from Blackburn and Bistro French was a fantastic spot for people to enjoy themselves. There was nothing flash about the place, which was typical of our squad day in day out on the training field, it was just a nice place where players, families and friends could all go together and have a good time and feel at home. The Drifters were on and I was the only one who was old enough to know all the words. I ended up on the stage with my tracksuit on while the others were dancing on the tables. What a great night.

My old mate Richard Quartly came up for the game and joined us at the Bistro French and had great fun on stage with me and the lads. The next day, on the Monday he was supposed to be going home to a marriage guidance counsellor as him and his missus were having some problems, but it never happened.

On the Monday the club had organised to travel to the ground on a bus and there was a big presentation at Ewood Park. A lot of us had been up most of the night and we'd arranged to meet at a pub in Blackburn. We're sitting there drinking at about 11am and Richard's chatting with the lads. There was about 50 pieces of football memorabilia going around for the team to sign. When it got to Richard I said, 'Just sign it mate. Nobody will know.'

Richard then says, 'I've got to be back to speak to my marriage guidance counsellor at 3pm.' I said, 'Mate, you're never going to get back for that.' He said, 'I'll get it put back an hour.' Then I said, 'Anyway. Who's more important? Me or your missus?' He never made that train and he got a divorce down the line.

I was fortunate to have played 21 times in total for Blackburn. Many people said when I got there I was like a new player and person, but I always said it was down to playing with better players around me, which is why I still wonder now how far I might have gone with a top club earlier on in my career and that's no disrespect to West Ham, who had some very good players as well.

When people ask the difference between the Boys of '86 and this Blackburn team, the simple way to answer is to just say they were different teams. We had a bad start that season at West Ham and I would probably say I enjoyed the football we played at West Ham better than the football we played at Blackburn. They were two very good sides, don't get me wrong, but that season at West Ham was just super special. I just wish that team had won the league, because they deserved it as well.

That season at Blackburn was almost like a fairy tale. From non-league football to Wembley and then becoming Premiership champions. I had no idea what the future held for me next, but I did know that I wouldn't be playing professional football for much longer.

Chapter 23

EAGLES AND MAGPIES

'Tony had just finished and was going to pack up. I said, 'Do you want to come in and help me with the coaching at Maidenhead?' He was on £150 per week, which was a top earner for us at the time. He played in midfield for me and just sat there, passing the ball around. His experience helped the younger players in the team.'

– Alan Devonshire

RAY HARFORD took over at Blackburn that summer from Kenny, but it was a bit hush-hush as nothing had been released to the media. He offered me a coaching role, but I'd been away from my family on and off for about 10 months and if I agreed to take the role I would have to pack up shop and re-school the kids up north, which wasn't fair on the family. I'll always appreciate Ray's offer of another season at Blackburn and although I often wonder how things might have unfolded in coaching, I'm happy with the way my future worked out.

I thought I had another year of playing left in me, especially as I hadn't played towards the end of the season and decided to head back down south. I started training again in the summer at Barnet FC and that's when Crystal Palace came in.

Ray Lewington approached me, Steve Coppell signed me and that's how I started at the Eagles. Steve was a really nice bloke.

He had managed Palace for years and they had that great FA Cup run when they lost against Man United. He was like Mr Crystal Palace. For me, it seemed like a good move, because they were a good team in the second division and trained in Mitcham which was local to me. Ray was there who I knew from my Fulham days and with him was Peter Nicholas, who were both coaches to Steve Coppell.

They had a firm old pitch at Barnet and I did my ankle tendon in and was having acupuncture, but I was dead straight with Ray and Steve and they took a risk and signed me with an injury. I had a medical to see if everything else was alright and when the results came back, Peter Nicholas asked me, 'What you been up to?' and I said, 'Eh?' He's then explained, 'There was traces of drugs.' I said, 'I've never touched drugs in my life.' He asked, 'Have you been eating bread with poppy seeds?' I said, 'Yeah.' Turns out that opioids, which are found in heroin and morphine, are also in poppy seeds. Mad, eh? Poppy seeds almost stopped me signing for Palace.

In addition to Ray, there were a few more familiar faces at Palace. I got reunited with Ray Houghton, Jeroen Boere and Iain Dowie. Iain is such a nice bloke and you'd struggle to find a more committed player. He used to say to me in training, 'I'm a handful, ain't I?' as his elbows were flying everywhere and I used to tell him, 'Calm down mate!' as we were both laughing.

The truth is though, I'd signed injured and they'd signed a dud. I spent all my time trying to get fit, because my ankle was killing me and I couldn't take off on it. The physio, Pete Maclean, was great. He used to keep me active and I'd be doing about a thousand sit-ups and push-ups a day, because that's all I could manage. Peter never gave up and made me exercise, trying to keep me mentally positive, but I was 35 going on 36 and I never did regain that fitness. In the end, I only played three games.

Once against Port Vale in the FA Cup in January 1996, then against Tranmere away on 20 February 1996, which we won 3-2, then Huddersfield away four days later and we lost that 3-0.

During that season Ray Lew and Pete Nicholas took over in February 1996 as interim managers and then after, Dave Bassett came in. I was extremely grateful to Ray and Steve for the opportunity at Palace, but it's just a shame the fans didn't get to see the best of me, as it's a great club. Thankfully about 25 years down the line I managed to reconnect with Selhurst Park through a friend of mine called Danny Imray.

Moving the clock forward, I first met Danny around 2010 at Hampton and Richmond FC as his mate Steve was the chairman at the time and Dev was manager. We clicked straight away and a few years down the line and many nights out later, Danny said, 'Tony, I'm looking for a one-to-one coach for my son, Danny Jr.' I said, 'I'm happy to mentor him, but my son Ant would be ideal to train him. Get him to play non-league football first and if he's any good, he'll soon get recognised.' Although it was a long drive from Romford to Surrey, Danny would drive his son over to see Ant during school time, summer holidays, weekends, you name it, and also did a bit of Zoom coaching with him.

By the age of 16 Danny Jr was in the squad at Chelmsford City and that's when professional clubs started getting interested in him. Then in February 2021, he signed with Crystal Palace from Chelmsford and is still with them at the time of writing. He's got the talent to be a top player and I wish him all the best for his future.

* * * * *

BACK TO 1996. Alan Devonshire had been managing a ladies side in Hampton when the opportunity presented itself to manage Maidenhead United alongside Martin Busby. Dev dived straight in and the pair became joint managers but then Martin left soon after and it was all Dev.

Straight after I left Crystal Palace he asked me if I wanted to play and I said, 'Not really, mate. Me ankle is playing me up and I'm doing a little bit of radio work now.' He said, 'Come down and see how you get on.' I said, 'I'm an ex pro and people are going to kick the shit out of me for fun.' He replied, 'Come down. If you don't like it, you can leave.' I couldn't really run and because I'd done my ankle tendon I couldn't jump off my left foot, which was my take-off foot. I had to learn to jump off my other foot, which was a nightmare changing it round after all those years. You know what though, I absolutely loved it.

The lads were terrific and I used to travel in with a guy called Trevor Roffey who was the goalkeeper and used to play for Sutton United. Trevor's dad Dave used to go to the games and then my dad got the bug and started to bring Anthony, which was his first introduction into non-league football and where he went on to do so well himself. I also played alongside my younger cousin Spencer Collins and his dad, while my uncle Terry would also come along, which reminded me a little of my schoolboy days when all the family would come down and watch you play on Sundays.

At the end of that season, Maidenhead won the league's Full Members' Cup in the Isthmian League, which was their first cup competition they'd won in about 60 years. The opposition teams we played were all respectful with me, but we couldn't swap shirts at the end of games because that was the only kit we had. Getting introduced to non-league football again was a great time of my life and I was only getting paid £150 a week. Who'd have thought?

I was also loving the coaching side of it at Maidenhead, but at the same time I'd been doing commentary with Jonathan

Pearce for the odd game here and there. Then when Jonathan started to ask me to commentate more regularly, I'd be saying, 'Can't do this Saturday or Tuesday because I've got games and I'm also coaching.' I loved the commentary and I knew this was something I could see myself moving into after football, but I hadn't fully committed to making the leap yet.

I made 42 appearances in 15 months playing for Maidenhead and really enjoyed it, but my ankle wasn't allowing me to train properly. One day, my mate Andrew Dickie came to see me play against Barton Rovers with his daughters and son and he noticed something different about my kit. Maidenhead play in black and white, which is where they get their nickname 'The Magpies,' and while everyone else had a white stripe down their black shorts, I just had plain black shorts because my arse was too big. When I put on the pair they'd given me, they looked like they've been sprayed on.

I came off after 70 minutes as I was struggling to move on this bone-hard pitch over at Barton Rovers and went into their bar. I asked Andrew what he thought about me in the game and he said, 'Can I be honest? Give it up. You're hardly running around, you're standing in the middle of the pitch playing it off and I know your ankles and Achilles are playing you up, so you're not doing yourself any favours.'

A few days before, Jonathan Pearce had called me. 'Tony. Do you want to come to the World Cup in France? If you come though, you need to be full-time.' I told Andrew about my chat with Jonathan and the possibility of working with Capital Gold, longer term and he said, 'I'd bite his hand off. You've had a good run, but don't look over your shoulder and regret this chance with Jonathan.' That was the push I needed.

After leaving the ground at Barton that day, I gave Pearcey a call then I went and spoke with Dev. 'I've got to pack it in mate. I've been offered a full-time job to go to the World Cup in France with Jonathan Pearce for Capital Gold.' He replied straight away, 'You've got to do it mate. This could be the next big chapter in your life.' He wasn't wrong.

Chapter 24

GOLDEN ERA

'As a co-commentator he was one of the best I've ever worked with because he'd tell you why the goal was scored, who was at fault and the technique behind scoring the goal. But not just that. He's one of two or three I've worked with who will predict what's going to happen in the next 15-20 minutes.'

– Jonathan Pearce

ALTHOUGH I joined Capital Gold full-time in 1998 with Jonathan, I'd been on the guest panel alongside him for a number of years before. One story comes to mind, around 1991 when I commentated at Fulham along with Bobby Moore and Leroy Rosenior, as we'd all played for Fulham. They were in Division Three and it was a poxy windy night and we're in the front row with all the ISDN units and I'm in between Jonathan and Mooro, with Leroy on the end.

This game gets going on and was complete crap. It was 0-0 after about 70 minutes and we've run out of things to say and that's when Jonathan starts getting out all the stats out like, 'This is the fifth game in succession that Fulham have been held to a 0-0 up to the 70th minute,' blah, blah, blah. Me, Leroy and Bobby are all looking at each other rolling our eyes. Next thing, one of the older players gets injured and goes down for a while. Jonathan goes off with his rhetoric, 'There goes the frustrated older player. He's gone down with an awful injury, clutching his ankle. We are looking at battleship grey skies over Craven Cottage, as they float over the riverside stadium and beyond the River Thames at the back.' He then says, 'As the older player is laying there, there goes a crisp packet blowing past him on this horrible windy night at Fulham.' Next thing I see Bobby is writing something down on a piece of paper. He passed it to me and I read it and laughed, then passed it to Jonathan. It said, 'Cheese and onion, or salt and vinegar?'

When I stopped playing football, it wasn't like falling off a cliff edge because I'd been overlapping the radio work. The only way I can describe it was like entering a new dressing room. When I went up to Capital Gold there was Jonathan, Rob Wotton, Darren King, John Curtis and Bill Leslie later on. Jonathan designed the show, but we all had an input into it, which is why it worked so well.

So many people came through Capital Gold that went on to do very well in TV as well, mainly due to Jonathan giving us all the opportunity. Jonathan is a top geezer, but he was also a really hard task master, who always wanted perfection on the airwaves. When we all went into TV at a later date it was a lot easier, simply because Jonathan's standards were so high. I'd never had any media training, it was more learning on the job. Jonathan would say things like, 'You're talking too much. Less is more. Don't take too long to get to the point.' Everything he said I took on board.

My very first interview was with Sir Alex Ferguson straight after a game. I was late coming down from the stand as I didn't know where to go. As I walked into the press room with the likes of BBC, Sky, Five Live etc, Sir Alex says, 'Tony. How are you mate?' He then turns to the other broadcasters and says, 'Turn your tapes off.' He then asked me what I was up to these days. I said, 'I've just started working for Capital Gold.' He replied, 'What? And all these guys started without you?' They've all looked at me. He then said, 'Let's start the interview again. Tony – ask me the first question.' What a top man.

I hit the ground running at Capital Gold and was moving up and down the leagues, similar to when I was playing football, in terms of going round all the grounds. I might be at Leyton Orient on a Tuesday, Arsenal for a Champions League game on a Wednesday and then off to Chelsea to do an FA Cup semi-final. It was busy, but that gave me the best understanding of anyone of London professional football.

We shared the duties of driving the Capital Gold van up and down the country and I even learned how to plug in an ISDN unit and get everything live on air, which for anyone who knows how much I hate technology, was a massive thing. Running off with a tape recorder to do some interviews, then coming back to do the phone-ins was full-on, but the buzz was absolutely brilliant. One year I did about 130 games.

When you're travelling around with someone as a co-commentator, you do a lot of miles and you need someone you can work with and have a lot of fun with. That was Jonathan. But it was also his knowledge about the game and his genuine love of football and all its characters which really shone through. Like for example when Teddy Sheringham scored the only goal for England in an international and he said, 'It's ready, steady Teddy, with a glass of sherry.' Here's a couple more classics.

Arsenal were playing 'The Owls,' Sheffield Wednesday and were having one of their great seasons. Jonathan said to me, 'Arsenal will be all over them but we've still got to paint pictures, even if it's one-way traffic, just to keep it going.' It came to half-time and it was 0-0. I said to Jonathan, 'It seems to me that we keep repeating ourselves.' He replies, 'I know mate, but we can't have any dead air.' The first 15 minutes of the second half was the same. Pass, pass, pass. I'm raising my eyes to him and he's saying, 'Keep it going, keep it going,' because you have to remember there was 250,000 listeners for that game who either couldn't make it, were at home, in their cars, in a taxi, whatever.

Then it happened. Arsenal got their first goal and it was a great passing situation. I'm making it up now, but let's say Jonathan said something like this. 'Adams to Bould, Bould out to Winterburn, Winterburn passes it into midfield, down the line to Pires, crosses at the far post and up rises Kanu to make it 1-0 for Arsenal! Surely this is going to raise the bar for Arsenal tonight. Sheffield Wednesday are going to have to come out of their shell. They've been parking the bus all evening.'

Now, Sheffield Wednesday start to come out of their shell a bit and it becomes easier to commentate. They miss a couple of chances, but then Arsenal did another movement almost the same and Kanu scores again. Jonathan comes out with the best one-liner I've ever heard. 'And it's Kanu with number two, to sink the Owls, twit twoo!'

The other was at Old Trafford against Chelsea. Man United is a pretty difficult place to commentate from because they put the London radio stations right at the back and you've got United supporters sitting a row behind you. There we are talking about this game and it's painfully obvious that I'm a Londoner and Pearcey's got a little bit of a London accent too. As Man United fans are going past us, they're calling us all sorts, then suddenly they score just before half-time and it's 1-0. I said to Pearcey, 'This is really handy because we're going to get out of here alive. If Chelsea get back in this game, we're in trouble.' He said, 'Don't worry about that.'

Midway through the second half it happened. Chelsea started to pick up and the commentary has obviously turned pro-Chelsea and I could feel things being thrown at my head like sweets and peanuts, and you could hear the muttering of the United fans behind. I'm carrying on with the commentary as fans were trying to knock our headsets off, when next thing, 'Dennis Wise to Di Matteo, into Poyet, slips it through to Zola, Schmeichel comes out and Zola dinks it over him. Goal!' Me and Jonathan are bouncing commentary between us and we're still getting things thrown at us, then Jonathan turns to the United fans and says, 'They think it's all Zola! It is now!' Jonathan did not give a shit.

* * * * *

PHONE-INS WITH the general public were always great. You never knew who or what to expect. Once we were doing a phone-in at Spurs and Tim Sherwood was being slaughtered by the Spurs fans after a particularly bad tackle. I'm on the line with this fan and saying something like, 'I played with Tim. He takes it, he gives it, but he's a really good player. He did however deserve the card he got from the ref today.' The producer says to us, 'Next caller. It's Barry on the line from Watford.' This bloke comes on the line while he's driving with a couple of his mates in his car and says, 'I think they're being a bit harsh on Tim Sherwood.' I've immediately mouthed to Jonathan, 'It's Tim.' Barry says, 'Sherwood's a fine passer of the ball,' and I've said, 'No he's not. He can't pass wind.' Barry's replied, 'But he can read the game well.' I've said, 'No he can't. My gran could read the game better than him.' This goes on for about a couple of minutes and in the end Barry from Watford says, 'Galey. When did you know it was me?' I replied, 'The minute you opened your mouth!' You could hear the laughter down the line.

One thing that didn't leave me from football was my banter and whenever a new person came on board, of course, we had to do something to wind them up. We had one lad called

Adam Leventhal, who is now on Sky and has had a great broad-casting career, and on Adam's first gig, Pearcey and I were at Spurs getting ready for the 3pm kickoff. I said, 'Pearcey, just for a laugh, whenever you speak with Adam on the radio, keep getting his name wrong.' A minute later it was, 'There's been a goal at the KC Stadium,' or wherever he was and Jonathan says, 'And it's over to Ardul Levonfort.' Adam obviously knew it was him, but didn't want to say, 'You got my name wrong,' so he gave his update all enthusiastically. A few minutes later, Jona-than's said, 'And it's back to the KC Stadium for an update from Adams Levenstile.' After about six times on the trot of getting it wrong, at the end we had to say to him, 'Adam. It was just a big wind-up! You handled yourself brilliantly, mate!'

However, a couple of years later, Jonathan ended up on the receiving end of wrong names. We were covering the European Championship in 2000, staying in Amsterdam at a place called The Big Cock hotel. I thought it was very funny, particularly when I was ringing home and telling everyone where I was staying, when they knew I wasn't the most well-endowed, which made them laugh even more. It wasn't a great tournament for England, but one of the highlights was that it was the first win against Germany in a competitive game since the World Cup final in '66. We were massive for it on the radio and Jonathan was shouting, 'We need people from the team of '66 to be on the show.'

We managed to get the late, great George Cohen on and Jonathan starts saying something like, 'It's a historic day for England,' blah blah blah, 'and I'm delighted to say on Capital Gold, Tony Gale and I are joined by 1966 World Cup winner, George Cohen.' He then did this great piece with George about the memories of 1966, but the whole way through, George kept calling Jonathan, 'Jeremy'. Obviously, I was sitting there with this massive grin on my face, but didn't say a word. Then as we walked out I said, 'Alright Jezza!' I still have Jonathan down as Jezza in my phone to this very day.

Then about a week later we were driving from Amsterdam to cover England against Belgium in Charleroi. We needed to get to Carpark P1, which was where the broadcasters were, but we had a really basic sat nav which wasn't getting us there. We could see the stadium floodlights from a distance, but we kept looping around it. The roads were getting shut off and it was three hours to kick off. Suddenly we see a sign for the car park, get to a roundabout, but a policeman wouldn't let us through.

There had been a bit of trouble with the fans and as a result the Belgian police were being very heavy-handed with us and that's when Jonathan hit boiling point. He's got out of the car, showed this policeman his pass, then starts swearing because we had media rights to get in and this guy didn't give a shit. While this policeman is standing there not budging, Jonathan's turned to us shouting, 'Can't they see we've got accreditation? This is ridiculous!' He was getting more and more angry and had steam coming out of his ears, while we're all packed into the car. He had his wife and young child in the car, and there was me and Bill Leslie also in there.

I didn't know Bill Leslie before Capital, but I immediately struck up a great rapport with him, because he's a really nice lad. I used to call him Lord Leslie, because he's got a posh voice. So, here we are with Jonathan blowing his lid on the verge of getting arrested and Bill's decided to get out to try and defuse the situation a little bit and tried to speak to the police, but they weren't having any of it. Jonathan in the meantime was about to self-combust and I lent out the window and said, 'Why don't you just tell them who you are, Jeremy!' That completely took the wind out of Jonathan's sails and everyone cracked up.

We clocked up some serious mileage that trip and I was lucky not to get done for speeding. Others weren't as lucky though. We were on our way from Belgium to Holland and I'd been driving for about three hours, doing over 100mph all the way and was knackered. I said, 'Bill, can you take over mate?' He used to call me, 'People's' because Jonathan used to call me the 'People's Pundit.' Bill replied, 'Alright, People's.' He jumps in the driver's seat and off we go. He's been driving about 10 minutes and was only doing about five miles an hour over the limit and some geezer on a police bike comes up and pulls him over for speeding. He got a €200 fine!

As lively as those episodes were, there's been other times when me and Jonathan were close to reporting a disaster zone, but thankfully it didn't fully materialise. Once we commentated on a game in Turkey which Arsenal had played in and next day were flying to Romania to commentate on another game. That night me and Jonathan were in this hotel bar in Turkey thinking, 'We'll stay up all night and go from the bar to the airport.' There's only me, Jonathan and the barman, who's whistling away cleaning the glasses with a tea towel, when all of a sudden the hotel starts shaking and our beers are slopping around for about 10 seconds. Me and Pearcey are looking at each other, while the barman is still there whistling away and I've gone, 'What's happening mate?' He's replied, 'It's a force 6 earthquake. Quite major.' Our initial response was, 'A fucking earthquake?', which was quickly followed by, 'Another round of drinks please, mate.'

Same year, we were out in Barcelona covering a game and we went into the old town the night before and found this lovely old traditional restaurant. Out comes the waiter and I've gone, 'Errrr, Sopa? Soupo? Soupi?' I've turned to Jonathan and said, 'I don't think this geezer speaks English, mate,' but the waiter then says, 'OK.'

The waiter comes back with the soup and I've said to Jonathan, 'He hasn't brought any bread.' I'm asking, 'Bread? Breado? Panno? Panne?' The waiter's nodded, then I've started with the butter. 'Burro con panno? Burro?' I've said to Jonathan again, 'This geezer's not speaking. He doesn't understand what I'm saying.' The waiter then says in perfect English, because it turns out he was from London: 'I understand what you are asking for, but what I don't understand is why you are asking for a donkey with your soup and bread.' It turns out burro doesn't mean butter!

In seven years at Capital Gold I covered over 750 live games, which included commentating on every play-off final, the League Cup, FA Cup, Cup Winners' Cup, UEFA Cup, Champions League, World and European championship playoffs, not to mention covering every single England international, home and away, and every major final and major playoff. But let's not forget covering the World Cup in 1998. Now, that came with some stories.

Chapter 25

BREAKFAST OF CHAMPIGNONS

'I had to organise that World Cup for the radio in the independent sectors, so all the stations around the country were taking our commentary. Early on in the tournament Tony pulled me aside and said, 'Listen. You're doing yourself no favours because you're so serious. Just relax.' I said, 'I'm bored.' It was like being in a dressing room before a game and that's how we ran it, like a football team. Tony loved all that and if I have to be honest, he was pretty good at it.'

– Jonathan Pearce

THE 1998 World Cup started on 10 June, but we left for France three days earlier. At the time there was that famous Nike television commercial which featured the Brazilian squad, so me and Jonathan decided to have some fun winding up my mate Mike Osman, who was a huge Southampton fan.

Oz was sat at the studios in London doing the breakfast show and he gets a call from me, saying that Jonathan and I are at Heathrow airport, heading to France. The truth is, we were actually at the Eurotunnel waiting to drive our vehicle on, but that didn't work for this story. I said, 'Mike, there's a massive story breaking from the airport, it's carnage here. You need to tell Howard Hughes,' who was doing the news for Chris Tarrant. 'Tell him to make sure he's listening live because this is a massive story. We're going to phone you back in 10 minutes.' Mike's spoken with Howard and they were waiting for this story which they were going to broadcast live on FM and AM radio.

Everyone at the Capital studio are running around like blue-arsed flies as Mike's on the radio saying, 'We're about to drop a breaking story from Heathrow airport with Tony Gale and Jonathan Pearce on the scene. Apparently it's a huge story. Stay tuned. It's coming your way very, very soon. It was coming up to the news and Mike's said, 'We're going to go live now to Tony Gale and Jonathan Pearce.' I've come on and said, 'Oz, it's all kicking off here at Heathrow. Hold on. Oh my God what's going on here? The television screens, the departure boards, they're all smashed and the X-ray machines are in bits. It's like a warzone.' I'd painted this picture of devastation and everyone back at the studio is thinking, 'What the hell is going on there?'

Mike then asked a straight question. 'What has happened? You guys alright?' I've replied, 'The Southampton team are filming the new Nike commercial in Heathrow and it's all gone very wrong!' Basically saying Southampton were lacking a bit in skills. Oz absolutely died of laughter. It took him about 30 seconds to get his breath back.

Jonathan had been planning this trip since England qualified for the World Cup and was in charge of our team, sorting out all the travel logistics all over France, getting the commentators and co-commentators all round the country to do each game, plan the journeys and book up the hotels. He also had to sort out all the flights, the train and bus times, the press conferences, accreditation and then, let's not forget, he also had to commentate! When we got to France I said, 'Now, you've got to enjoy it, mate. This is when everyone sees what you're good at. You're the best radio commentator in the country. Let's hear it.' He was absolutely outstanding that whole World Cup.

We were mainly based in Avignon but driving around France. Bill Leslie was back at base at Capital in London and had to record bits with us for various shows, doing all the prep, bulletins and basically all the boring stuff, while me and Jonathan were living it up in France. Dominic Johnson, a very good reporter, was part of the team with me and Jonathan and I started calling him Paulo. Everyone kept asking, 'Why is he calling him Paulo?' Throughout the World Cup, Dominic had pretty much worn the same shirt and one day I said to him, 'Don't you have any other shirts?' I think it was his favourite. That's when I nicknamed him 'Paulo one top,' having a spin on words, with Wanchope.

Avignon was brilliant. What a lovely place that was. Jonathan booked these beautiful rooms for one night at this hotel where the French president had stayed, which was incredible, however, in the earlier part of the tournament we travelled together all over France in this big motorhome sponsored by Capital. First night we got to Avignon we went to the opening game of Brazil against Scotland on 10 June at the Stade de France in Paris, and then we travelled down immediately to Bordeaux to see Italy versus Chile, which was a right old schlep. I said, 'Where we going to stop to sleep?' Jonathan said, 'We'll find a car park or service station.' I've gone, 'We can't stay there. We'll get attacked or murdered.' Jonathan couldn't stop laughing, while I was being serious.

We spent quite a bit of time in the motorhome and we'd be describing our journeys from here to there and everywhere. There was me, Jonathan and Dominic Johnson, so after a while I said to Jonathan, 'Can't we tell a few porkies and get a train or a plane? Living in this thing is driving me mad.' After about a week we started sleeping in it less and less, because we knew the tournament was six weeks and that was not doable. Thankfully Jonathan gave in and I really don't think he was unhappy sleeping in a proper bed and taking a decent shower.

Reporting at the games themselves was something else. Two of the outstanding fixtures were England against Argentina, and Holland against Argentina. The Dutch game was played at the stadium in Marseille, which had one of the most stunning backdrops to a ground with all the mountains and was decided by a beautiful goal from Dennis Bergkamp. England's game of course, was famous for Diego Simeone getting David Beckham sent off, which we saw live. However, there's another side of media you don't see at these tournaments. In my time commentating, I've never ever been late for a game or pulled out ill apart from one match where I had a sore throat and couldn't speak. I have had to adapt on a few occasions though. On this occasion, I did one commentary off a rooftop in Paris because I couldn't travel due to having food poisoning and a really bad case of the shits. I had a telly wired up with an aerial on this rooftop where I could just about get a signal, sitting there in my shorts and vest commentating on a game that I wasn't at, but pretending I was there, while Jonathan was in the south of France.

After the semi-finals on 8 July, there was three days before the third place play-offs and on 10 July, Jonathan organised an evening I'll never forget. He managed to get us tickets to see The Three Tenors in concert, under the Eiffel Tower. Of course, I made all the jokes like, 'How much were the tickets? Thirty quid?'

Pearcey was wearing jeans and a t-shirt and I'm wearing a tracksuit and I asked, 'How we dressing tonight?' and he said, 'Like this is fine.' Well, our tickets were about six rows from the front which was incredible, but as we're going through our section we were seeing ladies in long dresses and blokes in bow ties. We looked like Del Boy and Rodney who'd gone to the fancy dress and got it totally wrong. We got a few odd looks, but what a concert. Honestly, I've never been to anything like it in my life. To see Carreras, Domingo and Pavarotti together was unbelievable. They sung everything from *Nessun Dorma* to *You'll Never Walk Alone* operatically, which had Jonathan in tears. Certainly the best concert I've ever been to and I've been to a few.

Back to the World Cup final. We did all our daily transmissions for the World Cup from the Chicago Pizza Pie Factory, which was on the Champs Elysées. David Speedie came out to do a couple of games and I did the World Cup final with Speedo, which was France against Brazil on 12 July. France win, then after the game we had to get back to the Chicago Pizza Pie Factory to do an end-of-tournament drink and a few transmissions and soundbites together about what a great tournament it had been. We fought our way through thousands of people on the Champs Elysées as France were celebrating and got downstairs at the Chicago Pizza Pie Factory, saw all the other commentators that were there and we had a nice drink.

About 4am, me and Speedo decided to head back to the hotel. We go upstairs and as you came out, you were bang on the Champs Elysées. We had to do a right to get to our hotel and there was nobody about now and I turned to Speedo and said, 'That's handy.' Then all of a sudden we hear this rhythmic noise and it was about five hundred French gendarmes all kitted out in their riot gear in a line, banging on their shields and spread across the Champs Elysées. I turned to Speedo and said, 'What the fucking hell is all this about?' Then we looked the other way and there was about two thousand looters who were nicking everything from the shops, which was why the gendarmes had been sent to clear them.

As we're standing there, the looters are moving towards the gendarmes and the gendarmes are walking towards them, with us in the middle. Speedo says to me, 'Which way shall we go?' and I said, 'Towards the police!' We walked over to the gendarmes shitting ourselves, with our hands up in the air and they parted their shields and let us walk through, like nothing had happened. What a memorable end to the tournament.

For whatever reason, I kept a diary throughout the '98 World Cup. My last entry read like this:

Monday July 13th – Up at 11:30 and onto the battle bus for the journey home. We arrive at Calais ferry and just missed one, but catch the next one an hour later.

I've saved myself all day for a fry up on the ferry, but unfortunately it's a choppy day on the water and I throw it all up down the toilet straight after, which makes the rest of the crossing terrible for me. A two-and-a-half-hour journey to Pearcey's house from where I get a cab home and I'm indoors at 9pm. Anthony answers the door and tells me to be quiet because Lyndsey is putting Alex to bed, so I just miss out on seeing her. A chat with Ant and Linz and I'm in bed for 11.30 and sleep until 12.30 the next day. Lovely. I'm home.

* * * * *

I'D MENTIONED that I pretended to be at a game in France but I was actually on a rooftop somewhere else, but the best story of any commentator to not attend a match, whilst pretending to be there, goes to Bonzo.

The year after the World Cup, Jonathan and I were working for Channel 5 out in Romania, but Capital Gold were also covering the same game of West Ham versus Steaua Bucharest. Dominic Johnson was going to be reporting live for Capital and he's said, 'Who's going to cover the game from London though? Who do you recommend? Do you think Billy Bonds would do it?' I said, 'Yeah. I'm sure Bonzo would love to do it.'

Bill had just finished managing and coaching, so I gave him

a call. 'Bill. Do you fancy reporting on the Steaua Bucharest game? You need to be up at Capital Radio studios and Darren the producer will look after you.' He said, 'I'm not going over to Romania?' I said, 'No. You'll be watching on the telly at the studios.' He said, 'That's fine.'

They put him in this room sitting behind the glass, with the producer on the other side and they gave him a light ale and some sandwiches. Dominic is commentating from Romania, while Bill is in the studio, but they can't let the public know that Bonzo is in the studio, because it makes Capital Gold look cheap and stupid. The producer has said, 'Billy. Make reference that you are there, but don't make any reference that you are not there. When Dominic asks you a question, you'll reply like any co-commentator would who's with him.' Bonzo's said, 'I've got it Dazza. Noooo problem. If Galey can do it, I can do it. Don't worry about it.'

The game starts and Bill's doing fine. Dominic Jonson kept referring to Bill by name in the commentary so he'd pick up. 'Billy Bonds, what did you make of that?' Bill replies something like, 'Shaka Hislop goes down on a slippery night here at Steaua Bucharest and makes a great save down on the right hand side and tips it past the post.' Dominic would keep asking the questions and Bill responded well. Then there's a run down the line and Dominic says something like, '….he goes round the left-back, gets it up to the far post and there's Rosu and bang, that's the opening goal for Steaua! West Ham go 1-0 down. What a goal that was, Billy Bonds. Do you think Hislop could have done better?'

There's total silence.

Dominic keeps the commentary alive and says again, 'Billy Bonds. You must have been taken aback by that goal, but do you think Hislop could have done better on this wet and slippery night here in Bucharest?' Still total silence from Bill. Dominic tries again, then next thing we hear Bonzo say live on air, 'Sorry Dom. Me telly's gone on the blink.' You have to love Bonzo!

Bill could never, ever tell a lie and he'd always give it to you straight, albeit, sometimes on the radio you can't always be that straight.

In one game, Paolo Di Canio went right up to the linesman's face shouting obscenities and it looked like one of them was about to do something. Jonathan made the comment, 'Do you believe there should be a certain yardage that football players need to keep from linesman?' I've put my case forward for a couple of minutes, because we were trying to pad out time and Jonathan's said, 'We've got Billy Bonds with us at the Reading game. Bill, you've been listening to this debate. If you were an official and Paolo Di Canio came up shouting in your face like that, what would you do?' Bonzo says, 'I'd just put one on him.'

That was Bill! I tell you what though, he loved that job which started to get him out and about again and it was great having a legend like him on board.

Chapter 26

LAST CAB HOME

'One of my proudest moments of my dad was when I watched him speak at my grandad's funeral. Seeing him stand up in front of all those people speaking about his dad, the bravery and the tone in which he spoke, while I could see the pain he was going through. He kept asking me if I was alright, because he knew how close I was to my grandad. Along with my dad, my grandad was my best mate.'

– Anthony Gale (Tony's son)

I WAS in Essex doing some coaching and I got a call from my mum as I was driving over the Dartford Bridge coming back to Surrey. 'Get to the hospital straight away. Your dad's there. He's got a chest aneurysm.'

I zoomed to the hospital and I managed to get to him before he went to the operating theatre. He was with his brother, Sid, who he'd called to say he was in pain. My mum was at my sister's looking after her kids at the time, so she couldn't get over in time before he went to the operating theatre.

My dad had a great sense of humour and as they were about to take him down I said, 'Pete, you alright?' He said, 'Feeling really rough, son.' My uncle Sid was looking at me as if to say, 'I don't think it's going to be alright,' but I said, 'There's football on tonight. Come on. Me, you and Sid watch the football down the club.' He said, 'Yeah. Don't count me out of that one,' and those were his last words. After the operation, he never came to and died on the ventilator the day after. He passed away on 20 January 2001 and was only 67 years old.

They gave me his valuables, which was his watch and wedding ring. I went to the lift to go downstairs and was looking at the watch and it made me think about all the things we'd done together, all the good times and what a great dad he was. Then I accidentally dropped the watch and the ring on the floor. The ring fell in the hole between the door and the floor, but thankfully it was 90 degrees the other way and was just sat there balancing for me to pick up. What's the chance of that happening? My son Anthony was with me and I said to him, 'He still lives on in me and you. Let's make him proud.'

On the day he died I was supposed to be commentating on Ipswich Town at Stamford Bridge with Jonathan Pearce, and my dad died near enough around kick-off time. I obviously had to cancel going to the game because I was at the hospital. I called up the radio station and spoke to Darren King, our producer and I said, 'Can you tell Jonathan that my dad has died, but not until after the game, so it doesn't mess his commentary up,' because Jonathan was also a good friend of my dad. Jonathan put out a beautiful tribute on air that my dad passed away, which was a lovely thing to have done.

My dad attended every one of my schoolboy games and not only took me home after in his black cab, he'd also drop the other kids back. If you asked any of the London taxi drivers who worked around Heathrow airport at the same time as him, they'll all know him. He's even on the cabbies wall of fame.

We had the funeral ceremony at St Saviour's church in Pimlico and they had to leave the doors open at the back because about 700 people turned up to pay their respects to him. When I got up to do the eulogy, I had a bit of a lump in my throat, but when

I looked up and saw everyone there, all I could think about was the laughter and the times I had with him. It was the first time I'd ever enjoyed being at a funeral.

Other cab drivers used to come and see my dad at their flat, because he used to get suits which had fallen off the back of a lorry. My dad's nickname at that time was 'Peter the whistle', (as in whistle and flute, suit). The first thing I said when I got up and spoke was, 'I'm not used to doing these eulogies, but my dad wouldn't help but laugh because half the people here today have one of my dad's suits on!'

I thought there was a lot of people at the church, but after, we went to the crematorium and for a quarter of a mile on each side of the road were black taxis and they were all there because they couldn't all park up at the church. The leader of the taxi union came up to my mum and said, 'This is for you Val,' and handed her five grand in cash from a whip round from all the cabbies down the airport. I said to them, 'Boys. We're going back to the estate to have the wake. You're all entitled to come.' I think we spent the five grand that night.

Every year since my dad passed away, a group of us have been going down to Richard Quartly's brasserie which he runs in the Cotswolds, by a lake. He was great friends with my dad and since 2001 we've been going down there and having a memorial for him. It's a combination of golf, horse racing and then we'd go back to the brasserie and have a few drinks with the music on.

The intention originally was that it would be a one-off for one year but it's been well attended by some great friends, including Strongie, who's never missed a year and does the after-dinner speech. We've lost a few dear friends along the way, including some of my uncles, but the cousins come now and we toast my dad at the end of it.

One of my uncles who's passed was Terry, who was always

up for a laugh and loved the weekends. One occasion, on the Saturday evening we were round Richard's and he said, 'Let's go round Cirencester and we'll have a curry.' We were always playing tricks on Tel, because he was the oldest one there. We'd eaten and as Tel went to the toilet I said, 'Quick. Let's pay the bill and get out.' We knew that Terry took his time in the carsey, so 20 of us paid up, ran out and went a couple of shops down and hid inside the door wells. Terry comes out of the toilet and the restaurant is empty. He says to the waiter, 'Where are they?' He replies, 'They paid the bill and left, sir.' He said, 'Without me?'

He's dashed out the door, looked left and right and couldn't see anyone and then he walked about 20 yards down the high street and we've all jumped out the doorway. He's shouted, 'You bastards! You know I'm losing it. You'll make me lose it even quicker.' RIP Tel.

Thankfully, the world of commentary continued to treat me well and as one door closed, another opened.

Chapter 27

SKY'S THE LIMIT

'The one thing that stayed with Galey is that dressing room humour, which you all miss when you stop playing football. The one-liners, the wind-ups. Galey brought them from the dressing room and into real life when he came to Sky.'

– Chris Kamara MBE

AROUND 2003/4 there was a big rights issue between local stations and TalkSport, who were just starting to come into the equation, which drove all the prices of the rights up. Capital Gold couldn't afford those prices, so I knew I had a year up to the end of my contract to sort something out. Jonathan also left in that last year, so I decided to go to the boss of the sports department at Capital and explained I was looking to work elsewhere. He said, 'I fully understand. What you can do is start to do a few games for Sky, just to put your toe in the water.' That's what I did and when my Capital contract came to an end, I started doing a lot more commentary for Sky.

Jonathan and Jeff Stelling both had radio backgrounds and when you go into TV it's so easy, because you need to learn to shut up now and again, whereas on radio it's got to be constant, because you can't have dead airtime. You prepare the same amount, but it's all live as opposed to commenting on everything in hindsight on TV. That's why Jeff's show was so good because the basis of it was kind of taken from the radio model.

At Capital Gold it started at 1pm and built up to the games, then

3pm live kick-off and then you'd be bouncing between different commentators at different grounds. That's basically what Sky did, but on TV and with four pundits around a load of tellies. You're still building up to the game, showing little clips from the grounds and then Jeff would go off to the four guys on the panel or to the grounds where one of us were at. Sky were the forerunners in that and Jeff did a great job leading the commentary team, even if I did take the piss out of him. At the time it was me and TC alongside each other on the punditry and Jeff used to call us 'The Chuckle Brothers.' First time I went on the programme I had Jeff and TC standing back to back to see who was taller. Jeff claimed to have a quarter of an inch over TC, which I think he did, but only because he had his Cuban heels on.

During my time at Sky I was lucky to have worked with some lovely people, who are still mates to this day, which made it that much more fun to go into the studio. Chris Kamara is great entertainment and he's exactly the same on and off-screen. We had similar lengths of careers as players and Kammy also did a bit of managing, but it's his on-screen presence that everyone loves him for, because he's funny, entertaining and you never know what to expect next with him.

What people maybe don't is how much charity work he does, such as a golf event in Tenerife he organised for 12 years raising money for Marie Curie, which I had great pleasure of travelling out for to lend my support. Kammy also had a share in an Irish bar in Tenerife called The Hole in The Wall, which served great beer and live music and had loads of ex-pros constantly visiting. There would be hundreds of people in the bar and they'd ask Kammy to sing and he'd say, 'No, no,' but then he'd sing straight away, *'Stuck in the middle with you,'* which is the only song he can sing!

Matt Lorenzo is another top bloke in media. His dad, Peter

Lorenzo, was one of the original voices of *The Big Match* and was the first commentator on ITV. Matt was a presenter at Sky and we used to do a regular slot on Sky Sports News at 8am on Fridays. He was like a steady ship. If anything cocked up in the presenting department, he didn't need the autocue, he could ad-lib. He was another one who gave me great advice both on the television and hosting charity events. I'd come with all these notes and he'd say, 'What do you need all that for? Trust yourself. Don't write and prepare too much. If say for example the dessert comes out late or the starter doesn't appear, you have to be able to adapt. Here's some advice – just remember what you're doing in the next five minutes. That's all you need to know.'

Then around 2007/08 we were together in a show called *Off The Bar*. It was a park-based Premier League preview show, with a bookie on it, which made it great to watch but made it almost impossible for Matt to get past Ofcom. It was fun while it lasted and we had loads of great guests including Ray Winstone, but unfortunately it was axed after two series. That however wasn't the end of mine and Matt's adventures.

In 2009 Matt was asked to do a talk on a cruise and was all set to go with his wife, when last minute she had to drop out. He asked me if I fancied going and I said, 'Yes,' of course.

We spent a night in Corsica, which is where we boarded the ship, then shared a room together on board, which Matt's still having nightmares about. Shortly after boarding I got chatting to some geezer from Liverpool and he said, while Matt was standing next to me, 'Why are you here with that bloke from the lottery?' which I thought was hilarious. Later that evening, as Matt's laying on the bed and I'm in the bathroom, I've shouted, 'Have you got anymore anti-perspirant? This one's finished.' He shouted 'What??' It was a roll-on. Some people are so fussy about the odd hair here and there.

Work-wise, we did two sessions on that ship. One was at 11am and only 20 people turned up in this gigantic auditorium at the back of the boat. We thought, 'Bloody hell. This ain't great.' We did the routine and then a couple of days later we had to do the same gig again, but in the evening. The thing about the boat is that it never shuts and with the drinks being all-inclusive we really gave it some. Two days later we've rolled back into this auditorium and were expecting 20 people or less, but this time 1,500 people turned up. Let's just say we gave a lively performance.

As far as Sky goes, I was privy to a load of great footballing moments and was fortunate to have commentated on Wayne Rooney's first goal at Everton against Arsenal, when it hit the underside of the bar and beat David Seaman. Another similar great memory from my Capital Gold days was commentating on Thierry Henry's debut and his first goal. He was the best player in the Premier League that I've commentated on without a doubt.

If you have a football career, you have a shelf life, the same goes with a radio career and any career. Do they want to see a grey-haired geezer talking about football? I might have more to say than many commentators and probably have more on-pitch knowledge, but aesthetically they want to have the younger people on there now, which is easy for me to accept. However, I can still do my commentary, because that's to do with voice and I still think I've got a decent voice and delivery.

You've got to be yourself, have a bit of a sense of humour, but you also need a basic understanding of the game and being in touch with everything football, at any given moment. Some of the pros used to come on there and say, 'It's easy.' I used to say, 'It's easy to do, but it's not easy to do well.'

*****

SHORTLY AFTER finishing with Capital Gold, John Lyall died on 18 April 2006 and hundreds of people attended the funeral. It was like the Who's Who of West Ham and Sir Alex Ferguson flew down and did part of the eulogy, which was brilliant.

Fergie mentioned that he'd offered John a job as director of football at Man United shortly after he got the manager's position, but John didn't want to move up north because he was already settled down south with West Ham. He looked at John like a mentor and when he was managing St Mirren and Aberdeen, he'd ring John all the time. John had a lot of time for young managers and he also had a bit of Scottish in him, so he enjoyed the banter with Fergie. Even when Fergie got up to the higher echelons, I think he still looked up to John and certainly never ever forgot about him.

A couple of years later there was a remembrance dinner at Upton Park for Ron Greenwood and John Lyall and Fergie flew down on his own especially for it. He was on a table with the likes of Sir Trevor Brooking, Graham Gooch and Parkesy, and I was in charge of introducing him up onto the stage. 'Here he is. The man that must be fed up with us. We stopped him winning the title when we were already relegated...'

Then he sat down. As he got up again I carried on and said, 'And we stopped them in the FA Cup when Fabien Barthez put his hand up appealing for offside and Di Canio went through and put it in the goal...' and he sat down again.

After a few more times, he's got his white handkerchief and started to wave it and said, 'That's enough, that's enough,' and then he came up and did the speech, which was brilliant. He got a standing ovation when he got up to do it and another when he finished.

Shortly after, he left and flew back the same evening as Man United were playing Wigan in the last game of the season to potentially win the Premier League, which they achieved. To come down for the dinner with all that going on, it shows the true colours of the man.

However, while some of us were enjoying the limelight, others were content with daylight, as I soon found out.

Chapter 28

FROM PUB BARS TO IRON BARS

*'It's called sunlight, Meehan. Think of it as a
privilege which can be withdrawn.'*

– Mr Burton in Mean Machine

TERRY CREASEY was one of Bobby Moore's best pals and is
a larger than life character, who used to broker tickets for the
Hammers. I met him shortly after joining West Ham and we've
become good friends and been to numerous parties and golf
days over the years.

Terry was like Ronnie Barker out of *Porridge*, which is appropriate because he ended up getting nicked and as he said,
'having a holiday,' at HMP Springhill in Aylesbury. Whilst
inside around 1989 he sorted out a football match at the prison
between almost the entire 1966 squad and a group of prisoners,
who Terry managed, which meant there was no way the '66
squad were getting beat.

They asked me to play, but I wasn't allowed to because I was a
current player for West Ham at the time. I did however go down
the nick and watch the game with my dad, which was surreal, as
Terry got the likes of Alan Ball, Martin Peters, David Webb, Paul
Roberts and Geoff Hurst to play, who were all good mates of his.
Bobby Moore was in India at the time and unfortunately couldn't
attend, but in the words of Tel, 'A good day was had by one and all.'

FROM PUB BARS TO IRON BARS

* * * * *

MARK WARD was a really grounded player who came from non-league, had no airs and graces about him and was a working-class boy from up in Liverpool. First time he came in at West Ham I thought, 'Wow. He really is short,' and he became the target for all the little jokes. One day he's walked in and gone to hang his jacket up and I've shouted, 'Do you want a box to stand on, Wardy?' and he's turned round and said, 'What did you say, you fat twat?' Me and him started to laugh and that was the beginning of our friendship. Alvin then said to Wardy, 'You've got to take him as he is. It's just banter with him and it doesn't mean anything.' He then said, 'Why do you all call him Reggie? Is he fucking hard?' Alvin laughed and said, 'He couldn't fight sleep! It's because he's that brutal with his tongue, that's why he's called Reggie, after Reggie Kray.'

After he left West Ham in December 1989, we always kept in touch, then in 2005 I got word that he'd been banged up. Everyone's made mistakes and Wardy paid a huge price for his one. He knew he'd done something wrong and didn't need people telling him that. Thankfully, the footballing fraternity got behind him and he received loads of correspondence from a number of different supporters. However, it was the fans from West Ham, Everton and Man City that contacted him the most and never once did he receive a letter from any of them trying to mug him off or accuse him of anything.

When he was at HMP Walton, Howard Kendall and Duncan Ferguson visited him and he got a few letters from players, like myself and Bonzo, which were like chalk and cheese. I said, 'Hello short arse!' Then it went on to give him some advice. 'Someone told me that you were planning an escape. I might suggest that the easiest way for you would be to crawl under the cell door.' I finished off with, 'If you've learnt how to write, drop me a line. I'd love to hear from you. All the best mate… from the best player you ever played with! Tony Gale.' Bonzo's letter on the other hand said, 'Dear Mark, thinking of you, Bill.' That was it. I call Bonzo the Clint Eastwood of football because he's a man of few words. I don't think the length of the letters mattered so much to Wardy, more the fact that people kept in touch and showed he had mates on the other side. Four years is a long time to be in prison and when he was down, those letters really helped him.

Wardy had never been in trouble before he went into prison, so, towards the end of his sentence they moved him to HMP Kirkham in Preston, which is an open prison and basically meant he was allowed back out into the community to do some work. One day my phone rings and I've answered, 'Hello?' Some geezer responds with this strong Scouse accent, 'Hello, Galey!' I've said, 'Alvin? Is that you?' He's gone, 'No mate. It's Wardy!' I've said, 'Are you out of prison?' and he's said, 'No. I'm in a church.' Now I was confused. 'What do you mean you're in a fucking church? Have you broken out of prison?' He's replied, 'No! I'm still in prison but working at a church in Liverpool for the prison, doing maintenance stuff. I'm doing a year of community service.' I pissed myself laughing, then asked, 'How did you get a phone?' He's laughed and said, 'I got one of the lads to get me a mobile, but because you're not allowed to have them in the prison, I stash it where all the lawnmowers are at the church. That's one of the reasons I'm calling. Can you do me a favour and send me some credit on my phone as it's 'pay as you go'?' We then both cracked up laughing again.

I made sure that phone had credit on it for the rest of the time he was at Kirkham, but me and the Boys of '86 also did something else to help him for the last year of his sentence. We might not have been on the pitch at that point, but that team spirit never left us.

The job he had at the church in Liverpool was about 30 or so miles from Kirkham prison, so he gave me a call to ask if we could help in any way, because firstly the travel was going to cost him a fortune and secondly, the conditions of being at an open prison meant he had to be back at a certain time to closed conditions. Wardy had no intention of breaking those rules and potentially extending his sentence, but without transport, he was stuck. At the time, we had a few quid in the kitty from different events we'd done and I said, 'Wardy. We'll send your brother Billy a couple of quid to buy a little car to get you to work and back. Don't let us down.'

We gave about a grand towards a little runabout from the Boys of '86 pool and he was unbelievably appreciative. It also meant he had a car to use straight away when he came out of prison. The only thing was, as everyone knows, Mark is a big Evertonian and was horrified when he picked up this car to see it was red. However, that car gave him the opportunity to work every day and come back at 6pm and the money he earned, which was minimum wage, went into an account in the prison. Then when he left the prison he had about five and a half grand in there, which was enough for Wardy to pay the deposit for a flat and pay a few months' rent. It gave him that fresh start he needed.

Wardy did his time as well as he could and when he came out in 2009, he was a totally reformed man. Well done mate. We're proud of you.

Chapter 29

STAG DO

'Just when I thought I was out, they pull me back in.'
– Michael Corleone, The Godfather

WHILE I'D been doing commentary for a couple of decades, I'd also been busy on another front. I never intended to manage a team or run a football club and what started off as a bit of help to a cousin turned into a 20-year labour of love.

My uncle Terry Collins was the one that got me involved in non-league Walton Casuals FC. His eldest son, my cousin Spencer played a lot of semi-pro football for Walton Casuals, Walton and Hersham, Crawley, Farnborough, Carshalton and a few others, then when he was 26 he sustained a double fracture of the leg and that was his career over. He started coaching the kids at Walton Casuals, then the reserve team manager left and they asked him to take on that role. Not long after, he started managing the first team in November 2002 when they were almost bottom of the league and he helped to get them out of trouble.

The next season uncle Terry asked, 'If you ever get the chance, maybe you could come down and give Spencer some ideas on training?' I said, 'Okay. No problem.' That's what kind of pulled me in and I ended up standing on the line with Spencer, doing the coaching with him, teaching him different aspects of the game and just trying to help him manage whenever I could. My title there was Director of Football, but I was already kind of starting to run the football club and then a few years down the line I was given the title of Chairman. Titles aside, from the outset it was all about fundraising for the club, getting more money for the players, getting some decent kit and improving the quality of the ground. From there it just developed and I've never been one to walk away from anything without finishing it properly. That first season of 2002/03 we finished 18th in the Combined Counties Football League. Although we were hovering around relegation, that first season gave us a good idea of what we could do the season after.

It was a real family affair with Anthony playing, Spencer managing and my uncles Terry and Ray as kit men. I got new footballs, some new training kit, but we also lacked some of the bigger equipment such as a watering system. Because of my job with the radio, I was around in the day and got a bit obsessive about wanting to have a good playing surface at Walton, so every hour and a half I used to change the sprinklers around to keep the grass green and the seeds growing. Then down the line, in the winter, we didn't really want to go on the pitch and mess it up and leave a crap playing surface, so I managed get the lads to use Fulham's training ground at Motspur Park, which has a giant indoor dome with a full size Astroturf pitch. That became the training venue for Thursday nights, which they loved.

Locally, there was Walton Casuals and Walton and Hersham, but Hersham have always been the bigger club in the town and we were like the poor relations. Then in the 2003/04 season we were up against them in the FA Cup preliminary round and we turned the tables. We even got my younger cousin Terry Gale out of semi-retirement because we didn't have a lot of experienced players at that time. What he lacked in fitness, he made up in skill and determination at centre-half that day. Despite smoking on the halfway line at half-time, which wasn't the most professional look, he played a belter of a game and won man of the match. He couldn't walk after, but he didn't give a shit. There's a nice photo of him in the changing room after, absolutely knackered, having a fag. We beat Walton and Hersham 2-0, which was the first time in history we'd done that. That win was a massive boost to the players and the club, and it kind of put us on the map. We proved that we were more than just a pub team who met just for a game of football and a beer.

Dave Symonds, nicknamed 'Jacko,' was the main man who used to run the football club before I came along, then when I joined we ran it together, along with our president, Graham James. Dave and Graham were great people and did so much for the club, and I can't talk highly enough about them, although when we played AFC Wimbledon at home that season, Jacko did have me worried. On the day, we had a crowd of about 3,000 and people were paying with cash through the turnstiles. It was our biggest ever take and every time we had a bag full of money, Jacko was running backwards and forwards to the boot of his motor dropping the cash in. I didn't know why he kept running away at first, then I asked, 'Jacko. What you doing?' He replies, 'I'm sticking the money in the boot of my car.' I've replied, 'What happens if someone nicks the car?' Jacko spent the rest of the game with one eye on the football and the other on the car. That season we finished seventh, but the season after was something special.

By the 2004/05 season we had a number of good players and the camaraderie was amazing. My son Anthony was playing left-side midfield for Spencer and it all came together nicely. We went on to win the Combined Counties League Premier Division, clocking up 138 points and gaining promotion to the Isthmian League Division One. We were clear by 26 points at the top of the table, with a goal difference of 99.

Getting promoted to the Isthmian League was great, but it came with its challenges because we had to raise more money, which involved getting more sponsors in. Terry Brown, the old West Ham chairman, sponsored the club for a number of years when I first arrived, then Antler Homes helped out for a couple of years. Initially though, we used that money from the AFC Wimbledon game to buy a couple of temporary stands on the far side, then we concentrated on upgrading our ground, which meant getting a tunnel and at least 150 seats.

The 2005/06 season didn't start great. We had a ground inspection from some guy at the FA and it was on a day that we had a kids game at the end of the season and this geezer couldn't get a parking space, which give him the right hump. When he arrived, he started ticking things off like, 'The loudspeakers ain't loud enough.' In the end they failed us because the tunnel wasn't good enough, which was bollocks and the second one was there were no numbers on the seats. Not that anyone sits on the seats in non-league football anyway. I wasn't at the ground, so I called him up and said, 'Can we get round that by putting marker pen on them until the little buttons arrive?' He said, 'No. The ground has failed.' I said, 'We've spent all this time trying to get up a division and you're not trying to give us a chance. I'm going to the FA.' He said, 'Do what you like.'

Me and Jacko decided to appeal and had this day at the FA to put forward our case. The bloke who'd failed us was there and these three guys on the board recognised me and said all upbeat, 'Hello Tony! How are you?' Two of the guys had been in Poland with me when I was in the England youth team back in the 1970s. I could see the assessor looking over thinking, 'Bloody hell. He knows them.'

I put our case forward and said, 'I've represented my country at youth level, played as a professional for decades and I've never heard anything so stupid in all my life. You cannot reward people from non-league who put so much time, effort and money in and fail them because they haven't got round to numbering new seats.' They explained it was the regulations and I said, 'Yeah, I understand that. But for a little oversight that was easily remedied, it was very heavy handed. You gave us no chance to make it right.' Long story short, we had to hang around for about half an hour and then they overturned the decision. We finished 15th that season, but winning that little battle was a success in itself.

*****

EVERY TIME I thought about giving Walton Casuals up, someone else came on board and it reignited my energy. I first met Duncan Saunders and his dad Paul around 2005. They went to a game on a Tuesday night at Walton Casuals and being ex-football players themselves, they enjoyed it. Afterwards they went for a drink in the bar and that's when I met them properly. They started to attend more regularly and not long after started doing sponsorship of the club and then got deeper and deeper into it. They worked closely with myself and were a big factor in keeping the club alive after Dave Symonds left.

Duncan and his dad had a family-run haulage business in the area for 70 odd years and were able to transform portacabins into dressing rooms and a new club bar for us, which in turn helped to attract more fans. On the back of that, as the club got bigger we could hold functions at the bar. They were good local people who wanted to give something back to the area, not just financially, but shared in our vision of seeing where the Casuals could go at that point. They wanted to help make the club into a household name in the local area, which, with limited financial resources, would always be difficult for a non-league club.

Duncan even used to wash the kit to help save money so that the players could have more in their pot.

People don't realise what goes into running a football club. It's okay me raising the money and things like that, but on match days you've got to be in there at 1pm, opening up the stadium, making sure you have all the float for the turnstiles and getting all the staff sorted. Then there's selling the raffle, the programmes, sorting out the chairman's lounge, who's making the sandwiches for the lounge and who's making the food for the players after the game? Then, in the chairman's lounge, you had to make sure you entertained them and there was tea and biscuits at half-time and then afterwards, making sure there's drinks for the opposition, the linesmen, the referee, the chairman, directors and the FA people who were coming down to assess. Then you had to look after the players themselves, making sure everything was out for them. It's a lot of hard work and Duncan did all of that horrible, shitty hard graft and was excellent in delivering.

I used to have some great chats with the referees and linesman, who generally made some brilliant decisions, but they also made some stinkers, like footballers do in games. After the dust settled, it was great to chat about our experiences. Some of them were young referees coming into the game and there's nobody for them to talk to and although I was chairman, I had to take this impartial view that I had a reputation to uphold and wanted no part in slagging off referees or anything like that.

They'd ask my opinion sometimes of their decisions and I'd be honest with them and we'd also discuss the impact of VAR, which is something that comes up all the time when I'm commentating. When it first came out, commentators all had to go up to Stockley Park and listen to a load of referees, showing us playbacks and explaining the rules. They showed examples of past goals which would have been allowed or disallowed, and when offsides are valid, explaining that as long as it's a goalscoring part of the body that's over that line, you are deemed to be offside. Matt Le Tissier was there and put his hand up and said, 'I've just worked it out that I would have had 25 goals less in my career.' The guy hosting the event says, 'How did you work that out, Matt?' He replied, 'I might have been offside by a nose!'

There were a number of times the opposing team's directors would start having a go at the refs and linos and I'd say, 'Hold on. These boys are doing a job. The game's been played and they've come up for something to eat, not for you to give a description of the game.' Once everyone started to eat and there was a relaxed atmosphere, our ground became one of the best in non-league to visit, without a doubt.

*****

THE FOOTBALL network is very strong and even though you have friends who've moved around and away, when you get chatting everyone still knows each other. Football is like a big village. An old friend I crossed paths with from my playing days was Martin Tyler, who is one of football's best known commentators. I first met him when I was a player at Fulham and he was commentating about me for ITV and *The Big Match*. He followed my career all the way through to Blackburn and then into Walton Casuals, where we became rivals in non-league football. Martin started helping a guy called Alan Dowson at Walton and Hersham and then later moved onto Kingstonians, and our clubs played against each other a few times, with the most memorable one being in March 2007.

On the day, one of the referees was a young lad and I saw Martin talking to him on the pitch, being all nicey-nicey and schmoozing before the game. I said, 'Oi. Don't listen to him. You've got to referee the game.' Martin's a really nice bloke, but if there's a little edge to have, he'll get it, because, like me, he's very competitive. When the decisions started going against us in the first five minutes, I turned around and went to Martin, 'Was that a nice chat with the ref before the game?' They beat us 3-1, but they were a much bigger club than us, so to get that far with them was great.

There was a lot of banter and competitiveness between the two benches, but after the final whistle we were all mates again. The lasting memory for everyone though was when one of our lads, Billy Mead, suffered a broken leg in a 50/50 challenge. The game had to be stopped for about 15 minutes before the ambulance took him off to the local hospital, which was very sad. Bill's a top lad and my son now trains his son.

At the end of the 2007/08 season, I got in touch with Les Strong, who was managing a Mauritian team called Petite Riviere Noire FC, which had won the Mauritian League the previous season under his management. As you can imagine, you had the likes of Chelsea and Man United all wanting to go out there and play friendlies and now there's me saying, 'Strongie. Can Walton Casuals come out?' He's gone, 'Alright then Galey. Bring the Stags over.'

The geezer who owned the club was an old school friend of Strongie's, called Mario Monte and he was Mauritian, but came from South London. They arranged for the Casuals to come out to Mauritius and play a friendly, but also visit the local little villages and coach the kids. Strongie got him to help his team as well, because Anthony wanted to become an international coach. Strongie said, 'Coach our team and you'll automatically become an international coach.'

We were staying in a five-star hotel and Strongie turns to me and says, 'I'll need to say a couple of words to the lads.' He turns to them and says, 'We're delighted you're here, but you're staying in a top hotel and people are paying an absolute fortune to be here, so we need you to behave yourselves.' They all nodded, but within five minutes of arriving at the hotel they were throwing balls into the swimming pool and doing diving headers.

When the Casuals and Petite Riviere Noire played, it was live on TV in front of a full stadium, which was a great experience for them. Then after, our friend Monty organised for us to go to the Government House and meet the Prime Minister and shake his hand, which was mad for the lads.

* * * * *

IN THE 2009/10 season Walton Casuals got to the third qualifying round of the FA Cup, before losing to Staines, then in 2011 we opened a new clubhouse and changing facilities. The next season we finished ninth place, but football wasn't at the forefront of my mind. My mum had a major stroke in December 2012, which was heart-breaking, but thankfully she pulled through. Then, towards the end of 2013, after 37 years of being together since the age of 15, mine and Lyndsey's divorce went through.

2014 was a mixed bag. In the summer, me, TC and Little Les (Les Lee) headed out to Brazil for the World Cup. We paid for our own trip to get out there, but managed to land some work going round to pubs doing speeches before the games.

One of my mates, Mark Snowsill, was a naturally great organiser. In the past he'd arranged a trip to the Miracle of Medinah in Chicago to see the Ryder Cup, which is one of the greatest sporting events I've ever had the pleasure of attending. A great group of lads went, including my good friend George Ruff.

Coming back to the 2014 World Cup, Mark had organised this wonderful itinerary about a year in advance including a stay in the Copacabana Hotel. Unfortunately, he passed away at a premature age about six months after organising the trip and never got to come out with us.

I'd like to say a few words about Mark. He used to pronounce his surname 'Snow-sill', and I used to pronounce it, 'Snozil', which led to me calling him Snoz. Through his businesses he became a generous sponsor and great contributor to Walton Casuals and was also someone who became a really good friend of mine. He was a mad Fulham fan who used to hire jets for him and his mates to go and see matches abroad, and for a good few years I loved going to see Fulham with him and Strongie. He absolutely loved life and I knew he was only looking to work a couple more years and then retire.

On this particular day, I was up in Newcastle, doing commentary and saw some old friends after the game, had a few drinks, got a little merry and then went to bed. About 2am the phone goes in my hotel room and when you've had a couple of drinks, you're in the middle of nowhere. It was Snoz's wife, Sandra. 'Tone. I thought I'd ring you up as I wanted to let you know. Mark's died.' I was numb and I said to Sandra, 'Mark's died?' She said, 'He came home from seeing Fulham, went to get changed and dropped dead.' That was one of the saddest moments of my life. RIP Snoz.

Going to Brazil was an experience. We flew into Sao Paulo and stayed in a nice hotel with a rooftop bar, but it was in an industrial part of the city with not a lot going on, so we decided to hunt down another couple of local bars. We were walking for about an hour and had got lost, because every street looked the same, when Les pointed to this rooftop bar and said, 'That looks lovely. Looks like there must be a bit of life going on over there. Let's go up.' TC and I said, 'That's our hotel, Les. We've done a giant circle!'

We were following the England games all over which meant we flew into Sao Paulo, then from there to Rio, where you were literally flying in between houses and it looked like the wings were going to clip someone's roof. You could almost look through someone's living room window, it was that close.

Inevitably, you're going to bump into the lads from back home. We saw Kammy out there and one night we're sitting there in the Copacabana Hotel having dinner and Alan Shearer walked in for a romantic meal with his wife. He came over and asked us, 'How did you get to stay in this hotel? I'm with the BBC and staying up the road at some other place which ain't like this.' We replied, 'Connections, son.'

We didn't realise the hotel we were staying at is where all the FIFA officials were staying. So there we were, me, Little Les, TC and my cousin Richard King, who by then had come out to join us, and the lift stops at a floor and in stepped the FIFA president, Sepp Blatter. Me and Rich immediately clocked who it was, but Les didn't have a clue. He just thought it was some random bald-headed geezer. Les goes, 'Alright mate. Over for the World Cup, are ya?'

This lift journey couldn't end fast enough, but because we were so high up it kept stopping at floors and it went on forever. I leant across to Les and said, 'Mate. It's Sepp Blatter.' He didn't have a clue but said, 'Ahhh. Right.' He turns to Sepp and says, 'Alright Sepp. If you like football, you must know Tony? He works on Sky.' Rich couldn't stop laughing.

From the Copacabana to East End car parks. When the 2014/15 season started back in England, my uncle Ray did all my driving and let's just say he's had a few 'moments' behind the wheel. The first game of the season we drove to West Ham who were playing Spurs. Ray drives us into the car park, finds a spot, parks up and then the parking warden asked if he could straighten his car up.

Ray got the hump, pulled out and went straight into a post, while all I did was stand there and piss myself laughing.

The season after, Ray's driven us to West Brom in his big, flash Lexus, which I used to enjoy stretching myself out at the back as it was like being in business class. We got to West Brom and pulled up and Alan Smith, the ex-Arsenal forward was there. He was walking past and I've opened the door and shouted out, 'Smudger!' Alan comes over and I said, 'Al. This is Ray.' They've shook hands and Ray is star-struck chatting with Al, then after a bit we go off into the media section. About an hour later we go to the gantry, I've put my headphones on and was all ready to start, when one of the staff comes up and says, 'There's a car downstairs which has been left running for about the last two hours. It's a Lexus. Would you know who's it is?' Don't think I've ever seen Ray move so fast.

On the Walton Casuals front, me and Anthony were appointed as caretaker managers in the 2014/15 season, then Anthony became first team manager the season after. The next few seasons turned out to be a bit of a rollercoaster with a number of highs, lows and a few unexpected episodes, which were out of our hands. However, certain activities have a way of grounding you and making you appreciate what's important to you in life.

Chapter 30

DOING MY BIT

'It's not fun talking about bowel cancer, particularly at dinners, but Tony Gale will always draw people's attention to it by being incredibly funny. He makes it OK to talk about it. The sort of events he talks at tend to be predominantly male, most of whom normally can't be bothered to listen and take care of their own health. Tony manages to get their attention very easily, in a way that I can't.'

– Stephanie Moore MBE

SHORTLY AFTER I started commentating on Capital Gold I got on the after-dinner speaking circuit at charity events. I'd been to a few functions, saw the impact it had on generating awareness and funds for the charities and thought, 'I fancy doing that.' However, I knew it wasn't as easy as standing up and cracking a few jokes, so I called a couple of mates, Richard Digance and Mike Osman, and they said, 'Come down and see us, tell us your stories and we'll go from there.'

They were both doing big television stuff at the time and Richard in particular had his own TV series and was on sell-out tours across the country. I had a work overlap with Oz at Capital Gold from about 1996 when I started doing bits and pieces for the Euros, but then I started going to a lot of functions and saw him doing impressions. He's that good it's hard to know sometimes if you're actually speaking to Oz.

So, there I was in front of an audience of two of the best

230

comedians in the history of British comedy and they said, 'What have you got Tony? Give us something to work with.' I told my first funny story and they sat there stony faced. At the end they said, 'Was that it? Let us know when we're supposed to laugh.' I told them another couple of stories and again they're both still sat there deadpan. They then said, 'Tony, we've got some serious work on our hands. We're gonna have to dig deep to make you funny.' I knew they were partly ribbing me as they started to laugh, but it's true, I did need a lot of work and it didn't happen overnight.

I did my very first after-dinner speech after a charity golf day. I was sat with former world boxing champions John Conteh and John H. Stracey and former heavyweight boxer Billy Walker. I got up and started telling this story and got a little bit stuck. Three seconds may not seem like a long time, but as I'm staring at my cue cards trying to get back into it, there was total silence in the room. I'm thinking, 'Oh shit.' All of a sudden, John Conteh, who'd done a lot of after-dinner speaking, jumped up and went, 'Yeah, but Tony...' and started like an on-stage conversation for everyone to listen to, which was brilliant. We did that for a few minutes, brought the house down and then I was able to deliver the rest of my story without any problems at all. I will always be grateful to the guys that hosted that day – friends of mine, Wes and Les Squibb.

It took me a little while to get to grips with what Richard and Mike told me and although they helped write some stuff for me at the beginning, after a few dinners, I was able to go it alone.

* * * * *

SINCE RETIRING, I've played a lot more golf and most of it tends to be for charity days. A few years ago me and Sir Trevor Brooking put up a charity prize of two people playing against us for a golf day in the Essex veterans league. This particular day was shortly before lockdown and it was these two business people from Essex who were proper blokes, against me and Sir Trev.

Trev is one of the nicest guys you'll ever meet and he never swears at all. So, there we were over at Thorpe Hall Golf Club in Southend and I started geeing everyone up saying, 'Come on. Let's bet a fiver for the match.' First geezer tees off and does a good drive, the second one not so good, then I hit a good drive and Trev's on last. He tends to take lot of time over his shots, including his practice swing. Eventually, he tees off and the ball goes up about a yard in front of him and lands at his feet. He looks at me and the other two didn't know whether to laugh, because it's Sir Trev. This was the first time I'd heard him say a four-letter word. He shook his head and said, 'Gosh.' I've said, 'Fucking gosh?' and we're all rolling around in laughter. That's about as annoyed as Trevor gets.

I can't speak highly enough of him, even if he does like winding me up about getting sent off in the semi-final against Nottingham Forest. In fact, years later I was supposed to attend a function with Trev, but when I found out Keith Hackett was one of the guests, I suddenly realised I'd double-booked with another event. Trev's footballing royalty, does an unbelievable amount for charity and I've never seen him turn down a photo, a chat or a request to sign something for a fan. There's a lot the younger generation of players could learn from him.

I try to do my bit for charity whenever I can, but there's two charities in particular I support on a regular basis. The Lily Foundation and The Bobby Moore Fund. When I started working with Jonathan at Capital Gold in the late '90s, his sister-in-law Liz Curtis was also working there and I soon got to know Jonathan's relations by going to his family functions. Then in 2006, Liz's daughter Lily tragically died at only eight months old from something called mitochondrial disease.

The year after, Liz and her husband Dave set up The Lily Foundation and they soon started to have fundraising events. I went to their first annual ball and supported Jonathan with the hosting and the auction, and since then I got more and more involved and try to attend as many events as I can in whatever capacity they need me. Sometimes it's golf days, other times events at local restaurants and sometimes I'll get a call asking if I can host the auction, source a prize, whatever really. I'm honoured to be able to help. With the generous support of a lovely man called Rob Burgess-Allen, we were even able to have the Lily Foundation on the Walton Casuals shirts for two seasons.

The charity has snowballed since they first started and I highly recommend attending their annual ball which is up at a big hotel in London. It's great fun and you can have a few drinks while helping them raise thousands of pounds. At the time of writing they've raised nearly £8.5million, which is incredible and it was no surprise when Liz was mentioned in the honours list in 2021 to receive an MBE. She went to Windsor with Dave and her family, and got awarded the MBE from Princess Anne, then she came back to a pub in London, where we all met her for a few drinks, with the rest of her team from her charity and people who she'd helped over the years. She said it wasn't an MBE for her, but for all the people who had helped her. She's an amazing woman and she also has an amazing husband in Dave who in my opinion probably deserves an MBE himself.

Shortly after Bobby Moore died, his wife Stephanie decided to set up a charity dedicated to bowel cancer research. With the help of former Fulham forward John Mitchell, who was also a great friend of Bobby, they started to do a few golf days and got massive support from sporting celebrities.

A few years after Steph started the fund, Imperial Cancer Research and the Cancer Research Campaign merged to become Cancer Research UK and gradually her team grew. By this stage they were doing all sorts of events like balls, dinners, sports quizzes, shooting days and various other events, raising a couple of million a year.

During that time, me and TC met Steph and started supporting her efforts in any way we could. Then in 2015 we started the Bobby Moore Memorial Golf Day, which has turned into an annual thing now. We have a shotgun start, with 120 people playing, and each team will have one footballer in the team, people like Graeme Souness, Matt Le Tissier, Glenn Hoddle, Ossie Ardilles, Alan Curbishley, Ray Houghton, Teddy Sheringham and the list goes on.

The golfers tend to be real down to earth people, usually contacts through our West Ham network. One of them for instance, Ronnie, is a straight talker who owns a skip firm in East London and has done really well for himself. One year, in the evening after the golf, we had the dinner and he went up to Stephanie after she'd done her talk and said, 'Stephanie, that was a lovely speech. I've gotta say, your Bobby was my hero. What happened to him at such a young age was horrible.' She said, 'Thank you so much.' He then said, 'The way you spoke tonight, I can understand now why Bobby got hold of you in the first place.' Steph pissed herself laughing and he didn't even know he'd been funny!

Me and TC try to help as much as possible with Steph, but there's been times where certain factors make it difficult to attend. In 2016 she asked us to attend a golf day in the Isle of Man which involved us leaving in the early hours of the morning to get a 7am flight from City airport in East London. There was me, TC and Little Les and as we're driving round the M25 about 4am, everything came to a standstill because of this horrendous accident on the motorway. There was helicopters and ambulances all up the M25 and around 6am we called Steph to let her know that we couldn't make the flight.

We were stuck there for about two and a half hours and when it did finally move we decided to head to a local golf course instead. As we're just getting into it, Steph's called. 'You have to come because I'm relying on you. You are our after-dinner speakers, you are our celebrities, people are looking forward to meeting you. There's a flight at 5pm from Gatwick and you could get that and be there in time for the dinner.' We dropped the golf and said, 'We're on the way.'

We got there about 7pm, did the after-dinner speech, met everybody and then decided to go for a night out at the local casino. Steph had this young lad with her from Cancer Research UK, who was very shy and had worked his arse off all night. Me, TC and Les said to him, 'Come on. You're coming out with us.' He said, 'No, no, no. I've got to go home.' Stephanie said, 'Go on! Go out with the boys. They'll look after you.'

We go down to the casino, played a bit of blackjack, had a few drinks and won about a grand between me, Les and TC. However, they paid us the money in the Isle of Man Manx notes, which is not accepted in the UK. We said bye to this lad from the charity and next morning, early hours we headed to the airport. I said to Les, 'See if you can change that money up.' He's gone up to the money exchange and they've said, 'We can't change that amount,' so we had to take it with us.

We go through the bleeper machines and next thing they've got the sniffer dogs all around us, as if we were drug dealers or something, because of this wedge of cash. We then got taken into a back room and searched like we were Pablo Escobar and had to explain we'd won it at the casino. Fun times.

You don't mind doing things for people if it's going in the right place and those are two charities I'll continue to support as long as they want me to. Liz and Steph are great people and they deserve all the success that comes their way.

On the footballing front, meanwhile, I was about to hit a crossroad and it was all about taking the correct turn.

Chapter 31

DECISION TIME

'Giving that football club up for me was one of the hardest decisions I had to make and bear in mind I run eight businesses. Me, my wife, my kids were in tethers for months. That's how much it meant to us.'

– Duncan Saunders

ALL GOOD things have to come to an end at some point and on 10 May 2016, West Ham played their last game at Upton Park against Man United. It was an evening match and my friend Little Les had a box which was supposed to hold 10, but on that night had about 30 people in there. Brian McFadden from Westlife and Keith Duffy from Boyzone were there with an Irish friend of ours called Ronan (not Keating).

After the game I asked photographer Dickie Pelham to take a photo of me and my daughter, Alex, as we were the last two people on the pitch at Upton Park after the game. Then we went into the tunnel and signed the wall. Alex wrote, 'Thanks for the golden days. Forever blowing bubbles.' Somewhere along the line I also knew that Walton Casuals had a certain lifespan, but there was a lot more to achieve before that day came.

I first met Ray Hole around 2016. My son Anthony, used to train his son and thought Ray was a man who could come on board and help Walton Casuals move to the next level. He invited Ray over and he attended a couple of meetings, then ultimately became a director of the football club.

I'd also like to mention a few other people from around this time who were incredibly helpful. Doug McClelland is an ex golf pro who's been in the trade all his life, ran Silvermere Golf Club and also ran an excellent golf day that contributed to our sponsorship. Doug was also responsible for bringing on board our accountant, a lovely man by the name of John Butler. Finally, there's Micky Johnson who started sponsoring Casuals from about 2015. All three of them were invaluable in everything we did and still have an active involvement with the Walton Casuals College to this very day.

In the 2016/17 season we reached the third qualifying round in the FA Cup, losing to Westfields, but it was the season after which was far more dramatic. We moved to the Elmbridge Sports Hub, which cost £17 million and had been built on the site of the Waterside Stadium, however, it was the way we finished the season that will forever go down in Walton Casuals history.

We only lost two games the whole season and then in the last 15 minutes of the last league game against Ashford United, we scored, which secured us a place in the playoffs. The semis were against Cray Wanderers and they were the favourites to go up, whereas we were one of the favourites to get relegated at the start of the season. I couldn't make it because I was commentating on that day, but straight after the final whistle, Ant called me to say they'd won 5-2.

The last game of the season was the playoff game against Corinthian Casuals in front of 2,000 people and so much hinged on it. Not just winning, not just promotion, but getting promoted into the seventh tier, which Walton Casuals had never done. I was commentating at Watford, but was calling people up to find out what the score was and after a goalless full and extra time it had gone to penalties. I was calling every 30 seconds and then there was this lull where nobody was answering their phones and getting back to me. I was getting the right hump. I thought, 'They've got beaten. They get all that way to the playoffs and they've fucking blown it.'

What happened was, there had been some crowd trouble, because some silly lads started fighting and it delayed the game by about 15 minutes. Then finally, Ant called me up. 'We done it!' When I saw him later that night I gave him a big hug. When I say 'We,' I'm referring to every single person who worked alongside that club from when I joined, brought the club from what was a Sunday morning team to a brand new club. New kit, changing rooms, the works. Don't get me wrong, from the beginning, it was always a labour of love and very tiring, but what we achieved over the coming years made it all worth it.

I was pleased for all of them but for Anthony especially, because he's the one that got stick if they lost and any little thing that went wrong. They'd say to me, 'You only appointed him because he's your son,' and all that bollocks. No, I appointed him because he was the best person for the job and his results confirmed that. I had two promotions at my time with Casuals. One with my cousin Spencer and one with Anthony. One was a record breaking year with Spencer, but getting out of that next league was a real tall order and Anthony did it and stayed in that league. Both Spencer and Ant should hold their heads high.

After a restructure of the non-league pyramid by the FA, Walton Casuals moved to the Southern Football League in 2018/19. In the last six games we had a good little run which kept us up, but we were punching well above our weight to be in that league and that was a great feat achieved by Anthony to stay there. We were playing the pretty game of football and about halfway through the season I had a chat with him and said, 'If you want to win some of these games, you've got to win them ugly', which he took on board. It was a great success story for him and the team to stay up in that league, but even more impressive that we went on to win the Southern Combination Challenge Cup for the first time in the club's history, beating Sutton Common Rovers 4-2 in the final.

In the background though, we were trying to get a new stadium built and I was involved with Elmbridge Borough Council trying to get it over the line. Walton and Hersham FC's ground at Stompond Lane was sold off by the council to build a big housing project and they wanted them to groundshare with us. The council then built a new stadium with two 3G pitches and an Olympic running track on the opposite side to it, and the idea initially was to amalgamate with Walton and Hersham, but we were three leagues above them and weren't really up for that idea.

I couldn't come to an agreement with Walton and Hersham's chairman, who was a really nice guy called Alan Smith. I wanted to run the football and was happy for him to become president, but we just couldn't totally agree on everything. In all honesty though, it was just getting too much for me by this stage.

During the COVID-19 period, we brought Stewart Lawson onto the board as an advisor with his experience in business. I first met Stewart about 2014 at a dinner charity event, but didn't really get to know him at that point. He's a big supporter of charities through his companies and around 2018 we crossed paths again at a charity lunch in Central London. We started to chat more regularly, became great friends and then two years down the line he became a very big sponsor and supporter of Casuals for two years along with his lovely wife, Marie. Stewart brought so much new energy to the club and got us doing the admissions online, as in getting people through the gate online, instead of paying at the turnstiles and also using drones to publicise our academy. He took the club to another level for two seasons, then after the pandemic, he just couldn't sustain it anymore. Also, he couldn't see the club going any further, which to be honest, neither could I.

The best thing that happened to me was letting it go. I didn't have the energy anymore. The task of fundraising for hundreds of thousands of pounds again and keeping it alive, at the age of 62, was becoming too much. Stewart's decision helped me make my decision. So, at the end of the 2021/22 season, we decided as a board that somebody else would be better to take the club on to greater things. Unfortunately, we couldn't find anybody either with the money or the integrity, so, sadly we all decided to fold the club honourably without any issues or problems. Ray Hole did it all professionally for us. If we couldn't keep our club to what it was accustomed to, then we didn't want to pass it on just to see it get run down. We also had a responsibility to the council, which we maintained, by keeping on with the academy (I'll explain more about this in the next chapter…).

In all my time during the 17 years we never owed one penny, whereas there's so many clubs nowadays that are flying by the seat of their pants, both league and non-league, but we never had the club in debt at any point. There's so many people who talk about what they do and don't do, but there's not a lot of doers. When the push comes to shove, players are players, but the people that are providing the grounds, the environment and all that, they are the proper non-league people. The doers. Players will come and go, so the loyalty is not to the players, but to the club. We did however keep the academy and that is a legacy which continues to do incredible things.

Chapter 32

GRASSROOTS...
STILL GROWING

'Tony did so much hard work behind the scenes with the academy and building sponsorship and what he did financially to keep that club afloat was incredible. You've got to pay the council to run a facility, then there's the budget to pay for players, kits, referees and staff. It's a hard job and he was doing that on the side of his commentary with Sky at the time. That was a real challenge.'

– Ray Hole

PEOPLE TALK about money trickling down from the Premier League to the Championship, but nobody talks about how grassroots football is funded, without all the limelight. I've been part of the Premier League, the Championship, Division One and also played non-league football, but the lower league football divisions, and especially non-league are so important in terms of what they stand for and what they achieve on and off the pitch.

I was at Walton Casuals for 17 years and I know in my heart it was the correct time to get out. All the sponsors who helped out, I had great friendships with and I'm so blessed to have friends like that who trusted me to put money into the club and make it work. Without them, there was no club. However, when it came to an end I didn't want everything to fall off a cliff edge. The Walton Casuals Football College started towards the end of 2018, but got off to a rocky start because of COVID. It was initially called an academy, but we thought it was a misleading term because players might think they were going to be professional footballers, so in summer of 2022 we rebranded to 'College.'

I'm chairman of the college, Ray Hole thankfully stayed on as managing director and Jonathan Pearce is el presidente. Ray's son Joss along with Justin Skinner are head coaches and Stewart Lawson has remained on board as a business advisor. If you're looking for success at the college, to me the real success is the fact that it still exists, because with COVID a lot of things disappeared. That shows we are sustainable, robust and resilient, which are all the things you need in football.

The college operates at the Excel Sports Hub and most of the kids are not going to be a pro, but they might enjoy a good career playing non-league football, where they will meet a lot of people and it's a great networking system. I love football, but one thing I've always emphasised is that, no matter how good you are, your football career is probably going to end in your 30s and you need a plan for the rest of your life. Our continued love of football development is very important at the college, but we push having education to fall back on as the most important thing.

At the college, we try to give them experiences they won't get anywhere else. At the time of writing we have around 30 people on our books and numbers are still affected by COVID, so we need to attract more students. Many 16-year-olds are looking to get into A-levels or generic qualifications and we'd like to give them the opportunity to get involved in something that will help them in the real world straight away. Our vocational course takes the kids through a two-year BTEC Level 3 in

Sports Coaching and Performance, while doing football at the same time. Then all of our students who pass the qualifications go on to either a vocation or university.

I act as a mentor to our students, but we also have a pathway programme, where we explain, 'If you want to be in sport, not just football, there's so many jobs to do.' We take them to professional grounds to show a little bit of the inside track of football and show them that whether they want to be a physio, a nutritionist, a groundsman, an accountant or play football at a semi pro or pro level, it's all available at a football club. We also bring in inspirational speakers from sport to pass on the spirit of winning and have even had some members of parliament involved.

Dominic Raab, who's the MP for Esher, really liked the idea of the college and came down to watch the students training, but also to present prizes to them. At the end I came walking onto the pitch towards him and he said, 'I know you. You're on the telly,' and I said, 'I know you. You're on the telly a lot more than me lately!' The MPs were on every day during lockdown, but especially him and Boris Johnson. They went from being politicians to household names. It was just after lockdown and everybody was very conscious, especially Dom, that you couldn't get too close to each other, so we had to have photos done apart and all that. I said, 'No problem. But how about we put a little bit of cheese and red wine in the middle and we can get a little bit closer then?', because they all got caught in the garden at Downing Street. He laughed.

I continue to raise money from functions I do alongside Len Herbert and give it to Ray to help with the kids and their education and that will never change. What better investment can you make than someone's future?

Chapter 33

THREE WEDDINGS, TWO FUNERALS AND ONE BIRTHDAY

'A wedding is like a funeral, except that you get to smell your own flowers.'

– Grace Hansen

IN JULY 2010, Scott Duxbury decided to tie the knot with his lovely wife Nicole. I first got to know Scott through troubled times at West Ham when Terry Brown had sold the club to the Icelanders in 2006. Scott was CEO of the club and got me involved in an advisory capacity, as well as helping on the corporate side and we instantly clicked and became really good friends.

Scott got married at Stoke Park and the choice for best men was either me or Gianfranco Zola, who was West Ham's manager at the time. I got the nod for best man and had to dress up in the whole top hat and tails while Scott and Nic arrived on a horse and carriage to a lovely wedding. My opening line for the best man's speech was, 'I do believe it was a spin up between me and Gianfranco for best man, and I'm very pleased that I won. It was only the fact that Mothercare didn't do his size in dinner suits.' Gianfranco laughed his head off.

Since leaving West Ham, Scott's become CEO and chairman of Watford Football Club, where he's done a brilliant job. My partner Dee and I often attend the games in the chairman's lounge and it's always great to see Scott, Nicole and his three wonderful kids. He's one of the best business brains in football and along with the owner of Watford, Gino Pozzo, has turned Watford's fortunes around and made it into a beautiful stadium at the same time.

2015 was a busy one. My old Fulham manager Bobby Campbell passed away which was obviously a sad occasion, but it was great seeing just how many people appreciated what he'd done for them. I was in the Fulham first team at 16 and captain at 18 and that was all down to him.

Bobby's got a lovely family and it was a super service which loads of people turned up for, but was less like a congregation and more like a gallery of superstars. Hundreds of people went to the church and then after we went back to his daughter's for the wake with some of the lads that I played with. We were all telling stories about him and what I hadn't realised was that what he did for me, he did for so many other football players as well. When you relay it all those years later, you realised just how great a man he was.

Same year, my vertically-challenged friend TC got married to Karen in Dubai and I was best man. In fact, TC actually only invited two ex-players, which were me and Frank McAvennie, and I reckon it was probably a coin toss of whether it would be me or Frank for best man. I probably won because nobody would have understood Frank.

Frank arrived a few days after me with his missus, Moya. They'd flown through the night from wherever he came from, had a few drinks on the plane, arrived, dumped their stuff and came down to meet us at the pool bar where we all were getting happily pissed. He'd just bought this lovely new flash watch and he's walked into the pool bar with his hand above the water so as not to get it wet. TC on the other hand had to have a snorkel up at the bar to get a drink. I did say to him, 'We'll pass you a drink by your lounger, because this pool ain't for kids.'

I said to Frank, 'What do you want to drink mate?' and he's said, 'Pint of lager.' I get him a pint and we're having a chat and Moya dived in the pool, comes over to us and pulls Frank. He's slipped and gone under the water, but somehow he saves his pint of lager from going under, but his other arm went in, which fucked his watch up.

I think I'm the only best man not to be in any pictures because it was not far off 40 degrees. TC's missus come up with a bright idea of us wearing a three-piece suit, which we were all fitted out for in Billericay. I'd even lost a load of weight to get in it. It was a jacket, waistcoat, shirt, tie and all that, but we had no idea how hot it was going to be and I hadn't accounted for eating like mad for 10 days and how difficult it might be to get into the suit. Let's just say, within a week that suit was tight as fuck.

I'm a big bloke and I sweat a lot. I said, 'Tone – how are we getting over to the wedding venue?' He said, 'We're getting a coach with all the other guests.' I said, 'I'm not getting on a coach, waiting for people to get on with the air con not working and we're all sitting there sweating. Listen, I'm gonna order a nice car which will mean that we'll go from the air condition-ing of the hotel and we jump in the car.' When I ordered the car, I said to the geezer, 'I want to be picked up at such and such a time. Have that air conditioning on full blast.' I went to the church to check it out and asked, 'Is there air conditioning?' and they said, 'Of course.' Same thing, 'Make sure it's on full blast by the time we arrive.'

The bride is supposed to be customarily late, but Karen got

seriously held up for some reason. I've gone to the front of the church and said, 'Don't worry, I've got this covered.' I then started playing the organ and singing, 'I'm forever blowing bubbles,' and everyone joined in. When Karen finally turned up, the wedding was really nice. After, we went back to the hotel for the reception, but then we had to walk to the part which was outside for the pictures and I thought, 'Fuck that.' Karen's going, 'Come on Galey, let's go out for some photos.' I said to Dee, 'It's going to be roasting. I ain't going out.' Anyway, I went out and exactly as I thought, after two minutes I had armpit stains under my suit and what looked like a map appearing on my back. That's when I snuck off.

We had the speeches by a swimming pool and they've got these big industrial blowers on us to keep us cool. Instead of doing the usual cheesy bit for the speech, I wrote a poem about TC, which was basically about him being short. Every other word was either, 'Short, little, small, tiny.' His mum who was sitting next to me was horrified. She was looking at me like, 'This is supposed to be a wedding, not a chance to destroy Tony.'

At the end of the poem, I got serious and said, 'There's a lot of people out here for the wedding, and it's great that we could afford to get out here, but some people who couldn't get out here for whatever reasons have recorded a little message.' Everyone's gone, 'Ahhhhhh. That's nice.'

I've turned to Richie who was in charge of the audio and said, 'You ready mate? Play it.' Rich hits play and on comes, 'Heigh ho, heigh ho, it's off to work we go.' It took everyone a split second to make the connection that it was the theme tune for The Seven Dwarfs and then everyone was pissing themselves laughing, apart from his mum who gave me the look of death. TC did his first dance with Karen and it was the worst choreographed dance I've seen at a wedding in my life. He's got two left feet, whereas Karen was really good, then shortly after everyone changed out of their gear, put their flip flops on and jumped in the pool, which was a right relief.

A few months later my good mate Richard Quartly got married in Cancun, Mexico and I was best man at that one also. Rich decided to splash out on a honeymoon suite in the hotel because it was obviously a big occasion for them, whereas me and Dee went for a double room.

When I'm in hotels, it takes something big to make me moan, but this room was doing my head in. Every time you'd be doing something, bang, the lights went off. I called Richard and asked, 'Do the lights keep going off in your room?' He's said, 'No. Why?' I've explained what was happening our end and after a few more power cuts in the room, I went to reception fuming and said, 'It's happened four times now and I'm best man at my mate's wedding. It's a lovely room, but the lights keep turning off.' They said, 'We haven't got any other rooms.' I said, 'You've got to sort me out. I can't deal with these lights going on and off. It's like a disco in there.' They were very apologetic and they've suddenly said, 'The only room we can give you is the honeymoon suite.' I said, 'Lovely!'

I've knocked on Richard's door and he was laughing his socks off. It turns out there was nothing wrong with the electrics, it was Dee's hairdryer. Every time she plugged it in, it blew the lights.

* * * * *

FOUR YEARS after TC got married, I got a phone call that stopped me in my tracks. TC had suffered a brain haemorrhage. Fortunately Phil Thompson, who was also commentating for Sky, was in the same hotel and he had immediately called the doctor.

Straight after I got the call, I rang his wife Karen, picked her up and headed down to West Middlesex hospital, down the road from the Sky studios. I went and saw him and tried to get his spirits up. 'TC. Just take a couple of Anadins. You'll be alright.' He was like, 'Don't make me laugh mate, this is serious.'

After West Mid he was transferred to Hammersmith hospital and we went up there and saw him every day as well. Thankfully, he didn't need to be operated on because the doctors were able to deal with the haemorrhage with medication. No pun intended, but TC's illness reminded me that life could be cut 'short,' in a heartbeat.

I think the hardest part for TC was the inactivity, because he lives at a hundred miles an hour and for the first six weeks after coming out he had to sit in a chair. I call him Captain Business-man, because nine out of 10 times I call and he's says he's in a meeting. Once I called him and he said, 'I'm in a meeting.' I said, 'What meeting?' and he said, 'I'm round me mum's.' I said, 'You're not in a fucking meeting, you're just round your mum's!'

Another one of my mentors and idols died towards the end of the year. On 19 November 2019, Teddy Weston passed away, which was also the date of my 60th birthday. I'd already done Perry Digweed's mum and dad's eulogies and Curtis, Teddy's son, who was the same age as me and Perry, said, 'I can't think of anyone better than you to do the eulogy. Can you do it on behalf of the family and our team?'

Usually, I write a little something down but on this occasion I didn't need to. When I looked at everyone in attendance there was all the boys that grew up under Teddy, who were now plumbers, electricians, ticket brokers, a few wheelers and dealers, you name it. A real bunch of characters, who were all in mine and Perry's lives.

It was an honour to do Teddy's eulogy, but of course I wanted there to be an element of humour in the church. Things like, 'There's Robin Carter over there. Good to see ya mate. You're back on the bench again.' Robin was always the twelfth man, but Teddy used to love him. Robin would be on the bench during a game and say, 'Teddy. We're 6-0 up. Can I come on?' 'Nah. Not yet Rob. Just gotta make the game safe.' At 7-0, Robin would come on for five minutes. Robin wasn't the best player, but Teddy looked after him as if he was his own kid and always made sure he was part of the team.

As far as my 60th goes, that was very memorable. Dee did an incredibly thoughtful job of arranging a surprise trip with family and friends, but hadn't said where the destination was and I thought it was just her and I who were going. Before meeting Dee, I was a bit of a creature of habit and I'd suggest holidays to either Tenerife or Tenerife, so I was looking for clues, asking her questions like, 'Is it going to be sunny? Cold? Because I need to know what to wear.' She kept saying, 'I can't tell you.' Then, two hours before leaving for the airport she tells me, 'We're going to New York,' which was somewhere I'd always wanted to go to.

We got to the airport early in the morning. We head over to one of the departure lounges and shortly after sitting down she says, 'I'm just going to take a look at the perfumes.' I said, 'Okay. I'm going to read me newspaper. Don't be late. Don't want to miss the plane.' Shortly after she's come back, 'Quick, quick. The plane is leaving.' I picked all the papers up and my bag, and we've run off to this gate. As we're running past this bar I hear, 'SURPRISE!' There was 14 of my mates there with their wives and they all had Tony Gale paper face masks on. My first thought was, 'Fuck me. I'm not paying for this lot, am I?'

What I didn't realise was that Dee had organised a fantastic itinerary and we had loads of different things to do each day. It was great to see everyone and it got even better when we got

251

out there. We went up to the bar at the top of the Rockefeller tower, which has beautiful views and as I'm looking out over Manhattan, I feel a tap on my shoulder and it was Les Strong and his wife. Next day we went to see the site of the Twin Towers and suddenly Scott Duxbury appeared. Then Richard Quartly, Stewart Lawson and his wife Marie turned up and by the end, there was 40 of us.

Always embrace the chance to create positive new memories, because if there's one thing COVID taught us, it's that everything can change in a day.

Chapter 34

GOING VIRAL

'Fishing. It does give you time to sit there and empty out things in your head as you watch the end of a tip of a float, while communicating with people either side of you, but only if they want to talk – because generally, they're talking a load of shit, mainly Frank and Galey.'

– Paul Parker

DURING LOCKDOWN I got a smartphone, which was a big thing for me as I'm shit at technology and I still miss my old Nokia! Dee showed me how to make a WhatsApp group with my mates and we had some great banter, which is what you needed during that time. The other big thing was walking and I ended up losing two stone during lockdown walking around the local area. Say for example, Little Les, who's in his late 70s and was particularly worried about how the virus might affect him. Me and Dee used to go for a walk and when I got to Les, she'd walk off and I'd stay and chat. Les only lives round the corner, so I'd see him about three times per week and I'd knock on his door and window and then go down the bottom of his path about 20 yards away and we'd shout to each other and have a chat.

I was still commentating on games through lockdown and was in a remarkably privileged position to be able to look forward to that once or twice a week when the football came back on during the pandemic. It was more the relief of getting out and having some sort of purpose, however, it was eerie. Driving to the ground, the roads were empty, but when you did arrive you weren't allowed in the ground until an hour before kick-off. Then you got your team sheet after putting your mask on and sanitising your hands 20 times, and had to stay away from other people before going up into the stand, where you'd commentate live on TV in an empty stadium. Going to West Ham that holds over 60,000 and having only 60 people present, which included the two sets of staff, was definitely something I won't forget.

Coming out of the restrictions was a massive relief for everyone and one of my first big outings was with my mate Stewart Lawson. He'd won a prize in a charity auction just before lockdown for 14 people to stay at Scotland's oldest working castle for about four days and it was absolutely beautiful.

There wasn't a lot to do outside the castle because you were in the middle of nowhere, so we made our own fun. We dressed up in all the Scottish gear, did a bit of clay pigeon shooting, had a murder mystery night and had a singer over who had never performed before and his machine kept going wrong. He couldn't get a note right, but we helped him through it.

The lasting memory of the trip was one night all the blokes dressed up in the kilts and I suggested that we stood in front of this big picture on the wall in this massive lounge and said, 'Wouldn't it be funny if every two hours, with the amount we drink, we take items of clothing off.' Thankfully for everyone in attendance, after eight hours, we only got down as far as our kilts.

Roll the clocks forward to 2022 and the COVID restrictions had been totally dropped. Stewart had started a company called Outdoor Pro a few years before, which is predominantly a fishing brand, but he quickly realised that if he wanted to compete in this industry he needed to heavily invest in other avenues. So he bought a TV production company and then managed to secure a three-year deal with BT Sport. That's when he came up with the idea of taking four ex professional footballers and trying to turn them into fishermen in a reality TV show. Through myself, Stewart met Paul Parker, Frank McAvennie and Paul Walsh and the first was a six-part series called *Angling Outlaws*, presented by Rob Hughes.

Before going on the show we'd barely picked up a rod before and had no idea what to do. If someone had said to us before lockdown that we'd be fishing at Four Lakes in Essex in a competition, we would have pissed ourselves laughing. However, it was an opportunity to do something which most people would never have, especially with the whole silver spoon service and with a load of ex pros having a laugh. It was great chatting about our time together and if we'd got one up on each other in certain games, we quickly brought it up. It was also great to just chat about what we'd all been up to since retiring from football, our families and how we were getting on in life.

I'd never lost touch with Frank since the West Ham days and he's still the great guy he was, even if I don't understand what he says. Walshy was different. I played against him many a time and also worked with him quite consistently at Sky, but he became a friend after football really. He was very good at his job at Sky and was a cracking football player, but he's also just a really good bloke. He had a bit of a drink problem years back and he addressed his issues. By doing that he had to go to regular meetings and now he's a counsellor to quite a few people who have gone through the same thing. I've got a hell of a lot of admiration and respect for him. On the fishing show he was always chirpy and like fishing, we were always trying to make each other get the first bite to make a comment. He's full of great, sharp one-liners, but I think I outdid him.

Paul Parker I'd kind of lost touch with. I was with him for a couple of years at Fulham, then we went our separate ways and he lived overseas for about a decade, then when he came back around 2018, we were living in the same town and reconnected. Paul was a prime candidate for this show because he didn't want to touch fish and definitely didn't want to touch maggots. Thankfully he didn't need to touch maggots and he slowly started touching the fish, although he didn't half moan about it.

Frank won the series and made sure he let us all know about it, while we all made out we didn't give a shit, but we did really. The second series was called *Speedy's Challenge*, named after Nick Speed, who was one of the best multidiscipline anglers in the UK. They got the four of us back together at a big fishing complex up in Doncaster called Lindholme Lakes, where they do a lot of the championships. This was a full-on week away with everything on site, including its own restaurant and bar, which came in handy. The four of us were in a team this time, working together instead of against each other. Nick Speed had seven days to get us into a position where we could take on another team. At that point they hadn't told us who the team was, but it turned out to be the England junior squad.

These lads were proper anglers and we'd only fished for a week in our lives. So, there we were along the riverbank and it was one of us, one of them all the way down the bank. Next thing, the klaxon goes to start the three-hour fish-off, to see who catches the most weight in fish.

Our four combined scores against the junior champions' combined scores. Paul Parker doesn't hear the klaxon go, so the geezer behind shouts, 'Paul, they've all started mate. GO, GO, GO!' He's then in a bit of a panic and pulled back his rod to cast his bait, but as he's pulled it back, his hook has got stuck up in the tree above him. The kid next to him straight away says, 'You fishing for squirrels mate?' Paul said, 'If I was man-marking him, he would have had one down the shin by now.' That was hilarious and sort of set the tone for the day.

It's all supposed to be a bit of a laugh, but the thing about it is that players don't lose their competitive edge. Me and Frank would wind each other up. If he got one, he couldn't wait to say, 'What you doing fatty? You got one yet?', knowing very well I hadn't. Then I'd say, 'Shut your noise.'

Frank won the first series, but I got the most weight of fish in the second series, even if it was a team event and I enjoy reminding the lads of that to this very day. Paul Parker said, 'When we played football and you got beat, afterwards did you go round telling everyone how well you played and the rest let you down?'

No matter what it is, of course I'm competitive, but I also think Frank lied about how much fish he caught in the first series. We gave a good account of ourselves and caught around 700lbs in weight of fish, which apparently wasn't bad, but we were never going to win it. Although we were competitive, we had some good laughs and the camaraderie between us was brilliant.

Chapter 35

CHIPS OFF THE OLD BLOCK

'My first childhood memory of dad's football that massively stands out for me was when I was five years old. I can still remember that feeling when hearing 'I'm Forever Blowing Bubbles' in the tunnel, before my brother and I walked out onto the pitch with dad for his testimonial at Upton Park. That moment will always hold a special place in my heart.'

– Alexandra Gale

YOU CAN'T push kids into sport. I used to go watch my son Anthony playing in the under-6s as goalkeeper, but he'd be sitting by the goalpost picking all the grass up off the floor, making it into a ball and throwing it. I was like, 'Try getting involved in the game. Come out on the pitch,' but the enthusiasm wasn't there yet. However, the Italia 90 World Cup is probably where Ant really fell in love with football. We sat together and watched pretty much every game, appreciating the stars like Roger Milla, Toto Schillaci and then the England team which had Gary Lineker, Paul Gascoigne and my old mate Paul Parker.

It didn't take Anthony long to get into the games at West Ham. My mum used to take him and there was all the chanting going on which always got his interest. After this one game he says to my mum, 'Tell Dad what they were saying about the referee.'

CHIPS OFF THE OLD BLOCK

She raised her eyebrows and said, 'Yes, Anthony. Terrible.' He then says, 'Dad. Why do they sing, "The referee's a vicar, the referee's a vicar?" My mum didn't want to tell him they were actually calling the ref a wanker, so we all went along with the vicar story.

By the age of six Anthony was playing for PD United in Whiteley Village on Sundays and I would help look after the team with a couple of lovely guys called John Green and a lifelong friend, George Ruff. The only times I couldn't be there was if I was playing for West Ham on the Sunday, but on those occasions, my dad would always be there.

Anthony started in defence with PD United, but he soon realised he didn't have a defensive bone in his body and wasn't going to be like his old man, and that's when he ended up playing as a centre-forward, scoring loads of goals. I used to get him things signed by players like Alan Shearer and David Beckham, saying 'To Anthony, keep scoring goals.' He's still got that memorabilia on his wall now. He then started getting his own bits signed by players when he used to come and see me play, but that wasn't always so straightforward. One game we played against Man United and it was the first time Paul Ince was playing for them. All the parents and kids were in the players' bar and you had to come out of the dressing rooms and through the gym to get there. Anthony came in a little bit weepy and my mum was sitting there with Paul's wife, Claire Ince and she was like, 'What's the matter Anthony?' He replied, 'Peter Schmeichel didn't give me his autograph.' Claire went up to the bar, goes up to Peter and said, 'Oi. Come and give this kid your autograph, now.' Peter comes over apologetic and says, 'I'm sorry. Did I miss you out?', then signed whatever Anthony wanted.

Ant got trials at Arsenal and was in the academy by 13 and then Crystal Palace as a 16-year-old. After Palace, Ant was out for two years because he had a serious knee injury which had to be operated on and he lost a quarter of his patella. They told him at 16 he'd never kick a ball again, but he proved them wrong. He got back and was playing with Dev at Maidenhead, then went on to play at Walton Casuals around 2002 and that's when we all got the shock of our lives.

One day, while working for Fulham FC on a summer coaching course, a lady came up to Ant and spotted a mole on his shin and said, 'I'd get that checked if I were you.' He replied, 'What do you mean?' She said, 'I don't want to worry you, but definitely get it checked.'

Ant came home and told us what had happened, which was obviously very worrying, then he went down to the local GP who said, 'Let's get you in and have a look because it's irregular in shape, raised and discoloured.' They got him booked in straight away, took a biopsy, sent it off for testing and said they'd give the results in two weeks.

When the results came through and they said it was cancerous, Ant broke down in tears. That news was totally devastating for the whole family. I said to Anthony, 'Come on. We can beat this. We'll get you in, they'll do whatever they need to do and you'll be back playing football again very soon.'

They needed to chop into his shin to get rid of the mole and also get into his lymph nodes in his groin to check the melanoma hadn't gone into his bloodstream. If they had operated a month down the line, the cancer may have gone into his blood and it could have been far more serious. Thankfully the tests showed it hadn't spread and six months later he was back playing football. I said to Anthony, 'Whoever that lady was who told you about the mole, you make sure you go and thank her.'

* * * * *

CHIPS OFF THE OLD BLOCK

AS A kid, we never used to let Ant go to the Millwall games, just in case it all went off and he got stuck. It's mad though, because he ended up working for Millwall for six years in their academy. My cousin, Scott Fitzgerald, was the academy manager and Ant said to me, 'I've got this opportunity at Millwall and it's too good to turn down.' I said, 'You have a real talent as a coach. Not all footballers became coaches and in fact, some of the most successful coaches took on their role because of early injuries in their footballing careers. You have to give it a go.'

Anthony had his UEFA B badge by the time he was 18 and did all the youth module badges which Scott put him through at Millwall. Sometimes he's felt he lives in my shadow as a footballer, and I told him once, 'You're not going to become as good a footballer as me, because your injuries won't allow you, but you've gone on to became a very good coach and much better than I could have ever been.' He did really well at Millwall and eventually, after six years he wanted to try management in adult football, which he got the opportunity to do at Walton.

Anthony now works at Nigel James Elite Coaching as well as doing his own one-to-one sessions where he's been fortunate enough to work with professionals like Declan Rice, Steven Sessegnon and Lyle Taylor. Without a doubt, he's a very good manager and coach. I always go back to Teddy Weston and say that he changed my life. He was my mentor. I now say to Anthony, 'Teddy changed my life. Football changed my life. Now you're changing people's lives and helping them more than you'll ever know. You're a coach to them, a friend, a brother and a dad in coaching.'

All this new breed of coaching where they stand on the line and they don't say anything is absolute bollocks. When a kid does well, there's nothing better than letting them know that and when a kid makes a mistake, don't have a go at them – explain why they've made the mistake and encourage and teach them to move on from it.

My daughter Alex has her own dance company which has done very well and sustained itself over the years and even worked through COVID keeping her academy alive online through Zoom. However, Alex may well have had a career in football. When she was about 12 she played one match at school and got a hat-trick. Considering she hadn't played at all, she was a natural. Me and Ant were like cheerleaders on the sidelines, so excited, but what we didn't realise was that a scout from Fulham had been watching her. Straight after the final whistle the scout has gone over to Alex and asked her to go for trials. Her instant answer was no, but Anthony didn't want to see her talent wasted and before she knew it, she had a pair of Adidas Predators on her bed from him. Ant said, 'Please. Think about this? Do you realise what you've been asked and what you did in that game?' As flattering as it was and despite being able to do 100 kickups, dance is where her heart was. How far could she have got with football? She'll never know, but knowing her competitiveness, I'm sure she could have played at a really good level.

Alex started dance school when she was five and when she left school at 16 she applied for a place at the BRIT School in Croydon, where Adele and Amy Winehouse went. They only took about 50 or 60 people from thousands of applicants. She went there for her auditions and didn't want anyone to know I was an ex-footballer or in the limelight and was insistent to do it off her own back and that I didn't try to pull any favours. Against the odds and people telling her, 'You should think about a proper job and career', she got a place.

When she received the letter saying she had been accepted, that was an incredible moment and we were all so proud of what she'd achieved. She attended the BRIT School for two years and at the age of 18 went straight onto performing professionally in the dance industry and trained for qualifications to teach dance with her aspiration to be a young dancer that taught, as opposed to a teacher that once danced. After six months teaching dance in gyms, she decided she could go on her own and the rest is history. She celebrated 10 years of the ADF Dance Academy (Alexandra Dance Fitness) in April 2022, after having started the company when she was only 21 and is now a successful dancer, teacher and choreographer. That's some achievement.

I was out at a sporting dinner once and this guy came up to me called Dick Best, who'd coached the England and British Lions rugby teams. He said, 'My daughter dances at your daughter's academy and I'd just like to say that Alex is so wonderful and I've never seen such a driven person in all my life. She's got a lovely way about her.' I was bowled over.

Since both my kids left school, they've never been a day out of work. They both left school without going on to higher education and immersed themselves in what they love to do, which is why they are so good at it. It's one of the proudest things to hear when a parent comes up to me and says, 'Your son/daughter really looked after my kids. They came here in their shell and now they've got confidence.'

I've been a player, pundit, commentator, mentor, chairman and more recently, an angler. However, the most important things to me these days are health, happiness and family. As a kid who grew up on a council estate in Pimlico, I'm grateful for every break I've been given and to everyone who has supported me.

I hope this book has helped to add a few laughs to people's memories. However, as my dad used to say, 'If you can't laugh at yourself, don't laugh at others.'

ACKNOWLEDGEMENTS

A BIG thanks to everyone who took the time to share some stories about my life, including Clive Allen, Ian Bishop, Liam Brady, Sir Trevor Brooking CBE, Terry Bullivant, Tony Cottee, Terry Creasey, Liz Curtis MBE, Gordon Davies, Sir Kenny Dalglish MBE, Alan Devonshire, Perry Digweed, Andrew Dickie, Paul Hardcastle, Vince Hilaire, Ray Hole, Ray Houghton, Danny Imray, Chris Kamara MBE, Stewart Lawson, Les Lee, Bill Leslie, Ray Lewington, Matt Lorenzo, Malcolm Macdonald, Tony Mahoney, Rodney Marsh, Frank McAvennie, Stephanie Moore MBE, Mike Osman, Gil Panayiotou, Paul Parker, Phil Parkes, Jonathan Pearce, Richard Quartly, Leroy Rosenior MBE, Duncan Saunders, Tim Sherwood, Jeff Stelling, Ray Stewart, Les Strong, Chris Sutton, Martin Tyler, Mark Ward and Robert Wilson. Big thanks to Steve Blowers, who is like the *West Ham Chronicle* when it comes to facts, stats and knowledge about West Ham. Thank you for taking the time to help out with the book, Steve.

Thanks to Dick Pelham and Richard Shenton for their fantastic photography.

A special thanks to my fantastic children Alexandra and Anthony Gale, my incredible partner Dee, my cousins Spencer Collins, Terry Gale, Steven Collins and my uncles Ray and Terry. Also, my cousin Jacqui Howes and my sister Joanne, who are the rocks in my family. If there's any problems, they're my go-to people.

In terms of all my fundraising functions over the years which were up in London and Silvermere Golf Club, I have to give a

ACKNOWLEDGEMENTS

special mention to Len Herbert and his family, who did all the organising. Len's a good friend and great man who I've known since retiring from playing football. Also, Tony Hoskins and Geoff Garner for all the charity events which they've run and I've participated in and Ian Morgan for the West Ham charity events he organises. Lastly, Dave Davies who was a big help in my early days of fundraising.

*****

I'D LIKE to say a few words about my ghostwriter, Paul Zanon. When Paul first approached me about doing a book, I was apprehensive. However, after we started the process and having spoken to him more than I'd spoken to anyone in the last six months, it's been a privilege and a pleasure to have met such a nice person. Forever a friend.

Finally, a big thanks to Steve Hanrahan, Paul Dove, Rick Cooke, Simon Monk and Claire Brown for their support and diligent editing and design to take this book over the line.